A Century of State Murder?

G000144431

A Century of State Murder?

Death and Policy in Twentieth-Century Russia

Michael Haynes and Rumy Husan

Pluto Press

LONDON • STERLING, VIRGINIA

First published 2003 by Pluto Press
345 Archway Road, London N6 5AA
and 22883 Quicksilver Drive, Sterling, VA 20166-2012, USA

www.plutobooks.com

Copyright © Michael Haynes and Rumy Husan 2003

The right of Michael Haynes and Rumy Husan to be
identified as the authors of this work has been asserted
by them in accordance with the Copyright, Designs
and Patents Act 1988.

British Library Cataloguing in Publication Data
A catalogue record for this book is available from
the British Library

ISBN 0 7453 1931 9 hardback
ISBN 0 7453 1930 0 paperback

Library of Congress Cataloging in Publication Data
Haynes, Michael, 1951–
    A century of state murder? : death and policy in
twentieth-century Russia / Michael Haynes and Rumy Husan.
        p. cm.
Includes bibliographical references.
    ISBN 0–7453–1931–9 (hardback) — ISBN 0–7453–1930–0 (pbk.)
    1. Mortality—Soviet Union—History. 2. Mortality—Russia
(Federation) 3. Life expectancy—Soviet Union—History. 4. Life
expectancy—Russia (Federation) 5. Soviet Union—Statistics,
Vital—History. 6. Soviet Union—Population policy. I. Husan, Rumy.
II. Title.
    HB1437 .H39 2003
    304.6'4547'0904—dc21

                                                        2003005379

10   9   8   7   6   5   4   3   2   1

Designed and produced for Pluto Press by
Chase Publishing Services, Fortescue, Sidmouth, EX10 9QG, England
Typeset from disk by Stanford DTP Services, Towcester, England
Printed and bound in the European Union by
Antony Rowe Ltd, Chippenham and Eastbourne, England

Contents

List of Tables

List of Figures

Preface and Acknowledgements

This book, our first to focus on a major social issue, follows a number of years of collaborative work between the authors. Previously our joint work concentrated on the economic history of the former Soviet Union and Eastern Europe, and problems of the transition. We have looked especially at how leaders in the region have, during the course of the twentieth century, alternatively used the state and market to attempt to develop and converge with the West, but without much success. Our aim here is to bring some of the costs of the failure to a wider audience. We have tried to draw as much as possible on the most authoritative sources in an area bedevilled by unreliable data. Where the data is weak and gaps exist we try to acknowledge this. The footnotes record our technical debts, but in a wider sense we wish to pay tribute here to the work of those specialists on whose discussion we often draw and without which this book could not have been written.

Our warm gratitude is due to a number of people who have helped us in differing ways: Jane Saunders at the Brotherton Library, University of Leeds and Nigel Hardware at the European Resource Centre, Birmingham University, both of whom located an array of relevant sources; David Appleyard and Mark Newcomb of the Graphics Unit, Department of Geography, at the University of Leeds, for help with the map and diagrams; Lyudmilla Alperin of the Moscow Centre for Prison Reform for providing us with unpublished data; Jonathan Sutton and Silke Machold for help with translation; Sue Blackwell for help in obtaining materials. The library of the Wellcome Institute in London is a major resource and the staff immensely helpful and knowledgeable. We should like to thank Roger Van Zwanenberg at Pluto for commissioning this book, and to the referees for their generous and encouraging comments. Julie Stoll has always been patient and supportive as the commissioning editor at Pluto.

We have generally followed the US system of transliteration from Russian but kept proper names in their most familiar forms. We have, however, not bothered with the apostrophe for the soft sign, as this is confusing for non-Russian readers. Russian readers will know where it should be. The footnotes record our technical debts.

The USSR in the Late Stalin Era

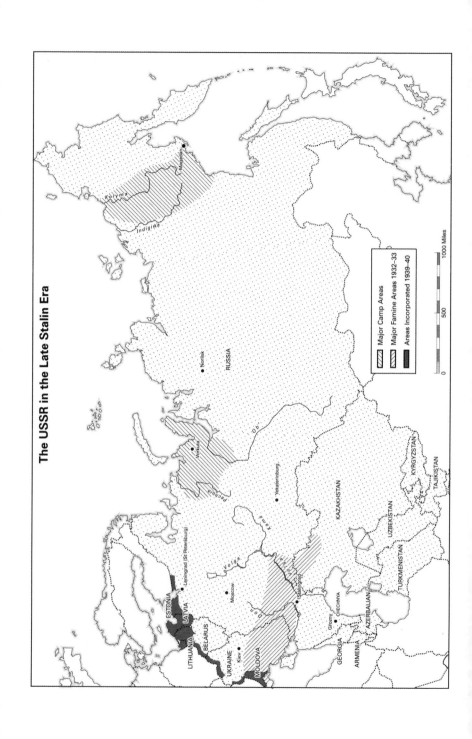

Major Camp Areas

Major Famine Areas 1932–33

Areas Incorporated 1939–40

0   500   1000 Miles

RUSSIA

KAZAKHSTAN

UZBEKISTAN

KYRGYZSTAN

TAJIKISTAN

TURKMENISTAN

GEORGIA

ARMENIA

AZERBAIJAN

CHECHNYA

Grozny

ESTONIA

LATVIA

LITHUANIA

BELARUS

UKRAINE

MOLDOVA

Kiev

Moscow

Leningrad (St Petersburg)

Stalingrad

Yekaterinburg

Norilsk

Vorkuta

Magadan

Kolyma

Indigirka

Ob'

Lena

Volga

Don

Pechora

The Four Great Mortality Crises in Twentieth-Century USSR-Russia

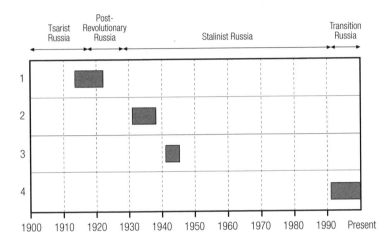

1 1914–21:   First World War (1914–17) and civil war (1918–21): military losses: 3 million;
                 excess civilian deaths: 13–14 million; birth deficit: 10 million (total population loss = 26–27 million)

2 1931–38:   Collectivisation and famine: 9 million; repression: 1 million (total USSR = 10 million).
                 Nazi-Soviet Pact in 1939 leads to expanded borders of USSR

3 1941–45:   Second World War: 43 million wartime deaths including 27 million excess deaths in USSR as a whole

4 1992–Present: Disintegration of the USSR in December 1991. Russia's shock therapy reforms:
                 2.6 million excess deaths between 1990 and 1999; 0.2 million war deaths in Chechnya between
                 1994–96 and 1999–2002

Glossary and Abbreviations

GLOSSARY

Cheka	Extra-ordinary Commission (against counter-revolution) (1917–22).
Congress of Peoples Deputies	Gorbachev-era legislative body, convened in summer 1989.
Federal Assembly	Twin-chamber Russian legislature deriving from 1993 constitution.
feldsher	A health practitioner qualified midway between a nurse and a doctor.
Gini coefficient	Measure of inequality of income distribution.
glasnost	'Openness' – increased liberalisation of public life under Gorbachev after 1985.
Gosplan	State Planning Commission.
guberniia	Province under Tsarist system of government.
Gulag	Often used loosely to refer to the prison camp system. Technically, the main directorate of labour camps established in 1930.
kulak	A member of the wealthier class of peasants.
nomenklatura	List of people with regime approval eligible for different posts.
oblast	Administrative region.
perestroika	Economic restructuring under Gorbachev after 1985.
residual principle	The proportion of the plan devoted to low-priority sectors (notably consumer goods and services) after allocations to high-priority sectors (heavy industry and the military) have been made.
samogon	A homemade alcoholic beverage.
State Duma	From 1906 to 1917, the lower chamber of parliament in Tsarist Russia. From 1993, the lower chamber of the Russian parliament.

Supreme Soviet	Formal legislature of the USSR. Corrupted version of that originally formed in 1917.
troika	Group of three. Used in various contexts in the Soviet era. In the 1930s, a three-man commission of secret police.
uskorenie	Attempt at accelerating the growth of the economy under *perestroika*.
White House	Russian parliament building in Moscow. Yeltsin's base in 1991. Attacked in 1993.
zemstvo	Local county council in Tsarist Russia.

ABBREVIATIONS

ASSR	Autonomous Soviet Socialist Republic
CIS	Commonwealth of Independent States
CMEA	Council for Mutual Economic Assistance (or 'Comecon')
EBRD	European Bank for Reconstruction and Development
GUIN	Main Directorate for the Execution of Punishments
IK OKChN	Pan-National Congress Executive Committee of Chechnya
ILO	International Labour Organisation
KGB	USSR 'Committee of State Security' (1953–91)
MCPR	Moscow Centre for Prison Reform
NEP	New Economic Policy (begun 1921)
NGO	non-governmental organisation
NKVD	secret police (People's Commissariat for Internal Affairs, 1934–46). From 1946 to 1954, MVD (Ministry of Internal Affairs)
OECD	Organisation for Economic Cooperation and Development
OGPU	United State Political Administration for struggle against espionage and counter-revolution (1922–34)
RSFSR	Russian Soviet Federative Socialist Republic
SIZO	pre-trial detention centre
SOE	state-owned enterprise
WHO	World Health Organisation

1 Demography – the Social Mirror?

Death is never fair but it comes to all of us. 'To every thing there is season, and a time to every purpose under heaven,' said the Old Testament author of Ecclesiastes, 'A time to be born, and a time to die; a time to plant and a time to pluck up that which is planted ....' But it is not this simple. Part of the unfairness of death is that too often it comes out of season, people are plucked away from us before their time. Perhaps its cause is the apparent randomness of the car crash, the glancing punch that sends a head reeling against a stone or a disease that is diagnosed too late. But dig a little deeper and a pattern begins to emerge. Chance can carry any of us away but looked at across populations we see that the unfairness of death is not random – there is a systematic pattern which derives from the societies in which we live. It is the unfairness of society that lies behind the unfairness of death – the poor die before the rich, the peasant before the lord, the worker before the boss. When conflicts come, their impact falls unevenly; famines carry away the weak and powerless, not the strong; repression hits the defenceless hardest. Indeed, in the pattern of death we can often see and even measure in stark relief the contested inequalities of the life of a society, its history of bad times and good times.

This book is about this pattern as it has applied to Russia in the last century. Many Russians did live and will live out their full time. But far too many others have died and will die before it as a result of what they suffered in this period, whether as part of the pattern of excess 'normal death' in peaceful years or the abnormal eruptions of waves of mortality produced by crisis and repression. Russia is not alone in having had such a great harvest of death. Such has been the record of most societies in the twentieth century – the optimistic vision of the past 100 years makes more sense from the perspective of someone in the advanced West that in any other part of the world. But Russia's record is especially interesting because it reflects a society at the centre of recent global history from its time as the Tsarist Empire to world war, revolution, degeneration, repression, an even bloodier world war, cold war, empire, collapse and transition to a supposedly new Russia on the verge of a new century.

The sheer scale of this defies our understanding. In the Second World War there were approximately 27 million 'excess' Russian deaths, meaning the difference between the actual deaths and 'expected' deaths under normal peacetime conditions. Note first that the number is approximate – we do not know exactly, no one knows. For Britain the figure is more precise: 264,000 servicemen and women actually died and 96,000 civilians. But what is the difference between 360,000 and 27 million? Both are big numbers but our minds find it hard to deal with big numbers. When Churchill met Stalin in the Second World War, Stalin reputedly said that 'a single death is a tragedy, a million deaths is a statistic'. There is a truth and an untruth here. The truth is that large numbers are statistics – numerical data collected on a more or less systematic basis, more or less accurately. The untruth is that large numbers do not count in the way that individuals do. Every large number is made up of individuals, every death out of season is an individual tragedy and 'a time to weep … a time to mourn' for those who are left behind. In this book therefore we will be concerned with both the big numbers – trying to set them out as accurately as possible, trying to put them in their context but we will also be concerned with the tragedies that lay behind, the hopes unfulfilled. Although we will offer pointers it will be for the reader to complete the connection between the two. But making that connection is important to understand what follows. You can try a simple experiment to measure what the difference is between 360,000 deaths and 27 million deaths. Don't just do this in your head, do it for real to get a sense of the comparison we want you to make. Find a long piece of string, a pair of scissors and a ruler. Now let 100,000 deaths equal one inch. You can cut off a piece of string that is 3.6 inches long to represent the British war deaths. Now for the Soviet deaths unreel a foot of string – that represents 1.2 million deaths – slightly more than the numbers who died in the siege of Leningrad. Now reel out another 21.5 feet of string without cutting it and put one end against the start of the British string and very carefully lay out the other 3.6 inches. That is what the difference means in terms we can all understand.

Why did we not want you to cut the string? Sadly the comparison does not stop here, we would like you to reel out another 17 feet – the figure cannot be precise. These extra feet do not measure deaths but children not born. Indirectly, therefore, they represent the continuing tragedy of the missing generation and the lives distorted by war. Whereas in Britain the wartime birth rate fell only slightly and then quickly recovered, in Russia the harvest of death was largely a harvest of young men. A generation of Russian women were destined to live and die regretting courtships and marriages barely begun or those which could never happen. Only when this war generation passed the end of their childbearing period and new generations grew up did this demographic effect begin to fade.

We do not pretend therefore that this will be an easy book to read for we are looking less at what has been given to us than what has been taken away. Nor will it be an uncontroversial book. In the 1990s in France a group of historians got together to produce what they called *The Black Book of Communism*.[1] This book was an attempt, part of a 1990s conservative crusade, to discredit the idea of a socialist alternative. It did this by lumping together the experience of Russia between 1917 and 1991 as if it was all of a piece. This experience was then merged with that of a motley assortment of regimes elsewhere in the world, imputing as many deaths as possible, however they were committed, to an ill-defined 'Communism'. Our book is explicitly *not* an answer to this. Its task is more modest but hopefully more compelling – to accurately set out the scale of the Russian tragedy with a sense of its wider context. Just because the contrast between the progress and barbarism has been such a characteristic feature of the twentieth century, we need the wider sense otherwise the picture becomes completely distorted.

But there is a reluctance to make this comparison save where it fits into the myth history that was part of the Cold War and is now part of the post-Cold War world. At the centre of that myth history is the idea that what happened in Soviet Russia was uniquely evil – comparable only to Nazi Germany and perhaps worse than it. We reject this view not because we seek to diminish the cruelty of the recent past of Russia but because the one-sided condemnation of one state effectively serves to legitimate the cruelties of another, and although this book is about sadness it is also a book born of hope that *wherever* injustice and exploitation exists, wherever it cuts people down, it should and can be fought. Focusing one eye on injustice in one place but keeping the other closed on injustice elsewhere does no service to anyone and least of all people in Russia. What has prompted this book has been the final tragedy of the twentieth century that exactly this type of thinking produced in Russia. In 1989–91 the system that had dominated Russia since 1928–29 collapsed to give way to a brave new world of market reform. The old regime fell discredited, deservedly disgraced. But the hope was that a new model could be found not by going beyond the failings of both 'East' and 'West' but by lurching from one to the other. The result has been another tragedy. Its contours were briefly set out towards the end of our period in 1999 in the annual report of the United Nations Development Programme:

> In 1989 about 14 million people in the transition economies were living under a poverty line of $4 a day. By the mid 1990s that number was about 147 million, one person in three ... income distribution has worsened sharply, particularly in the former Soviet Union ... the stress is showing in the declining or stagnating life expectancy and sharply worsening adult mortality. Today, for example, the probability that a 15 year old Ukrainian male will survive until his sixtieth birthday is a mere 65%, down from 72% in 1986. The Europe and Central Asia region is the only part of the developing world with rising adult mortality rates. Even Sub-Saharan Africa, with its AIDS epidemic, is seeing a reduction in adult mortality.[2]

This is a damning admission but the words are chosen carefully to avoid the obvious comparison that needs to be made with the tragedies of the past.

LIES, DAMNED LIES AND STATISTICS?

To measure and capture the scale of these processes requires us to use a lot of statistical data and the sceptical reader might fight shy of this because there are two things that everyone knows about statistics – that there are 'lies, damned lies and statistics' and that 'you can prove anything with statistics'. Fortunately neither of these statements is true.

In the first place it is not statistics that lie but the people who use them. Statistics can be more or less accurate, with greater or lesser degrees of error. The real problem arises when they are misused and the possible errors ignored. This is well brought out in a short and often funny book by Darrel Huff which has achieved 'classic' status – How to Lie with Statistics.[3] Readers who are inclined to a completely hostile view of statistics should read Huff to see how the techniques of the 'statistical liars' are worked. Hopefully they will emerge, as

Huff intends, with a desire to continue to use numbers but forewarned against some of the shabby tricks that daily continue to be played by advertisers, politicians, and even the occasional author.

Measuring social processes is an intrinsically difficult thing and in this sense we are never likely to have perfect data that commands universal support. But more data is available to us today than at any time in history. In a very real sense the development of our consciousness of numbers and statistics has been a product of the development of capitalism. Counting and numbers did not have the same function in pre-capitalist societies that they do in capitalist ones. The Domesday Book, for example, was a registration of the land and the people and animals on it rather than a census or social survey. A thousand years later we can reconstruct it in these terms but they were not the terms of the time. So far as we know the compilers did not even use it to try to get a reliable estimate of the overall population of England.

With the emergence of capitalism the relationship between the economic process and numbers, counting, statistics, and even mathematics became closer. The needs of merchants encouraged the development of accountancy; navigation required more complex calculations; centralising states required more detailed accounts and needed a sense of population numbers, the first insurance companies began to worry about risks and mortality rates. Capitalism also operated in less obvious ways by integrating and unifying economic processes so that they could be measured. Even in the late eighteenth century, for example, a country as small as Switzerland had 60 different solid measures systems, 81 different liquid measures, 11 currencies with some 300 separate coins all disrupting economic unity and making comparative measurement difficult.

Over time local particularities like these were swept away by reforms and revolutions such as 1789 in France which encouraged the development and generalisation of more rational systems of measurement like the metric system. Then in the nineteenth century needs widened further and the fascination with numbers spread more to the development of social processes – often stimulated by the desire to reform the moral and political character of the lower orders. In the last century this growing concern with numbers has become internationalised as business and states have grown in size and globalising forces have encouraged attempts at comparative international measurement through organisations like the League of Nations, the International Labour Organisation, the United Nations, the World

Bank, the IMF, the OECD, and others too numerous to name. In this way a mass of data is generated which reflects our need to know but which is also moulded, even at the level of basic concepts, by the narrower and even mystificatory needs of businessmen, advertisers, bureaucrats and politicians who run the system.

But this does not mean that we cannot pull out from this mine of data incredibly valuable material. Nor does it mean that the second objection – that anything can be proved with statistics – is valid. Because statistics exist in relation to one another, they cannot simply be isolated and pulled out of the air. We can therefore ask questions about their plausibility and test their consistency against other bits of data we have. And this is especially true of demographic data. As Alain Blum puts it, 'it is very difficult, in truth impossible, to manipulate complete demographic series'.[4] Demographic processes are underpinned by certain regularities. If one bit is falsified then it becomes inconsistent with the other bits – but the data is so detailed that making the falsification consistent becomes virtually impossible. The most notorious example of this, which relates directly to our interests in this book, was the attempt to hide the scale of the population losses in the 1930s in Stalin's Russia. Three major censuses were held after the revolution – in 1926, 1937 and 1939.[5] The 1926 census does have data problems but it was a product of the enthusiasm of the revolutionary generation. Frank Lorimer, who wrote the first major Western study of the population of the Soviet Union, said that it was 'one of the most complete accounts ever presented of the population of any country'.[6] Published in 56 volumes, its results still remain to be properly explored by historians. On the basis of this we can, allowing for likely changes in the birth rate and death rate, project forward the likely population into the future for the next decade or so. But of course the population in Russia in the 1930s bore little relation to such projections because collectivisation, famine and repression had killed millions. The gap between the real figure and the estimated figure was therefore a measure of the catastrophe created by Stalinism.

To obscure this disaster, the population had to appear to be growing. Stalin resolved this problem in 1934 by announcing that the population had been 168 million at the end of 1933, a significant increase over 1926. The statisticians were horrified. 'How great was our shock when, at the 17th Party Congress Stalin spoke of a population which surpassed our own estimates by 8 million people'. One later recalled:

At my request the director of the population and health department – at the time, the Hungarian émigré Sikra, asked Osinsky, the director of the Central Statistical Office of the time, to find out from where Stalin had drawn the figure. I was told later that Osinsky had a conversation with Stalin on this theme and that Stalin told him that he knew himself what figure to cite.[7]

The problem grew in 1936–37 when it was decided to hold another census which, like that of 1926, was to be carried out in great detail (albeit to an agenda heavily influenced by the centre). This census showed a population of 162 million. The gap was obvious and the statisticians knew full well its scale, and where the missing people had 'gone'. But if the real figure could not be revealed, neither could the mass of the underlying data because, from that, it would be possible to work back to the real figure. So in September 1937 it was announced that the census had been abandoned because it had 'deeply violated' both the instructions of the government and 'the elementary bases of statistical science', its organisation had been 'unsatisfactory' and the materials 'defective'. The key statisticians were arrested, imprisoned and, in some instances, shot. A new census was then announced for January 1939 to give what *Pravda* called 'an exact and truthful image of life in the country of the Soviets'. But this one encountered the same problems. The solution was to declare a figure of 170 million for 1939 which created some apparent consistency with Stalin's figure but then accentuated the contradictions with the underlying data – most of which had then also to be hidden. Even so, looking at what bits of data that did emerge and, working forward from 1926, and backwards from 1939, it was possible for demographers to estimate the likely error.

Since accurate data was needed for other purposes the best policy was therefore not to publish detailed data at all. This was in effect what happened on a wide scale in Russia in the 1930s across most aspects of life. Blum suggests that this led to a paradox in terms of the demographic data. In a technical sense the demographers were becoming better over time, struggling to improve their procedures. But they remained subject to the political imperatives of the regime and its secrecy. They therefore found themselves in the peculiar position of being 'at the interface of society and power'.[8] If they looked one way they could see the various catastrophes starkly revealed in their population tables and charts. If they looked the other there was the Stalinist regime masking its brutality with its fairy tale image of a happy, contented and rapidly growing people.

After the death of Stalin the amount of statistical distortion became less in Russia. In the Eastern European countries that were integrated into the Soviet bloc, it was never as intense as it had been in Russia in the 1930s although, of course, it was still present. Rapid economic growth and modernisation helped in the long run to raise the standard of living, producing less extreme demographic patterns and this, combined with an easing of repression (though subject to ups and downs) meant that more data could be collected and published. Censuses were held in Russia in 1959, 1970, 1979, 1989 and 2002, which created a much more secure basis for an understanding of the population. Censuses were also held regularly in Eastern Europe. Of course much of the data remained secret and some problems remained, but they were nothing compared to the 1930s. However, in the late 1970s these regimes began to experience economic difficulties. These difficulties soon began to be marked in the basic demographic data and especially in their mortality figures. But when attempts were made to disguise what was happening, the same dilemmas created by the interconnectedness of the data began to emerge. In 1976, for example, infant mortality data ceased to be openly published in the USSR. Then, to help cover the tracks even more, in 1978, publication of age-specific mortality data was suspended. This was followed in 1985 with the suspension of data on the causes of death. Alarm bells started ringing straight away. But, fortunately, the development of *perestroika* and *glasnost* after 1985 meant not only that this data became available but also that the whole of the demographic history of the Soviet Union (and Eastern Europe) became open for detailed investigation.

Since then the problem has been less the availability of data than the refusal to use it and integrate what is known. Of course, data problems still exist. Throughout the book we shall continue to draw attention to these. But since 1991 the central problem has been that, as in the 1930s, the propagandists of a transition driven from the top have marginalised or ignored the costs. Occasionally a glimpse of them appears in publications of the main global economic organisations. Sometimes a particular research project on them might even get funding. But in general it has been left to organisations like UNICEF, the World Health Organisation and demographers and health professionals to draw out the full implications of the tragedy that has been developed and even their often remarkable efforts have not always been able to throw light into every corner.

MURDER MOST FOUL?

If preventable death occurs should anyone be blamed? The question is both a practical and a moral one. Consider an example. In late 1962 the Soviet magazine *Novy Mir* caused a sensation by publishing Alexander Solzhenitsyn's story, *A Day in the Life of Ivan Denisovich*. For the first time in the 'official' literature of the Soviet regime, a realistic depiction of life in Stalin's camps – the Gulag – had been allowed to appear. One woman wrote to Solzhenitsyn that she had seen queues of all kinds – to watch *Tarzan*; to buy butter, women's knickers, chicken giblets and horsemeat sausages, 'but I cannot remember a queue as long as the one for your book in the libraries ... I waited six months on the list to no avail.' But not everyone was impressed. Solzhenitsyn received letters of condemnation from loyal Stalinists and he also received letters from existing prisoners. One of them, a V.E. Milchikhin, had been imprisoned for a 'criminal' offence and then murdered a fellow inmate. He was annoyed by Solzhenitsyn:

> [Y]ou writers are discovering the injustices of the days of Beria. But why does not one of you touch on the life of non-political prisoners? ... For example, why are we, murderers, inside? ... People who have hanged and executed Soviet citizens were released under article 58, while we have to stay in prison ...[9]

Milchikhin's question is an important one. Why is the murderer of one person or a small number so often treated more harshly than larger-scale murderers? Why should both those who give the orders and those who carry them out so often both escape unscathed? If those directly involved in the deaths of many walk free, why should not the isolated murderer? But if the isolated murderer should be jailed, then should not the larger murderer too?

The questions do not stop here. Mass deaths tend to have a systematic character. They are usually the products of groups of people operating through institutions which, in turn, depend on systems – there is a division of labour in which responsibility is spread across a chain of participants. The ethical problems this poses have been analysed at length in the study of the Holocaust. But the broader way in which this division operates, in both war and repression, has been set out by the philosopher Jonathan Glover in his *Humanity: A Moral History of the Twentieth Century*.[10] Glover's account focuses on death as a result of war and direct repression. But his discussion misses some important aspects of the argument about mass death. Glover does not systematically consider the way in which the economic system, economic processes and policies underpin the barbarism that his book recounts. This leaves him with the view that there is a struggle between the technology of death and human psychology and, since the technology of death is now so advanced, the solution lies with psychology. This omission of a systematic integration of the economic is not only questionable in terms of any analysis of causation but it also unnecessarily narrows the way the question of humanity and inhumanity is posed. Famine provides an important example. The term does not appear in Glover's index but most accounts of the crimes of Stalin would include the collectivisation-induced famine of 1932–33. We do not have to go to the extremes of some Ukrainian nationalists and see this famine as a deliberate act of genocide. Even if the charge is, as we think it should be, that Stalin's policy helped to turn a harvest failure into mass starvation and that he and his policy makers then stood by and did nothing to remedy the situation – the potential indictment remains formidable. As we shall see in Chapter 3, the numbers of dead run into millions. But how do we integrate this type of disaster into any discussion of responsibility?

One way has been suggested by the historian Stephen Wheatcroft in an essay which compares deaths attributed to Hitler and those that can be attributed to Stalin. Wheatcroft has been at the forefront of the advance in our knowledge of both Soviet demography and the debate on the patterns of repression.[11] Inevitably this means that he has had to confront the Hitler–Stalin comparison not only in terms of number and system but also in terms of responsibility. He tries to resolve the latter problem by making a number of important distinctions in the way that we should think about mass death. These derive from the fact that systems of justice usually distinguish between different kinds and degrees of unjustifiable killing. Murder usually involves intent – in the famous phrase, 'with malice aforethought'. Manslaughter on the other hand can involve killing by reckless or negligent behaviour. These distinctions are not totally hard and fast but Wheatcroft suggests that they can be extended to the mass level.

Developing his discussion we can divide mass deaths into those that were *deliberate and purposeful*, arising from conscious action and those that arose less from conscious action than irresponsible acts and neglect. This, Wheatcroft points out, is broadly equivalent to the distinction at the level of the individual between murder and manslaughter. The purposeful category can then be divided into what he calls *'murder'*, deaths which are outside of the legal structure of the regime (e.g. Hitler's mass extermination programme) and *'execution'*, deliberate deaths that have some semblance of being subject to a legal order, however dictatorial and unjust the regime is that gives rise to this order (e.g. Stalin's Russia).

Deaths from less purposive actions can perhaps then be divided into those that were the product of positive action and policies where there was an irresponsible failure to consider consequences, and policies of inaction where opportunities existed to save lives but these were not taken. These would be equivalent to *mass manslaughter* by reckless action or neglect.

We do not pretend that these distinctions are easy ones and Wheatcroft is primarily concerned to use them to analyse the deaths that can be attributed to Hitler and Stalin. Overall he argues that (excluding the issue of the war) Hitler was responsible for fewer deaths than Stalin. But deaths attributed to Hitler were primarily state murders, carried out with no semblance of legality, even within the perverted norms of the Nazi state. By contrast the Stalin regime maintained, in its own no less perverted terms, a semblance of legal process and therefore many of the smaller number who died directly at the hands of Stalin's secret police were subject to state execution. However, Stalin was also responsible for a much larger number of other deaths than Hitler. These arose from the wilful policies that led to collectivisation, famine, mass deportation, etc., and the inaction that allowed the tragedies of starvation, malnutrition and disease to carry away so many millions.

Wheatcroft's distinctions seem to us to make a lot of sense but there are some fairly obvious implications that he does not pursue. For example, policy-induced disasters like famine and policy indifference in the face of them are not restricted to Soviet Russia. It has been the fate of many to die of malnutrition and disease with help only a short distance away but barred to them. Nor is it of much help to lay the blame on 'God' or 'nature' because what appears at first sight as 'natural disasters' turns out on investigation to be socially constructed crises. A notable example of this occurred in 1943 in

Bengal when the harvest failed in the midst of the Second World War. This exposed not only British policy within India but also the wider choices made by Churchill and the British War Cabinet. Churchill took the decision to order sailings in the Indian Ocean to be reduced 'to sustain the Mediterranean campaign'. As A.J.P. Taylor put it, the result was that 'imports of food were urgently needed and did not come. Perhaps 3 million Indians died of starvation for the sake of a white man's quarrel in North Africa.'[12] If Stalin and his policy makers have culpability for the deaths in Russia in 1932–33, then do not Churchill and his policy makers have some culpability for the deaths in India a decade later?

But pursuit of this line of thought leads in another direction too. Many different kinds of crises can lead to death. The most interesting here are economic crises and the policy context in which they occur. This is not a new argument. After the Second World War, a form of analysis developed of economic choices, which became known as cost-benefit analysis. Choices were considered in terms of the flows of costs and benefits that were usually thought of in narrow economic terms. Should a bridge be built here or there? How do the costs and benefits of one project compare with those of another? But since economic actions often have quite predictable human consequences, it was not hard in principle to extend this assessment to include a human cost element too. How many lives might be saved or lost as a result of the action undertaken and at what cost? On a larger scale, the same ideas can be applied to economic policy as a whole. If cuts are made here or expansion develops there we can trace how this will affect not only the economy but also the human beings who are its objects. If a plant is closed down, for example, the costs will include not only the unemployment pay of the workers, but the associated costs of social dislocation and individual ill health and perhaps an increase in premature death. Thus it is difficult for policy makers to hold up their hands and say 'We did not know the likely consequences of our actions' because, whether in a vague or more precise form, they often did know and, if they did not, they should have known. This issue, of course, bears not only on the distant past but more recent events of the transition that forms the basis of discussion in the second part of this book. Those who presided over this disaster cannot shuffle off responsibility for what we might call a new 'harvest of sorrow' visited on ordinary Russians in the late twentieth century. Policy makers within Russia, and their Western advisers, cannot hide behind smart suits and equations –

for their culpability is direct. They quite deliberately and consciously ruled out other alternatives and designed, assisted, and propagandised the course of change that for millions has gone so badly wrong.

A CENTURY OF POPULATION CHANGE IN RUSSIA

With these ideas in mind let us sketch in the basic features of population change in Russia in the twentieth century. This will enable us to outline the major trends and to introduce some of the basic ideas of population analysis around which much of this discussion will revolve.

Table 1.1 shows how the population of Russia grew in that century. The statistics in each column are based on different versions of the borders of the USSR-Russia. The first column shows the population of this entity at the dates indicated. The figures for 1913 and before are for the Tsarist Empire, the figures for the interwar years are for the post-civil war Soviet Union, that for 1941 incorporates the border changes that followed the Nazi-Soviet Pact of 1939. The remainder until 1991 reflects the population within the USSR's postwar borders. The figures after this date reflect Russia as it became after the collapse of the USSR and the effective independence of each of the 15 republics that made it up and amongst which Russia was the biggest and most important. This column reflects the USSR-Russia as it was for the people who lived in it at those dates and these figures are important for that reason. But with borders changing so often, we cannot use the sort of figures that appear in column 1 to analyse trends. For this we need a sense of what was happening in a constant geographical unit. Column 2 therefore shows the population of the USSR as it was, assuming that the borders that existed after the Second World War had always existed. This data has been recalculated by demographers and statisticians who have used census and other data to adjust earlier figures and so create a consistent set of statistics. It is this type of data for this version of the USSR-Russia that will be most often used in the first part of this book. Column 3 shows the population of Russia as it existed on the reduced borders after 1991 and as if they existed before 1991. Detailed earlier data for both Russia and the other republics can be derived for their population history before 1991 from the Soviet statistics and sometimes we will refer to this – though in the future the use of such reconstructed data will become more common as the fragmentation of the former USSR is consolidated.

Table 1.1   The Population of USSR-Russia 1900–91

	USSR-Russia Contemporary Borders	USSR (1989 Borders)	Russia (1992 Borders)
1897	129.2	124.6	67.5
1913	178.4	159.2	89.9
1920	–	136.8	88.2
1926	147.0	143.8	92.7
1937	162.7	–	104.9
1941	–	190.7	111.4
1959	208.8	208.8	117.5
1970	241.7	241.7	130.1
1979	262.4	262.4	137.5
1989	286.7	286.7	147.4
1991	148.5	29.0	148.5

Sources: Dillon 1897; Ransome 1928; Lorimer 1946; Goskomstat 1998, pp. 32–3.[13]

How accurate are these figures? All statistics have a margin for error. Over time, as administrative agencies improve their work, this margin of error diminishes, but it never disappears even for the most accurate data such as a census. Moreover, if, for whatever reason, administrative turmoil increases, then the margin for error can rise. In Russia we know that, despite the brave efforts of the census agencies calculating the population in 1897, 1926 and 1937 the margin for error was significant and this can complicate matters of detail. Over time things did improve so that statistics like these of the total population (and its components) can be relied upon to give as faithful a picture as possible of what actually happened. Enormous efforts have been made to understand the limitations of these data and to correct for its deficiencies. This was initially the work of Western demographers. But within the USSR unpublished attempts were also made by official demographers to identify problems before, in the *glasnost* era, discussion was opened up. It is this data that we will draw on and document in the main body of this book.

It is clear from Table 1.1 that over the century, despite the horrific crises that Russia experienced, the population grew strongly, albeit at different rates at different times. Three factors can cause a population to change – migration, a change in the birth rate, and a change in the death rate. Migration is often ignored in discussions of Russian population change but at some points it was significant though usually in the form of net emigration, that is, emigration exceeding immigration. The most important influences in Russia, however, have been changes in the birth rate and death rate. The accuracy of these will ultimately depend upon the adequacy of the registration of births and deaths – if they are not registered then they cannot be counted and in the earlier period registration was weak and crises undermined it further. At various points we will have to have regard for this. But once again we can gain a sense of the possible margin for error and with this in mind we can more confidently analyse the real trends. Note that these trends are based on a discussion of *rates* – not the absolute numbers of births and deaths. Obviously more people will be born and more will die in a population of 250 million compared to one of 150 million. But the key issue is whether the rate is different. We therefore measure birth rates, marriage rates and death rates per 1,000 population to get a sense of this. If the birth rate is more than the death rate then (ignoring migration) the population will grow, and the bigger this gap, the faster will be the growth of population.

The death rate measures all deaths against population but there is another death rate that is especially interesting – the infant mortality rate. The infant mortality rate measures deaths of infants aged under one *per 1,000 live births* (the child mortality rate measures deaths of children aged under five). This is the period in all our lives when we are most vulnerable and it is therefore a much more sensitive indicator of how people are being treated.

International agreements under auspices of the World Health Organisation, in theory, determine that all countries should calculate these statistics the same way so that they should be comparable over time and between places. However, the problem of weak administration can interfere with this and, in the 1990s, in the former USSR, administrative systems did weaken significantly. But before 1991 the USSR did not always follow WHO guidelines. This was especially a problem for the infant mortality rate. Remember that this measures infant deaths against live births. Many of these deaths cluster in the first days, even hours, of life. Sadly, many pregnancies also end with stillbirths. But the difference between a stillbirth and a very early infant death needs to be precisely defined. If, for example, a definition of a stillbirth is allowed which extends to include a period of life outside the womb, then this will bring down the infant mortality rate but raise the stillbirth rate. Comparisons over time and between countries of infant mortality will therefore be more hazardous. Unfortunately this is what happened in Soviet Russia.

There is another crucial indicator – life expectancy. Life expectancy is usually measured from birth but it could be measured from any age. It simply reflects the average length of time a person can expect to live from birth or, say, at age 20 or 40 or whatever. Poor societies have low life expectancies. As countries develop, the rate of life expectancy increases. This is what happened in Russia until the mid-1960s. But low life expectancy does not mean that there are no old people or that no one lives to a great age. Life expectancy is the average of the age at which different people die. But if the infant mortality and child mortality rates are high, then life expectancy will be low because a large minority will not live past their early childhood. The Bible famously described the human lifespan as 'three score years and ten' and even in very poor societies it is not uncommon for those who manage to survive the first years of life to get close to or perhaps exceed this. This is not to say that the very long lifespans sometimes claimed are true – in societies where births were not properly registered fallible memory sometimes added years to create the illusion of significant numbers living to 100 and beyond. In Soviet Russia this was something picked up and used by the state as propaganda to show the positive impact of the system in areas like the Caucasus where quite extraordinary and unfounded claims were supported.

Three score years and ten is not, of course, guaranteed after childhood. At different times in a person's lifecycle they will be more or less vulnerable, and we can also look at death rates and life expectancy for different age groups. Historically, for example, the child-bearing years have been dangerous for women; men have fallen more to work-based accidents and injuries. One of the central peculiarities of the transition crisis of the 1990s will require this more specific type of age–sex analysis, for the new 'harvest of death' has unusually fallen heavily on men in later middle age.

Age is important in another way. Populations will vary in their age structures. Some will have more old people, some more young people. Demographers represent this in terms of age pyramids. If there is a preponderance of young people in a society, then the birth rate will be high relative to the death rate, and vice versa. In neither case will the simple birth rate and death rate be an indication of social conditions – it will reflect more the age composition of the population. But demographers can take account of this by calculating standardised mortality rates where the different age structures are taken into account and they can look specifically at the mortality rates for different age groups or cohorts of the population. These calculations are not complicated but their exact form need not detain us. The important thing is to be aware of this factor for the analysis of population.

THE MIRROR OF SOCIETY?

But how closely does population in general, and the death rate in particular, mirror social conditions? The answer is very closely. At the broadest level, the data in Table 1.1 are the result of what is called the 'demographic transition' in Russia.[14] Historically, pre-industrial societies have had low population growth because though the birth rate has been high, so too has been the death rate. With development, living conditions improve and the death rate falls and (with or without the help of contraception) people begin to control the number of children they have. This brings down the birth rate. Eventually this results in a society with low population growth because both the birth rate and death rate are low. But in the intervening decades the death rate tends to fall faster than the birth rate causing rapid population growth. Shorn of all important qualifications and detail, this is what has happened in Russia over the last two centuries as indeed has happened in all advanced countries.

But beneath this general pattern lie much more interesting trends between and within countries. It is social inequalities and state policies that exercise a central influence on the particular way in which factors such as the death rate move. In the nineteenth century, generations of statisticians cut their teeth trying to make sense of the way in which industrialisation was affecting mortality amongst different groups and in different places. The question even became important for census takers. The British census in 1911, for example, introduced a rough concept of social class based on occupation. In the twentieth century the analysis became more precise as detailed surveys conducted by both demographers and medical specialists tried to tie down connections between social position, wealth, health, and mortality in all its forms. In Russia too, before and immediately after the revolution, statisticians and doctors were no less concerned with these relationships. Indeed the revolution stimulated a more radical spirit of enquiry with a view to improving conditions and helping to build a new society. However, with the victory of Stalin and rapid and forced industrialisation, all such investigation was banned or took place in secret.

All of what we have said relates to what we might call the *normal pattern* of death. But part of our interest in this question has been stimulated by the *abnormal patterns* created by the great crises. A mass of data exists on the years before 1928. Interpreting the impact of war, revolution, civil war and the early famine of 1921–22 on society is not hard and it was carried out in detail at the time. Thereafter, until *glasnost*, discussion in public of the tragedies of peace and war was not allowed. Even the estimates of the number of deaths in the Second World War changed by enormous amounts, Stalin quoted a figure of 6 million, Khrushchev one of 20 million. The figures were never subject to any detailed published scrutiny. For the 1930s, the silence was even more eerie. The French sociologist Basile Kerblay pointed out, for example, that 'by a sinister paradox, we are better informed as to the losses to Soviet livestock ... than about the regime's opponents who were exterminated, such as kulaks (1929–1934) or those who died in the course of Stalin's purges (1936–1939)'.[15] But, from the 1950s, a trickle of published data began to appear in both the statistical and medical press and if this did not explicitly deal with social inequality, indirectly it did throw light on it until the era of *glasnost* after 1985.

To help make sense of the data in the discussion that follows it will be helpful to think through some of the general implications of the social analysis of patterns of death. We can think of 'normal deaths' as those ordinarily arising in the vast majority of instances under 'normal' circumstances (i.e. without war, repression, famine, or 'natural' disasters – the main types of 'abnormal' deaths). There are three layers of determining factors of these normal deaths. The most basic are the *macro determinants* – the broad, political, economic and social factors that ultimately determine real income and living standards. We make the explicit assumption that the higher the average real per capita income of a society, the higher should be the average life expectancy at birth, and hence the lower will be the average mortality rate.

Figure 1.1 provides a diagram that attempts to set out the macro determinants of the normal mortality rate. Increases in income and living standards should result in declining mortality rates and rising life expectancy; conversely, declining incomes and living standards will tend to result in increased mortality rates and falling life expectancy. As the diagram shows, there are a number of determining factors of real income per capita. Development is affected by the international environment, which is an external factor usually beyond the state's control. The stronger or larger the economy, the more it will be able to withstand a deteriorating international economic environment, and the opposite will apply to weak, smaller economies, assuming that they are open market economies. But the international environment also involves other forms of competition and pressure most notably military and great power and imperial conflicts which can also have an impact on internal politics and priorities.

Figure 1.1   Theorising the Macro Determinants of 'Normal' Mortality Rate

Clearly the economic policy of any state has an important effect on economic development. But this will be dependent on the nature of the political system. The more power is dispersed, the greater the degree of democracy, then the greater the likelihood of implementation of strong welfare policies, and policies designed to lead to widening and deepening of development and the lifting of income per capita. The opposite effects are likely the greater the level of authoritarianism. However, the nature of income distribution is also crucial, particularly at higher levels of development. Evidence suggests that an unequal distribution of income accentuates health problems and consequently has a deleterious effect on life expectancy and the converse is the case for a more equal distribution of income.[16] An article in the *Financial Times* by Michael Prowse, inspired by the ideas of R.G. Wilkinson, provides a clear summary of the consequences of inequality:

> Economic inequality is correlated with status differentials, with declining civic participation, and with lack of control for those at the bottom of hierarchies. Such adverse social environments create high levels of stress, anxiety, and insecurity as well as feelings of shame and inferiority. And these, in turn, cause higher rates of serious illness and death, including death as a result of violent crime.[17]

In regard to employment policies, we will also more contentiously suggest that a more proactive 'interventionist' state may better be able to minimise levels of unemployment and generate employment. Another crucial factor which determines not only real income per capita but also directly has an impact on the normal mortality rate is what can broadly be defined as 'social welfare policy' (the sum of health, sanitation, education and welfare policies). Universal expenditure on healthcare, education, housing, social services, environmental pollution, unemployment benefits and pensions all affect mortality rates. Along with these, the provision of clean water, and acceptable levels of sanitation and sewage services also contribute towards lowering mortality rates. These policies, however, are directly affected by the nature of the political system – again, the more genuinely open to popular influence it is, the more the likelihood of expenditure on social welfare.

The next layer of determining factors is that of *'meso' factors*. These are set out in Table 1.2 under four broad categories. Though there is an element of arbitrariness, this does help to delineate the categories and it allows us to focus on the determinants of each type of mortality. We can divide meso determinants under physiological (that provide the majority of normal deaths and may be thought as being 'internal' to the person), behavioural, psychological and environmental determinants. The latter three determinants can be considered as being 'external'.

Obviously, there is a degree of overlap. For example, stress (a 'behavioural' determinant) can lead to increased alcohol consumption that may, in turn, generate diseases such as cirrhosis of the liver (a 'physiological' determinant); or it may also be the catalyst for alcohol-induced acts of violence such as murder (a 'psychological' determinant). The third layer of factors are the *'micro' determinants* which ordinarily refer to the 'immediate' cause of death. Table 1.2 shows that each meso determinant can be divided into micro determinants as follows: physiological determinants can lead to death from ageing (e.g. organ failure) and disease; behavioural determinants can cause death due to accidents, stress, work and violence; psychological determinants can lead to acts of suicide or murder; and finally environmental determinants can work through the effects of pollutants.

Table 1.2   Typology of 'Meso' and 'Micro' Determinants of Normal Mortality Rate

→ Meso Determinants	Physiological	Behavioural	Psychological	Environmental
Micro Determinants	Ageing Disease	Accidents Stress-related Work-related Violent	Murder Suicide	Pollutants

All these micro determinants can be further categorised into ultimate physiological 'causes' that end life. So, for example, for any particular disease we can ascertain the exact bacterium or genetic abnormality responsible for death. Though these 'final' determinants are of great importance to medical science, we do not dwell on them here. The precise 'ultimate' determinant provides only a partial understanding of an overall explanation and trends of mortality. The point was forcefully made by Lewontin in his discussion of the causes of tuberculosis.

It is certainly true that one cannot get tuberculosis without a tubercle bacillus ... [b]ut that is not the same as saying that the cause of tuberculosis is the tubercle bacillus ... Suppose we note that tuberculosis was a disease extremely common in the sweatshops and miserable factories of the nineteenth century, whereas tuberculosis rates were much lower among country people and in the upper classes. Then we might be justified in claiming that the cause of tuberculosis is unregulated industrial capitalism, and if we did away with that system of social organisation, we would not need to worry about the tubercle bacillus.[18]

The idea that we should not worry about the tubercle bacillus may seem strange. After all, who wants to get tuberculosis? And if we get it, then shouldn't we go to the doctor to be cured? But medical intervention was not what brought down tuberculosis rates. It was, as Lewontin suggests, social improvement and the battles to limit 'unregulated capitalism'. And now tuberculosis is re-emerging in Russia – what has brought it back is not medical failure but political and socio-economic failure.

After the Second World War, the World Health Organisation famously defined health not negatively, as the absence of disease, but more positively, as 'a state of complete physical, psychological and social well-being'. Across the world, investigators who have explored this idea have found what are often called 'steep class gradients' in the ability to attain this state. The closer to the bottom, the more incomplete the state of 'physical, psychological and social well-being', and the converse is the case for those the closer to the top. This is because the physiological, behavioural and psychological factors affecting our capacity to enjoy a healthy life and survive to an old age are all socially determined.

Low incomes, poor education, inadequate housing, lack of employment, bad working conditions as well as polluted and unpleasant environments all come to be reflected in the gradients of disease and death. Indeed, they become marked in the bodies of the living from birth since the worse the conditions the greater the chances of low birth-weights, congenital abnormalities, etc., even when the baby survives the problem of infant mortality. Then mild nutritional differences for large groups also affect physical development having their consequences in terms of height, weight and even the age of onset of puberty so that the human body itself becomes a carrier of the marks of development as well as social differences between classes. A growing historical literature now exists on this and the techniques used to chart and analyse these patterns in the West are now being applied to Russian history too.[19] Pressure and stress affects people more at the bottom than at the top. This is because their lives are more subject to uncertainty (e.g. threats of unemployment and related poverty); because they have fewer resources to fall back on (e.g. savings) and because they lack the power to make themselves heard. The second element – the behavioural – also reflects the way in which lifestyles are socially constructed as patterns of eating, drinking, smoking, leisure activities, political activities, etc., vary across social groups.

If we take these elements together, we find overwhelming evidence of not merely a socially constructed pattern but a pattern which mirrors the basic divisions of society in a sharp and illuminating way. The pattern of death reflects vulnerability to early death from illness and disease, and vulnerability to violence, whether in the form of work-related or non-work-related accidents, suicide or murder.

'Normal' deaths, as we have noted, apply to relatively stable, 'normal' conditions. In more volatile conditions, as the years of transition in Russia and beyond, peculiar results have arisen with a significant rise in the death rate. The increased *formal* democratisation and the move towards multi-party parliamentary democracy have not necessarily led to economic and welfare policies designed to improve the material conditions of the majority. Under conditions of economic and institutional dislocation, reform policies of an ostensibly more democratic regime, but one built on profound demoralisation, have led to a deterioration in the level of development and decline in real incomes and living standards – and, in consequence, a negative effect on mortality rates. Why did ostensibly more democratic governments wilfully launch into policies that were likely to lead to such a damaging effect on their populations, on the very people who elected them? Such an intensely perverse result can only arise because the replacement of the authoritarian state has led to a very curtailed democratic system in which real power has not been opened up to popular control.

The premature death that arises as part of the 'normal death rate' usually gets less attention than the 'abnormal' crises of mortality. But in terms of the total deaths, those which occur year in year out (albeit with variation in rates) can add up to the greatest number. This leads to another word of warning. In analysing normal death, there is a natural tendency to be drawn to what appears to be spectacular – the epidemics of cholera, typhoid, smallpox or whatever. Such clusterings of deaths leave an indelible mark on public consciousness and therefore on the historical record. But they usually make a small mark on the mortality figures. Premature death from more banal causes can kill so many more – whether it be the death of a baby from diarrhoea or the adult from tuberculosis which is endemic in a society. But since death of this kind seems to be 'all around' it tends to be taken for granted as part of the inevitable lot of the poor even though the devotion of a relatively small amount of resources to the problem could remove it completely and therefore eliminate the waste of life and hope. This is not a mistake that we wish to make or to encourage the reader to make. The day-to-day tolerance of premature death speaks not to the indifference of those who experience it, but of those who have the capacity to change it but do not.

Let us now consider 'abnormal deaths'. Abnormal deaths come in waves – the death rate shoots up creating intense periods of mortality. This can be a product of war, which, in the twentieth century, affected Russia more than most states. It can be a product of dramatic crises, like drought, famine and earthquakes. We often refer to these as 'natural disasters' but in a world of abundance the question should rather be why more resources are not devoted to avoiding them and protecting people from their consequences. This too is something that is class structured. The well-built houses of the rich tend to survive earthquakes. The buildings of central government tend not to collapse. In famine, wealth and power protect. Amartya Sen writes, for example, that famine 'usually affects less than 5 to 10% of the population. Because those who starve are also amongst the poorest, their share of income or food is often between 2 to 4% ... a famine may wipe out millions but it rarely reaches the rulers.'[20] The same applies in respect of civil unrest, civil wars and wars, and state repression. Wealth and position enable people to avoid direct participation, they enable them to buy themselves a greater degree of relative security, even if it is only the security to flee within or outside of the country.

Nothing that has been said so far has been particularly radical. It has been part and parcel of a sociology of health and death that has been known for generations. The economist Amartya Sen was even awarded a Nobel Prize for Economics in 1998 in part for his work on 'the economics of life and death'. For Sen,

> Mortality data provides a gauge of economic deprivation that goes well beyond the conventional focus on income and financial means. The assessment of economic achievement in terms of life and death can draw attention to pressing questions of political economy. This perspective can help in providing a fuller understanding of famine, health care and sexual inequality, as well as poverty and racial inequality, even in advanced societies ... [21]

Yet, and here is the paradox, little of this creeps into the everyday analysis of the world, especially in economic analysis, even though it takes us to the heart of contemporary controversies over wealth, power, poverty, exploitation, and alienation. A cynic would say that this is no coincidence. Despite the efforts of influential theorists such as Sen, it is thought best not to examine these connections too closely, to keep things separate and to avoid embarrassing links. But they cannot be avoided and not least in the history of a country like Russia. Rather than being reticent about such connections, we explicitly aim to bring these to the fore in this book.

2   The Revolt Against Class Society 1890–1928

'We all depart, we shall all die, monarchs and rulers, judges and potentates, rich and poor and every mortal being', say the words of the Orthodox funeral service. In the grave, 'man is bare bones, food for worms and stench ... What have we become? What is a poor person, what a rich? What a master, what a free? Are not all ashes?'[1] In Russia before 1914 death was commonplace. With a population of some 170 million the high birth rate meant that over 5 million new lives were created each year but over 3 million were taken away, most prematurely and many as infant and child deaths. We should never underestimate the pain of loss. The rituals of death can help give meaning to a person's life. But the dead cannot hear the words. They are meant to comfort the living – 'blessed are those who mourn for they will be comforted'. But they were comforted by a deception. Whatever the equality of the grave, it is the inequality of life that matters. And that inequality determines when and how we go to the grave.

The funeral and burial of a Tsar, for example, was a 'scenario of power'.[2] Alexander III died on 20 October 1894 in his Crimean Palace of Livadia. His funeral train arrived in Moscow on 30 October. Then, after due ceremony, it arrived in St Petersburg on 1 November. On 7 November, before his family, his courtiers and the crowned heads of Europe and their representatives, with the forces of bodily decomposition outrunning the leisurely pomp of state ceremony, Alexander was buried.[3] Each year, lesser scenarios of power were also played out. Some who had this choice did not want it. Leo Tolstoy wrote in his diary in the 1890s that he should be buried where he died and if this were in a city then 'let it be in the very cheapest graveyard and in the very cheapest coffin, such as beggars are buried in, without flowers, wreathes or speeches'.[4] But for the mass of Russians there was no choice. Their passing was marked with the simplest of ceremonies in the 'cheapest graveyards' or village plots with the 'cheapest coffins'.

An orthodox funeral by law had to be taken by an orthodox priest. The service had also to be in the appropriate language lest the ceremony mark a rejection of the Russifying policies of the state. When Tolstoy actually died in November 1910 there were meetings and demonstrations, even strikes, across Russia to commemorate his life and some 7,000–8,000 escorted his coffin to his estate at Iasnaia Poliana. Political funerals in cities could escape the control of the authorities – allowing opponents of the regime to establish in public the place of the deceased in the 'martyrology' (it was their term) of those struggling politically for a better life in this world. The government was no less anxious that its individual victims – political prisoners, for example – should, if possible, be buried at night in unmarked graves. And this could occur collectively on a vaster scale. The coronation of Nicholas II on 18 May 1896 resulted in a huge tragedy at Khodynka Field in Moscow where hundreds of thousands had gathered to celebrate and receive gifts. The crowd surged and panicked and officially 1,389 were killed and many more injured. Responsibility was laid at the feet of Grand Duke Sergei Alexandrovich, the Governor General of Moscow. A battle took place for the ear of Nicholas. While one Grand Duke warned the emperor that it should not be said that 'the young Tsar danced while his murdered subjects were taken from the Potter's Field', Sergei and other Grand Dukes convinced Nicholas that it would create an equally bad impression if the celebrations ended early. He needed to show 'less sentimentality'. Ever sensitive to his position, Nicholas chose to go on. In royal circles the incident soon passed. But the stain remained, its victims buried in a mass grave in the Vaganovskoe cemetery in Moscow, 'forever a blot on your reign' as a more liberal Grand Duke had warned Nicholas.[5]

On the night of 9–10 January 1905 another blot was added as more victims were quietly buried in another mass grave in the dead of night in the Preobrazhenskoye cemetery in St Petersburg. These were bodies of demonstrators shot on Bloody Sunday as, led by a priest Father Gapon, they had marched to the Winter Palace to petition the Emperor. More than a 100 were killed and 2,000 wounded when troops opened fire. 'Lord, how painful and how sad!' wrote the Tsar in his diary, and then he added: 'Mama arrived from town straight to Church. Lunched with everyone. Went for a walk with Misha. Mama stayed with us for the night.'[6]

In both 1896 and 1905 the speedy and anonymous burial of the victims in mass graves while relatives and friends still searched and hoped, denied the dead a clearly known resting place. But the graveyards of Russia did generally record the place of rest for most of the population dying in any year. But the divisions of life continued to be reflected in the places of burial and their monuments. In the countryside, wealth and power in death might be near neighbours of poverty and degradation. But in the large towns a more appropriate hierarchy was maintained. In St Petersburg the Romanov Tsars were buried in the Cathedral of Saints Peter and Paul in the Peter and Paul Fortress. Orthodox patriarchs, on the other hand, were buried in the Uspenskii Cathedral in the Moscow Kremlin. Those with wealth, power, and fame continued to find places of honour in the central cemeteries of the two cities. The memorial art, the tombstones, famous sculptures, and epitaphs marked out in death those who had position in life. Across most of Russia and especially in the countryside, remembrance was simpler. Wooden crosses recorded the dead and then rotted. But it was no less, and perhaps more, genuine as the living came to the smaller cemeteries, often fenced or railed, where even today they sit and sometimes picnic amidst their memories.[7]

MORTALITY IN TSARIST RUSSIA

'In terms of the size of its population Russia occupies first place amongst the civilised countries of the world' boasted the first issue of the Tsarist government's new statistical annual published in 1905.[8] But on almost every other indicator of human welfare it was last. In 1916, in a pioneering analysis of the death rate and life expectancy, the demographer S.A. Novoselskii wrote that 'the Russian death rate is generally typical for countries that are agricultural and backward in sanitary, cultural and economic relations'.[9] But backwardness is not an inevitable state. Novoselskii and other contemporary commentators on Russia's high death rate well understood that death in Russia was socially determined. 'There is nothing in the nature of man that would force us to accept disease as man's inevitable destiny,' said Friedrich Erismann, one of the pioneers of public health in Tsarist Russia. 'We find that the mortality of man is most intimately connected with the imperfection of our mode of living.'[10]

During the nineteenth century Tsarist Russia had been drawn more closely into the international capitalist economy. Russia did begin to move forward, albeit not fast enough to begin to close the gap with the advanced European states. Output per head expanded, industrial growth occurred and urbanisation intensified as can be seen in Table 2.1.

Table 2.1   Population and Urban Growth in European Russia 1811–1914 (000s)

	Population	Urban	% Urban	St Petersburg	Moscow
1811	41,805.6	2,765	6.61	335.6	270.2
1838	48,825.4	4,577*	9.27	470.2	349.1
1863	61,175.9	6,105	9.98	539.5	462.5
1885	81,725.2	9,964.8	12.19	–	–
1897	93,442.9	12,049.3	12.89	1,264.9	1,038.6
1914	121,780.0	18,596.8	15.27	2,118.5	1,762.7

*The urban data refer to 1840 and not 1838.

Source: Rashin 1956, pp. 98, 11.

In 1913, the Russian Empire had the lowest per capita income in Europe save for the Ottoman Empire but it was the world's largest grain exporter and the fifth largest industrial power in the world. It also had a huge army, a growing navy which Russia's rulers needed to uphold its position as a great power and to achieve imperial ambitions of their own. While poverty and lack of development therefore kept the death rate high this was not an innocent effect, it reflected the way in which capitalism was developing in Russia and the priorities of those who controlled the Russian state and society.

Economic change was occurring in an empire which occupied 22 million square kilometres, 74.6% of which was in 'Asia'. This was one-sixth of the globe. The 50 provinces of European Russia alone were 16 times the size of the UK and to them must be added much of modern-day Poland, Finland, the Central Asian states and the vast expanses of Siberia. Growth was necessarily uneven. 'Every stage of civilisation is represented,' said one contemporary journalist, 'from that of nomads who prepare and cook their meat using it as a saddle during the day's ride, to the *blasé* Franco-Russian readers of the *Figaro* on the banks of the Neva and Moskva.' Tsarist statisticians saw themselves as part of the modernising process. The first ever national census was held on 28 January 1897. Inevitably it had many deficiencies but it was also the largest household questionnaire based census then held anywhere in the world. The weight of the questionnaires issued was over 1,000 tons and most were filled in by an army of enumerators who questioned the largely illiterate rural population themselves.[11] The detailed data allowed the first calculations of relatively accurate statistics of issues such as life expectancy.

Table 2.2 sets out the basic demographic data for late Tsarist Russia. It shows us a society with a high birth rate, a high death rate and low life expectancy which was just beginning the first stages of the demographic transition.

Table 2.2   Birth and Death Rates and Life Expectancy in Tsarist Russia 1868–1912

	Birth Rate per 1,000	Death Rate per 1,000	Infant Mortality per 1,000 Live Births	Life Expectancy at Birth in Years	
				Male	Female
1868–72	49.7	38.4		27	29.5
1873–77	51	35.1		28	30.2
1878–82	49.6	36.7			
1883–87	50.3	34.9	261	29	31
1888–92	49.6	36.5	279		
1893–97	49.7	33.8	266	30.8	32.6
1898–1902	48.9	31.8	260		
[1896–97]				31.32	33.41
1903–08	47.2	30	247	32.4	34.5
1908–12	44.7	28.6			

Source: Novoselskii 1958.

The crude death rate was highest in the countryside, but this is misleading. Calculated on an age-standardised basis, the towns were less healthy, acting as 'reservoirs of disease'. Novoselskii calculated that the standardised death rate was 32.09 per 1,000 in rural areas, 35.53 in small towns and 36.75 in towns with populations of more than 1,000.[12]

But there was variation across the empire. In European Russia in 1899, only three provinces (in the Baltic) had crude death rates of less than 20 per 1,000; 23 had crude death rates below 31, and 23 had rates of 31 and above, with one more province having over 40 per 1,000. The rural death rate was highest in the overpopulated and heavily agriculture-dependent *guberniia* (a province under the Tsarist system of government) of the central black earth area and the eastern *guberniias*. It was lowest in the western and north-western *guberniias* and the more developed areas that later became Poland, the Baltic States and Finland.[13]

Table 2.3 puts the main causes of death into three largely self-explanatory categories – those arising from infectious or communicable disease, those arising from degenerative disease and those arising from violence in the loosest sense. Less developed societies are characterised by a heavy loss of life from infectious disease. 'In no country in the world are infectious diseases so mortal as in Russia', said one contemporary.[14] As the demographic transition takes place, so it is underpinned by a disease or epidemiological transition. Infectious diseases eventually decline to less than 5% of all deaths – the majority of which come increasingly from degenerative disease and violence of all types, but before 1914 this shift was barely beginning in Russia.

Table 2.3   Main Causes of Death

Infectious-Communicable Disease	*Chronic Degenerative Disease*	*Violent Deaths*
Air-borne: Tuberculosis, measles, whooping cough, smallpox, pneumonia, influenza, diphtheria *Water- and food-borne*: Diarrhoea, typhoid, dysentery, cholera *Vector-borne*: Typhus, malaria, plague, rabies, anthrax *Personal contact*: Venereal diseases, leprosy	Heart disease, cancer, strokes, arteriosclerosis diabetes, cirrhosis, ulcers	*Accidents*: Home, workplace, at large *'Criminal'*: Infanticide, suicide, murder *Political violence*: Civil violence War

Table 2.3 also shows the main causes of death from infectious diseases by means of their method of transmission – air, water and food, vectors such as lice, and personal contact as in venereal diseases and some other diseases. The greatest number of cases of disease and usually death derived from airborne diseases, followed by water-borne and then vector-borne, but in crisis years the role of water-borne and vector-borne diseases increased most sharply.

As noted in Chapter 1, it is epidemic diseases that usually get the most attention. Local and national epidemics were regular occurrences, often stimulated by harvest failures.[15] There were few cases of plague (3,500 cases were recorded between 1905 and 1914) though it produced intense fear. Cholera epidemics were more regular. That of 1870 was part of a global pandemic. Cholera struck again in 1892 and again just before the war. In 1909–10 over 100,000 died of cholera.[16] Typhus was known as the 'famine disease'. Registered typhus cases averaged 82,000 a year between 1897 and 1917 but they had a clear cyclical pattern.[17] So too did typhoid. The smallpox rate varied between 45 and 118 per 10,000 between 1890 and 1913.[18]

Diarrhoeal diseases, especially in infants, leading to dehydration and death are an obvious example of endemic diseases, although they could also accompany crisis. Such diseases can arise directly from a lack of food but they are also associated with a cluster of other factors associated with poverty. It has also been suggested that fungal diseases especially affecting rye – the bread grain of the poor – also encouraged basic diarrhoea infections. No adequate statistics exist of the tens of thousands of infant lives lost each year to such a basic infection.[19] Tuberculosis is another major endemic disease that is better recorded for the towns where the statistics showed rates typical of early nineteenth-century Western Europe.[20]

The dominance of infectious disease also determined the age distribution of death. Figure 2.1 sets out deaths by age group for 1899. The most susceptible to death were babies and young children and the key indicators of the mortality problem were therefore infant and child mortality. In countries like Russia, the great horror of modern society, for the parent to have to bury the child, was the norm before 1914. Most children did not survive beyond the age of five and this accounts for the very low life expectancy. If they did survive then life expectancy was better. Some 60% of those who reached five could expect to live beyond 40 and over a third could expect to live beyond 60.

The imbalance between male and female deaths in the first years is partly a function of the greater resilience of female babies and partly the probable skewed under-recording of infant deaths. The greater share of female deaths between the ages of 15 and 40 reflects the ways in which reproductive health and infectious disease interacted, with some women dying in childbirth of complications, and others of infectious disease shortly after. Crisis years also change the age structure of death. Bad years might increase mortality by killing more children but a cholera epidemic might kill off proportionally more adults.[21]

Life and death also had a strongly seasonal pattern, especially in the countryside. Figure 2.2 shows how marriages were clustered at

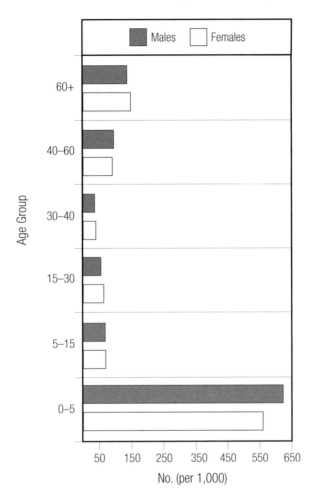

Figure 2.1   Deaths per 1,000 by Age Group in 1899

Source: Calculated from Tsentralnyi statisticheskii komitet 1905, p. 109.

certain times of the year, conceptions had a seasonal element and
so necessarily did births.[22] Death too came unequally as the annual
cycle passed. These fluctuations reflected several elements. The
amount of food available varied throughout the year, so did the
demands of agricultural labour and seasonal work in the towns.
Religion accentuated this seasonal pattern by discouraging marriage
and sex at certain times of the year. As a result, the high level of

infant mortality partly made the seasonal death rate a reflection of the pattern of marriage, conception and birth. But the pattern of death also reflected the uneven pattern of disease. Diarrhoeal diseases were most common in the late spring and summer months. Louse-borne typhus was more common in winter and early spring as people lived in overcrowded conditions, and so was TB. Hidden within the seasonal pattern were also work-related deaths: agricultural work-related deaths in July and August, for example, when harvest work was most intense.

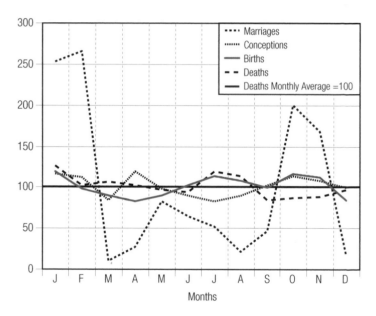

Figure 2.2   Monthly Cycle of Life and Death in 1889

Source: Calculated from Tsentralnyi statisticheskii komitet 1905, p. 108.

THE CLASS PATTERN OF DEATH

An examination of the causes of death in Table 2.3 easily shows that some self-evidently fall more on one class than another. Accidents at work will tend to befall the employee, whether worker or peasant, and not the employer. Infanticide, murder and even suicide are more often found amongst the poor. In civil disturbances it will be less likely for the rich and powerful to suffer. Degenerative disease we will set aside here since at this point it is less significant, though it will figure prominently later. The key issue that needs further exploration is the incidence of infectious disease.

By definition this is not completely exclusive. The rich come into contact with the poor at work, in the street and at home through their servants. Tchaikovsky died in still-mysterious circumstances in 1893, possibly the most famous victim of the cholera epidemic of the early 1890s. Chekhov, a doctor, succumbed to tuberculosis. Many doctors employed by the *zemstvos*, the *de facto* local government organisations, died from infectious diseases and especially from typhus.[23]

But infectious disease, and mortality from it, still has a clear class pattern because exposure to infection and susceptibility to it tend to follow the pattern of inequality and, therefore, tend to be disproportionally present in some parts of the population and not others. 'Cholera, just as typhus, is the disease of the "proletariat", for, of course, diet and misery are the important etiological factors in the disease', said one doctor.[24] Figure 2.3 (overleaf) shows the three basic elements involved. The pattern of infectious disease (morbidity) is a function of two elements – social conditions in which the microorganisms flourish and the susceptibility of the human body to infection which is itself a function of general well-being. Mortality from the infection is then a function of well-being and the care received. It is important to distinguish between medical care which, for large populations, probably had a minimal impact and the general care in the home which supported the physical and mental well-being of the sick person, and therefore created a better chance of recovery.

Given the thin layer of other social classes in the countryside, the crude death rate there tended to closely measure the death rate of the peasantry. How much differentiation there was within the peasantry remains controversial. To the extent that gaps existed, then the weight of death most likely fell on the poorest and, especially in the crisis years, on the small peasant, the landless peasant and the labourer.[25] But how far class gradients of death existed within the peasantry as opposed to between them and the middle and upper classes remains to be explored.

All the larger towns exhibited sharp internal variations in the spatial pattern of disease, general mortality and infant patterns. In Moscow, for example, the crude death rate in 1911–13 in the Prechistenskii area was 13.8 per 1,000 compared to 36 per 1,000 in Miasnitskii which contained the notorious Khitrov market slum. While the typhus rate was 12.1 per 100,000 in the former, it was 122.2 per 100,000 in

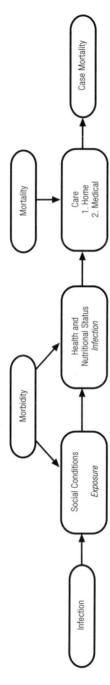

Figure 2.3 Relationship of Class, Infectious Disease and Mortality

Miasnitskii. Such gaps in the larger town regions were apparent in St Petersburg too. In 1913, the death rate average was 21.1 per 1,000 for the city as a whole. However, in the better-off Admiralty, Kazan and Litieny regions, it did not rise above 13.1, while in the poorer Alexandro-Nevsky, Moskovskii and Narva areas it rose to above 26 per 1,000, and the gaps were even greater on a more micro-basis.[26]

Vigdorchik carried out a pioneering investigation of the infant mortality rate amongst workers and showed, as is clear in Figure 2.4, how increases in basic income reduced infant mortality. He also related it to childcare since in families where the mother worked, the infant mortality rate was 19.5, but it was 25.9 per 100 where she did not.

Perhaps the best study, however, was by Novoselskii who took data from the 1910 Petrograd city census allocating the different administrative areas to seven different groups depending on economic indicators. He then related these to the pattern of deaths in 1909–12. The standardised death rate in the poorest areas was over twice that of the richer, and the infant mortality rate nearly 2.5 times as high. He then extended the analysis by examining 20 causes of death. Only

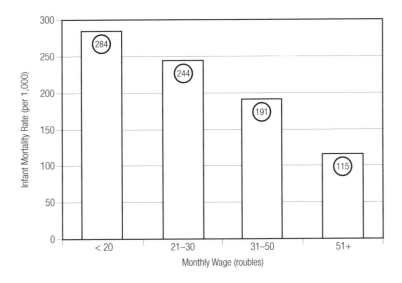

Figure 2.4   Relationship of Infant Mortality Rate and Income Amongst Workers in Pre-War Petrograd

Source: Vigdorchik 1914.

suicide and appendicitis, he suggested, showed little relation to economic conditions.[27] Today the dismissal of a link to suicide would certainly be contested.

These class gradients of death were not simply a product of the low level of development but of class itself. The formal social divisions of Tsarist Russia with its landed aristocracy and bureaucracy, its craft workers in traditional industry, its factory workers and miners, and its mass of peasants are well known. The economic dimension of these divisions is less well understood. Wealth – the *stock* of land, capital, and other assets – is always more unevenly distributed than income, which is defined as a *flow* over time. In Russia the state held enormous resources as did the aristocracy and the emerging capitalist class, but the majority of the population died with the barest of possessions. But income too was highly concentrated. According to one contemporary estimate, 0.9% of the economically active population accounted for 22% of income.[28]

All this came to be reflected in contrasting standards of living, access to sanitation and clean water and a wider healthy environment, patterns of education and behaviour and the availability of medical care. The relationship between social inequality and death was therefore more than a simple correlation, it was a product of an active relationship in which those who laboured in the fields, workshops and factories produced a wealth that they were not allowed to enjoy. This was well put in 1905 by the Bakers' Union:

> Petersburg society does not know that, in the basement under the floor of beautiful pastry shops and attractive bread stores, truly penal labour is going on ... Where else do people work eighteen to twenty hours a day? Nowhere; only we do. Where else are holidays unknown? Nowhere; only among us. We know neither Easter, nor Christmas, nor New Year's Day. Where else do people sleep in crowded, filthy housing? Where do they sleep in shifts, with no time for cots to cool? Here amongst bakers.[29]

The details of the story could vary across the lower classes but the point was valid for all.

But some improvement was taking place before 1914, as is evident from the slight falls in the death rate and infant mortality. Novoselskii was able to show that a perceptible decline in the recorded amount of infectious disease lay behind this, as can be seen in his calculations reproduced in Figure 2.5.[30]

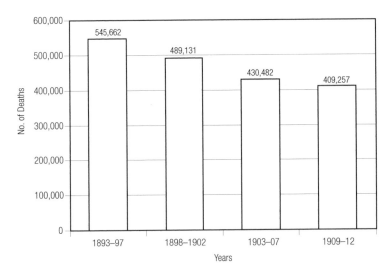

Figure 2.5   Deaths from Acute Infectious Diseases

Source: Novoselskii (1958), p. 72.

Yet this hardly supports a benign interpretation of the capacity of
capitalism to develop Tsarist Russia.[31] The improvement was slow
and uneven. This was partly because the overall rate of growth of
the Tsarist economy was uneven. But it was also because the benefits
of this growth were unevenly distributed, as they were elsewhere,
because of the social divisions built into the system. Simply waiting
for time and the market to solve the problem of health and death
ignores the way in which even as some improvements occur, the
class gradients of death are reproduced.[32] Left to their own devices,
markets reproduce what is sometimes termed a pattern of 'inverse
care'. Instead of resources flowing to where they are most needed,
the very poverty that creates ill health denies the poor and the sick
the ability to 'buy' a solution. Breaking this cycle requires not only
an increased standard of living but also massive investment in public
health that markets are notoriously unable to provide. Challenging
this in Russia before 1914 therefore needed a wider challenge to class
division and to the priorities of Tsarism. Presiding over a capitalism
marked by its combination of advanced and backward forms, the
leaders of the Tsarist state consistently showed that the welfare of
the mass of the population figured much lower in their scale of
priorities than other concerns.

WAR AND REPRESSION

Not the least of these priorities was Russia's role as a great power. Military expenditure made up some 57% of central government expenditure in 1913 compared to 7% spent on health and education. Judged as a share of national income, national *and local government* spending on health and education was 2% compared to the 5% spent on the military.[33] Yet each year the majority of recruits called up had to be sent back because they were unfit and many of those who enlisted subsequently turned out to be unhealthy. Conditions in the army often did little to improve their health, as the annual army health reports made clear.[34] But armed forces exist to fight. There was still an occasional need to deploy them to consolidate 'internal' expansion – most notably in Turkestan and the Fergana Valley in 1896. But it was war with Japan in 1904–05 which brought the greatest clash before 1914. Here the weak great-power imperialism of Russia came into conflict with the emerging junior imperialism of Japan. Historians happily denounce incompetent generals, and badly supplied war efforts and defeated states invite condemnation for their failure. But the inevitability of war is generally accepted. Deaths in battle then become part of the small change of history. Many accounts do not even record this. Yet in this war some 52,500 Russian soldiers died and perhaps 77,000 Japanese.[35]

There was little real glory in any of these deaths. 'My God, how the wounded groaned now!' remembered one sailor of the Battle of Tsushima where much of the Russian fleet was sunk. 'The fitter sailors trampled them underfoot, mercilessly stamping on them as they struggled to get out. There were so many people crowding the hatches that they could go neither forward nor back. Many crawled over other people's heads.' And what was it for? A little later Afanassiev, a non-party deputy, told the post-1905 Duma (parliament) that:

> In the Japanese war I led a number of mobilised soldiers through estates of the squires. It took us forty eight hours to reach the meeting place. The soldiers asked me: 'Where do you lead us?' – 'To Japan'. 'What for?' – 'To defend our country'. They replied: 'What is that country? We have been through the estates of the Lissetskys, the Besulovs, the Padkopailovs ... Where is our land? Nothing here belongs to us'.[36]

Let us allow Afanassiev a degree of poetic licence – the point was still powerful, and it would be no less powerful once the early enthusiasm for another war in 1914 wore off.

The 1905 revolution

Not far behind the priority of external power was that of internal order. In theory, the Tsarist state was an autocracy where all power flowed from the Tsar himself. In practice it was a state of the landowners and the bureaucracy. Their great concern was to manage the tensions that arose from the way that the inequalities of the new capitalist society were merging with the inequalities of the old landed one while surrendering as little power as possible. It took revolt in 1905 to help create a Duma and even then its role was hedged with restrictions, and before and after even moderate challenges could be met with repression.

Despite its authoritarian character the Tsarist regime claimed a more liberal approach to criminal legislation, especially in respect of capital punishment. But for long periods much of the country was ruled under exceptional legislation which effectively suspended civil rights and allowed executions.[37] Moreover, prison conditions were poor for many prisoners. 'How could a prisoner in jail protect himself against phthisis when the prison authorities feed him badly and keep him in a damp cell without air and light'? asked Erismann.[38]

Communal tensions, especially anti-semitic, were rife. Such conflicts were the less troublesome to the authorities because they divided the population against one another and because the authorities shared many of the popular prejudices.[39] The peak came in 1905–06 and especially after the Tsar was forced to retreat before demands for change. The violence of the Black Hundred gangs against socialists, workers, and especially Jews seemed to the Tsar no more than they deserved. He approvingly wrote of his 'loyal people' that they 'had become enraged by the insolence and audacity of the revolutionaries and socialists, and because nine tenths of them are Yids, the people's wrath turned against them', and then gave his public support to the political face of the gangs – the Union of Russian People, with its credo of 'Tsar, Faith, Fatherland'.[40]

No such benign views were extended to peasant, worker, and national revolt. When these came together in 1905, the response of the authorities was harsh. Despite its reputation as a 'liberal revolution' the events of 1905 led to several times the number of deaths in 1917 itself, though neither number has been properly quantified. National revolution erupted in Poland where some 300,000 troops had to be stationed. On 27–28 January 1905, 64 were officially killed and 29 died later in the putting down of a general strike in Warsaw. The real figure is thought to be nearer 200. In Lodz and the Dabrowa basin, a further 200 were killed and wounded by the military and tension and bloodshed continued throughout 1905–06.[41] Peasant revolt peaked first in 1905 and then in 1906. Punitive expeditions were sent into the Baltic area, Poland, and along the route of the Trans-Siberian Railway to reinforce order by sacking, burning and, if necessary, killing: 'Don't skimp on bullets, and make no arrests', was the instruction from the top.[42] In the towns where radical consciousness grew quickly and the first Soviets were formed, there were also serious clashes. 'Bloody Sunday' in St Petersburg was quickly followed by more shootings in Riga. Smaller incidents occurred throughout 1905 but two larger incidents stand out. One was in June in Odessa in the midst of a general strike where violence flared between strikers, reactionaries, and the local authorities while the crew of the Battleship *Potemkin* mutinied in the harbour. As many as 2,000 were killed and 3,000 wounded in the fighting and communal violence.[43] Then in December 1905 came an uprising in Moscow which was put down with over 1,000 dead, many in the Presnia district which was shelled by the army.

Having defeated the revolution the Tsarist authorities reimposed order in policies that were especially associated with the Prime Minister, Stolypin. Field court martials executed more than 1,000 in 1906 and by 1909 they had sentenced 2,694 men and women to death.[44] One response to this pattern of repression involved the assassination of key officials. The most prominent victim had been Alexander II in 1882, but in the new century a succession of assassinations followed before 1905.[45] After it, the most prominent came in 1911, when Stolypin was killed by a police agent-cum-revolutionary.

But such assassinations did less damage to the state than their perpetrators imagined, and in the years between 1906 and 1914, socialists led a struggle for the soul of the popular movement. Though they were divided on other issues, they were united in trying to build on the positive developments that had occurred in popular consciousness in 1905. Their aim was to pull workers away from both the pogrom mentality and from ideas of individualistic revenge in favour of a collective and militant political response. In this they eventually had some success. The labour movement began to recover from repression from 1912, stimulated in part by protests against a massacre of some 200 workers at the British-owned Lena Goldfields. A new strike wave developed and, in the first half of 1914, nearly 1.5 million workers struck, many in July, as the crisis in the Balkans was leading to world war.

The First World War

Russia's entry into the First World War began the first (and second most intense) of the four great mortality crises that marked its history in the twentieth century. The pioneering demographer Frank Lorimer said that this first crisis was the most cataclysmic Russia had seen since the thirteenth-century Mongol invasion.[46] It also is perhaps now the most controversial. The numbers are more confused.[47] Rasputin had foreseen 'a whole ocean of tears, there is no counting them, and so much blood …'. Later Hindenburg had written of Russia's losses in the First World War alone, 'imagination may try to reconstruct the figure of these losses, but an accurate calculation will remain forever a vain thing'.[48] But the bigger question remains the politics of these deaths. The crisis began as a barbaric war fought for disreputable motives using the European population as cannon fodder. It produced an attempt to halt the slaughter and overthrow the regimes that produced it. But this in turn led to a second wave of death amidst huge social crisis as the revolutionaries tried to defend themselves.

A number of attempts have been made to calculate the total demographic losses by comparing the actual trajectory of the birth rate and death rate with what might have been expected in the absence of war. The results differ, as does the allocation of losses between 1914–17 and 1918–21/22. Table 2.4 reports the leading set of estimates.

Table 2.4   Estimates of Demographic Losses 1914–22

	1914–17	*1918–20*	*1921–22*
Military losses	c. 2 million	1 million	–
Excess civilian deaths	←	13–14 million	→
Total Deaths	←	16–17 million	→
Birth deficit	←	10 million	→
Emigration	←	2 million	→
Population Loss	8.9 million	← 19.6 million	→

Source: Lorimer 1946.

An alternative approach is to track the deaths that occurred. Table 2.5 sets out the major components that must be considered for the years 1914–17 and low and high estimates for the numbers involved. It can be seen immediately that some categories are more speculative than others.

Table 2.5   First World War Actual Deaths in Russia 1914–17[49]

	Lower Estimate	Higher Estimate
Immediate battle and front deaths	657,000	729,000
Subsequent deaths from wounds, disease, etc., in rear	430,000	1,279,000
POWs dying in captivity	182,000	285,000
Total Military Deaths	*1,269,000*	*2,293,000*
Civil losses as a result of military action	318,000	318,000
Losses from punitive action	100,000	100,000
Additional losses from diseases	386,000	501,000
Total Russian Deaths	*2,073,000*	*3,212,000*
Non-Russian POWs dying in Russia	52,000	
Other possible losses		
Army missing	200,000	797,000
Not returning from captivity	238,000	238,000
Losses from emigration	200,000	200,000

Sources: *Naselenie Rossii* 2000, p. 78; Kohn 1932.

In addition to the peacetime army of 1.4 million, 13.7 million troops were mobilised. This strained the ability of the state to equip troops, and some went into battle with no bullets in their guns, some with no guns at all. As Table 2.5 shows, there is rough agreement on the number of battle deaths. Figures for death from wounds and disease vary by a factor of five but would seem likely to lie between the extremes. To these must be added the deaths of Russian POWs in captivity. Estimates of POWs vary (from 2.4 million to 3.75 million) and so do the number dying.[50] Civilian deaths arose from the shelling of towns and villages and people being in the wrong place at the wrong time. There were also deaths from punitive actions of all sorts. The more fluid nature of the Eastern front meant that deaths here were much larger than on the Western front. Other civilian deaths are more difficult to estimate. By 1917 there were over 5 million refugees – most in a stream from Poland and the Baltics but a second stream came from Galicia (then part of the Austro-Hungarian Empire but today Poland), and a third stream in the south were Armenians fleeing Ottoman Turkey.[51] Kohn suggested that these refugees were 'dying at an incredible rate'.[52] To these must then be added the deaths of civilians away from the front as a result of increased mortality. The crude death rate figures do not suggest that this number was large but these are not reliable, as registration systems weakened and their base became narrower. They also reflect the sharp fall in the birth rate and therefore infant mortality. On an age-standardised basis the death rate therefore must have risen. How much is unclear. Rural conditions were improved by good harvests and the cessation of the international grain trade, government support for soldiers' families and the ban on alcohol. But there were also counter-trends. The urban data for St Petersburg and Moscow shows slight increases in crude and infant mortality rates. Account must also be taken of the 2 million or so foreign POWs held in Russia by September 1917. The statistics suggest that only 51,608 died. Fortunately, many prisoners were employed as agricultural labourers. Even so, it is difficult to imagine that the proportionate losses of foreign POWs in Russia were less than those of Russian POWs abroad, especially as their camps acted as 'foci of epidemic diseases'.[53]

The Tsarina became a figurehead nurse, but the mitigation of social problems was due more to the efforts of the Union of the Zemstvos and the Union of Towns than to central government. But the government then held these organisations at arm's-length and refused to allow their leaders to influence the wider war effort. This was part of its downfall. So too was the continuing repression of dissent. The biggest single example, reminiscent of what would happen later, was the suppression of conscription protests in Turkmenistan in 1916. Over 1 million people disappeared. Most probably fled but several hundred thousand may also have died directly and indirectly as a result of the state's actions.[54] This further exposed the sheer brutality of the Tsarist regime and helped to weaken its support, especially on the periphery of the Empire. But the most significant individual death was perhaps that of the Tsar's adviser Rasputin. The image of his malign influence at the centre did much to undermine confidence in the regime, and when he was killed by a group of aristocratic plotters, 'the bullet', said the poet Mayakovsky, 'went straight to the heart of the regime itself'.

REVOLUTION AND THE VISION OF THE FUTURE

Social and political tensions came to a head in February 1917 when strikes in Petrograd turned into revolution as it became obvious that

Tsarism had lost all legitimacy. The fall of Tsarism radicalised the country but February was far from bloodless. Casualties numbered well over 1,000 with at least 400 dead and perhaps more. Perhaps the greatest single demonstration of 1917 was to honour the dead killed in Petrograd, 180 of whom were now buried in a place of honour in the Field of Mars in the city on 23 March. The new provisional government reflected this mood, abolished the death penalty and promised to carry forward the spirit of the time until proper democratic foundations could be laid for a permanent government. February produced a surge of creative thinking and organisation across the whole of Russian society. In the health sphere an 'All Russian Union of Professional Association of Doctors' emerged from the Petrograd Union of Doctors founded in May 1917. Meeting in April 1917 the Petrograd Congress of Dentists was even inspired to call for the organisation of community dentistry and the radical reform of dentistry education. Then in June 1917 the provisional government established a Central Medical Sanitary Council to bring together those working to alleviate the current problems and to help look to the future. But such efforts were undermined by several factors.

The most important was the war which continued to drain life directly at the front and indirectly in the rear. In June–July, for example, partly responding to Allied pleas and partly to internal pressures, the government launched a new offensive which led to 6,905 deaths and 36,240 soldiers being wounded.[55] Splits also took place over how radical a transformation of society was needed. Radicals were insistent that health reform, as with other social changes, required an attack on private property and the role of market competition and the reallocation of health resources to match need. This position threatened the privileged position that many doctors had established under the old regime and brought tensions to the surface between their professional and social positions. The medical profession also split horizontally with *feldshers* (midway between a nurse and a doctor) and nurses proving more radical than many doctors. These arguments were far from abstract. As social conditions worsened during 1917 so the death rate began to increase and political order began to fall apart. Z.P. Solovev, a Bolshevik doctor and editor of one of the leading medical journals, argued in August 1917 that 'we have inherited from Tsarism an indifferent, hypocritical medical bureaucracy, an impotent zemstvo and urban medical system, the weak shoots of a workers medical system and a clear sense that the country, step by step, is on the way to degeneration'.[56]

Deserting troops, brutalised by the war, often acted cruelly to the local villages that they encountered on their journey home. On occasion there were large-scale pogroms such as that in Gomel' in September 1917. But it was the 'popular violence' of the workers and peasants acting more politically that caught attention then and since. In fact much of this violence was low scale and symbolic.[57] By contrast, killings by the state tended to be indiscriminate and wanton. Perhaps the most famous example of this – which helped to push the revolutionary process forward – were the deaths of up to 400 in Petrograd in the July Days. The dead were mostly protesters killed by government troops. But popular violence helped polarise views. Liberal and conservative forces, fearing the mob, increased their support for 'order' whereas radical and left forces stressed the way that the government was turning against the people whom it claimed to represent. In the weeks that followed the July Days there was a shift to the right and politicians now looked to the new Commander-in-Chief General Kornilov to create order. Then in late August he tried to move on Petrograd in what appeared to be an attempted coup before his troops were dissuaded from advancing by workers and soldiers sent out from the city to argue with them. Their commander General Krymov committed suicide in despair.

By September–October, cooperation between the socialists and liberal middle-class parties proved impossible but there was uncertainty as to how to resolve the contradictions. In the end it was the Bolsheviks who, provoked by more half-hearted attempts by Kerensky to restore 'order', made the decisive move with support from the Left Socialist Revolutionaries. 'History', said Lenin, 'will not forgive us if we do not seize power now.'[58] Concretely, what Lenin was vehemently arguing for was an end to the war and to move society beyond the limits of the capitalist system that had given rise to it. Today, most interested commentators (East and West) would no doubt pour scorn on Lenin's actions and would reverse his conclusion by asserting that 'history has not forgiven Lenin for seizing power in October 1917'.

But no one in 1917 had any illusion that they could succeed in building an alternative to capitalism in Russia alone. Rather, the argument was that revolution there could initiate a wider process of change which would encourage workers in other states to overthrow their governments and end the world war and the class war. We now know that they failed. Under Stalin a system emerged that, as we will show, was just as much conditioned by class and which was one of the most repressive regimes of the century. But contrary to conservative accounts which stress the inevitability of this defeat, we would suggest that it makes more sense to see not only the aspirations of 1917 but the social forces that made it being unravelled by the extreme pressure that the revolution came under in the next years, and not least from those forces that sought to destroy the revolution.

In the short term the seizure of power in October led to a dozen or so deaths in Petrograd, but in Moscow there was bitter fighting and as many as 500 may have died. It took until February 1918 for the revolution to consolidate itself in the rest of Russia with many towns going over peacefully, but there were serious clashes in some – especially in the Volga cities. Yet, for all this, the revolution was a generous one – foolishly generous, some thought – as its first opponents were set free on the promise of good behaviour. This generosity was in sharp contrast to neighbouring Finland, freed from Russia by the revolution. There, in early 1918, blood flowed as revolutionaries were slaughtered by counter-revolutionary forces.

Living, as Arthur Ransome said, 'on enthusiasm, sandwiches and weak tea', the revolutionaries were more concerned to lay down markers for the future.[59] These included the eight-hour day, social insurance, medical funds, etc. A special decree on infant mortality said that 'in Russia two million lives which had hardly been kindled were annually extinguished because of the ignorance of the oppressed people and the inertness of the bourgeois state. Every year two million suffering mothers shed bitter tears while filling with their toil hardened hands the early graves of those made the innocent victims of the gruesome state system.'[60] But serious attention then had to be paid to building a new order amidst the developing chaos. The war was temporarily halted by a cease-fire, but under German pressure the Treaty of Brest Litovsk only brought more permanent peace at the expense of the loss of a large part of territory, immensely complicating the social and economic situation – as did the resistance of some professional groups, including doctors.

In health it was quickly realised that there was a need for more coordination and a Central Council of Medical Boards was established in January 1918. Six months later a Congress of Medical and Sanitary Boards met and called for the creation of a Commissariat of Health. On 11 July 1918 this came into existence with N.A. Semashko, a Bolshevik and former *zemstvo* doctor, as Health Commissar and Z.P. Solovev as his deputy. This was the first Ministry of Health anywhere in the world. Its long-term aim was to build out from the prevention of disease to the creation of a free, planned and unified system of medical care for all. The immediate task was to use the few resources available to try to deal with the emerging catastrophe of the civil war that was now under way. It was this civil war that would intensify the first great mortality crisis and force up the graph of death to new heights.

Civil war: armed conflict

The civil war all but destroyed revolutionary Russia and led on to a major famine in 1921–22. It is now commonplace to describe the deaths of these years as 'Lenin's deaths' and to compare them to 'Stalin's' and perhaps later 'Yeltsin's'. Yet this comparison is misleading, and deliberately so. The deaths of the time can only be laid at the door of one side if the historians implicitly assumed that all guilt lies with those who challenge the established order while that order emerges from history guiltless. In fact the civil war was a bloody attempt by the old order to restore its reign, an attempt that was supported by Western intervention. In a century marked by Western colonialism and subsequent neocolonial interventions, which led to direct and indirect deaths that are still not properly accounted for, it ill becomes the historian, least of all the Western one, to ignore the contribution that intervention made in Russia in these years – especially in terms of general support to the counter-revolution. Moreover the West perpetuated a crucial innovation in warfare. This was the blockade. In his book *Humanity* Jonathan Glover argues that the British blockade against Germany in late 1918 and early 1919 marked a major step in the barbarisation of warfare.[61] It was deliberately targeted at civilians and so it paved the way for later developments. But he is seemingly unaware that the blockade against Soviet Russia was more complete and lasted from 1918 to 1920, preventing even medical supplies passing to the revolutionaries.

Then what of the fact that this was a civil war with deaths occurring on both sides of the lines? No serious historian in their detailed discussions absolves the anti-Bolshevik of their cruelties, so what sense does it make to do so at the aggregate level by a statistical sleight of hand? Finally, most of the deaths in these years were disease deaths. While the scale of these clearly derived from the dislocation of the era, should they be laid at the door of the established order which started the war or the revolutionaries which tried to stop it?

On a day-to-day basis the civil war was a confused conflict. While the revolution was unified, 19 different governments are reckoned to have existed at different times and in different areas amongst the revolution's opponents. Some places were continually fought over – Kiev changed hands 16 times. Formally it was four sided – the revolutionary Red Army versus the counter-revolutionary White forces with their Allied supporters. A third force of peasant-based 'Greens' saw the Whites as the main enemy when they were the greater threat but were in conflict with the Red Army when the White challenge diminished. The fourth side was the new Polish state which, encouraged by the Allies, invaded Russia in 1920, so prolonging the agony of these years. But behind this 'formal' conflict was a messier fight. Each side had to cope with widespread banditry, which was sometimes politicised but often not. This was intensified not only by the lack of order but also by widespread desertion from the armies. More serious still was peasant revolt which produced high levels of demonstrative and retributive violence on both sides. This revolt was prompted by attempts to conscript men and requisition food or to change the local revolutionary land settlement (or to prevent one). More politicised opposition was also encountered by each side from different urban groups.

Most accounts ignore these issues and simply indiscriminately lump together deaths. Given the problems faced by the Bolsheviks in defending their base in a starving Russia, it is possible that there were more violent deaths at their hands. In the crucial area of food supply, for example, requisitioning was necessary because the starving towns had nothing to offer in return. But the balance between the different elements and sides has yet to be properly accounted for and White brutality was as notorious as anything laid at the door of the Bolsheviks. 'I will say two eyes for an eye, a set of teeth for a tooth', said the White General, Dobrovskii.[62] Yet in the end the Bolsheviks won because they retained more coherence and support than their opponents. The dominant conservative historiography tries to explain this away by pointing to good fortune and strategic luck as decisive factors because it is reluctant to engage fully with the deficiencies of the Whites (or simply says 'a plague on both their houses') and because it does not want to admit that morale and politics were also decisive factors. It is worth reminding ourselves therefore that it was not Marx but Clausewitz who said of war that 'we might say that the physical seems little more than the wooden hilt, while the moral factors are the precious metal, the real weapon, the finely-honed blade'. In the end the fact that victory lay with the Bolsheviks derived more from their greater capacity to mobilise, improvise, and generate sacrifice. This in turn reflected a confidence and commitment to a better world that was lacking in the Whites who, when they were not looking backwards, were looking forward to a world closer to fascism than any semblance of democracy.[63]

No proper assessment has been made of the violent deaths that took place in fighting. Direct combatants died at the front, and later, from wounds and from disease. Civilians died as casualties of battle and from punitive actions of organised forces. Tracking the components of violent deaths at this time requires us to consider (allowing for double counting):

- deaths in and at the hands of the Red Army
- deaths in and at the hands of other Soviet units (e.g. food requisition units)
- deaths in and at the hands of White units
- deaths in and at the hands of organised peasant 'Green' units
- deaths in and at the hands of German, Austrian and Turkish intervention forces in 1918
- deaths in and at the hands of Allied intervention forces
- deaths in and at the hands of irregular forces
- deaths in communal violence
- deaths in and at the hands of Polish forces in 1920.

It should be clear from this how misleading it is simply to present undifferentiated figures laid at the door of 'Reds' and 'Whites'. Most of the violent deaths did indeed come in and through the actions of the two main sides and some estimates are set out in Table 2.6. But this does not mean that deaths from some of the other categories (e.g. communal violence) were not considerable.

Table 2.6   Estimates of Red and White Military-Related Deaths in the Civil War 1918–21

| | Combatant Deaths | | | | Civilian Deaths | |
	Front	Wounds	Disease	Total (m)	Battles	Punitive Actions
Red Army	259,000	617,000		1.1–1.25	n.k.	n.k.
Other Soviet		200–300,000			n.k.	n.k.
Whites	n.k.	n.k.	n.k.	0.9–1.3	n.k.	n.k.

Sources: *Naselenie Rossii* 2000; Krivosheev 2001, p. 149. (n.k. = not known.)

The loose attribution of deaths to 'terror' is no less of a problem. Two issues are at stake here. One is the direction of causation – were the Bolsheviks reacting to events or creating them? The conventional historiography suggests that violence arose from the ideologically driven programme of the Bolsheviks which unleashed, as did the earlier French Revolution, a vicious circle of violence. We would reject this attempt to disconnect violence from its social and economic background and see it simply as a product of ideas. But even if violence is so disconnected then, as Arno Mayer has pointed out, the argument can be easily stood on its head. Violence, he suggests, was 'fuelled above all by the resistance of forces and ideas opposed to [revolution]'.[64] The second issue is the relationship of the violence of revolutionaries to their opponents in the civil war and, later, that of Stalin in the 1930s. Historians often play a trick here by appearing to eschew a political judgement. But unless the historian rejects all forms of violence in all circumstances then judgements have to be and are made. In the Russian Revolution the conventional approach ends up siding with the established order because it fails to differentiate Stalin's later violence from that of these years and it ends up supporting the established order of the time. We would suggest, and will try to show later, that there is a world of difference between Stalin's use of violence against his own population to recreate a class-based and exploitative society after 1928 and the attempt of these years to end such a society. No less there is a difference between the violence deployed by the Bolsheviks, whatever the corruptions that occurred, and that of their opponents who were seeking to defend a system that had brought the world to barbarism and would do so again. Forced to defend itself, Lenin said, the revolution should offer no apologies for meeting violence with violence. 'To all complaints and accusations that we practice terror, dictatorship and civil war – we will reply – yes, we have openly declared what no other government has been able to declare – yes, we have started the war against the exploiters.'[65]

As problems mounted in 1918, and encouragement from outside and intervention emboldened the counter-revolution, the original generosity of the revolution gave way to a harsher response. The shooting of the royal family in July 1918 to prevent them becoming figureheads of opposition was a manifestation of this. Problems intensified even more with the revolt of the Left Socialist Revolutionaries – the Bolsheviks' partners in government, threats from the White armies, localised revolts and a number of assassinations including an attempt on Lenin's life. This led to the Decree on Red Terror of 2 September 1918 which was an open declaration that counter-revolution would be met with as much violence as was needed to defeat it. This direct repression involved a mixture of calculated harshness and panic. Dzerzhinsky, head of the *Cheka* (Extra-ordinary Commission (against counter-revolution)), said: '[T]he Cheka must defend the revolution and conquer the enemy, even if the sword falls occasionally on the heads of the innocent.' There is no doubt that some *Cheka* units got out of hand but there were also attempts to rein them in. Then the problem was that this was a fight with no quarter. While most accounts note the Decree on Red Terror in September 1918, for example, few record the massacre on 10 September of more than 1,500 peasants by the troops of Ataman Annenkov or the massacre at Maikop of 2,500 peasants on 18 September by troops of another White General, V.L. Pokrovskii.[66]

Civil war: hunger and disease

'Within a few weeks [in 1918],' said Arthur Ransome, 'the territory held by the Soviets was only a small part of Russia, consisting for the most part of districts in normal times either not self-supporting or barely capable of self-support. The revolution was cut off from the main sources of iron, cotton, oil, meat and bread.'[67] The population of Petrograd fell from 2.4 million in 1917 to 700,000 in 1920, and that of Moscow from 1.85 million to 1 million. A Petrograd trade union report of the process of decline in that city said:

> We can and know how to work. But few of our metalworkers have stayed in Petrograd. Some died in the fight for freedom, others have gone to the front, still others have left the Red capital during the evacuation, and still others have dispersed all over the country in search of bread for themselves and their families ...[68]

The sharp decline in the availability of food brought widespread malnutrition. As bodies weakened, women ceased to menstruate. Amenorrhoea (the suspension of menstruation) was 'observed everywhere, reaching up to 50–70% in certain towns'.[69] But weakened bodies also found it harder to fight disease so that fatality rates from infection increased significantly. Health was worsened by fuel shortages which not only brought intense cold to homes but also contributed to the collapse of the urban infrastructure as the existing water and sewage systems failed. Diseases of all kinds rose, but water-borne disease saw a big jump as typhoid, dysentery and even cholera spread. But the biggest jump was vector-borne diseases. A malaria epidemic which was already in place intensified dramatically. Although there were fewer recorded smallpox cases its higher level of mortality made it the bigger killer.[70] In 1918 the rise in typhus cases that we have already noted began to explode into what has been called 'the greatest typhus epidemic in history ...'.[71] The officially recorded number of cases was 6–7 million but Tarassevich, the contemporary expert, suggested 20–30 million was more accurate with deaths perhaps running at 2–3 million. Typhus affected all the fighting forces alike – even the White General, Baron Wrangel, caught it. Refugees carried it around the country and especially along the overcrowded railways and into the towns where it wreaked havoc on a malnourished population. Measures to control it were most systematic on the side of the revolution. Lenin in 1919 said, 'either the louse defeats socialism or socialism defeats the louse'.[72]

The available diseases figures are depicted in Figure 2.6. They are better indicators of relative changes than absolute levels because of the massive under-recording.[73]

Disease mortality rates varied between areas and towns, especially in relation to the food supply. Traditionally, grain had moved from grain surplus areas to the south of Moscow, northwards. Now little food moved. It was people who moved from town to country and broadly from north to south. The situation was made worse the more isolated the town or city. Petrograd suffered especially badly and the death rate hit a first peak of 90 per 1,000 in March–April 1919. Then it fell somewhat but rose again in November 1919 to April 1920 with another peak of 90+ in February 1920. In Moscow the peaks were lower but the pattern was similar.

This wave of disease was not met passively, at least not on the Bolshevik side. Despite the absence of almost all resources attempts were made to fight it and to restructure priorities. Doctors, *feldshers*, nurses, half-trained medical workers and untrained ones, all threw themselves into the struggle. Statisticians, themselves malnourished but freed from the shackles of the old system, sought to count and measure every conceivable thing including the wider contours of death. This creative impact of the revolution, continuing and in some senses intensifying from 1917, despite the dire circumstances, was another qualitative factor that distinguished the revolution from the counter-revolution.

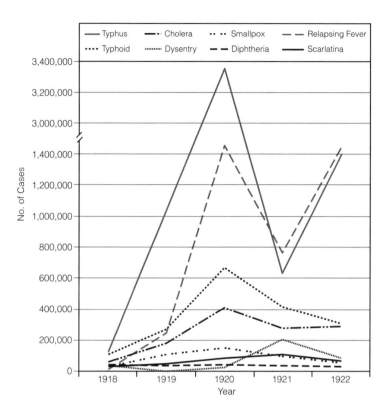

Figure 2.6   Registered Cases of Major Diseases in Russia 1918–22

*Readers should note the discontinuous scale for typhus.

Sources: Dobreitsera 1923, pp. 121–30.

But the cost of victory when it came in 1920–21 was high in both political and personal terms. 'The thought of another agonizing winter of war was unbearable. We had to make peace', said Lenin of the conflict with Poland. The base of the regime had been undercut by the urban-industrial collapse and in early 1921 the regime was faced with peasant revolt, workers' protests and revolt in the naval base of Kronstadt. Some of the best revolutionaries were dead. Most of the others were physically, mentally and politically debilitated. To recoup the situation it was necessary to move away from the war-induced centralisation, but this shift too would have shorter- and longer-term consequences that pushed the revolution in contradictory directions.

Famine and the Early New Economic Policy 1921–22

The New Economic Policy (NEP) was an attempt to create a space in which a shattered Russia could be rebuilt through the use of more market mechanisms than were possible in the war economy of the civil war years. It is often assumed that the recovery began immediately and that the market was a universal panacea. But this is not so. The shift to taxes in kind and then money and the freeing of prices eased tensions in the countryside and increased trade through more orthodox channels, but it also had negative consequences that were sharply apparent in 1921–22. Enterprises put on a self-financing basis struggled to survive and cut back employment; some went bankrupt. The number of workers continued to fall until the late summer of 1922. Self-financing also affected the state sector. In late 1921 and early 1922 medical provision was moved to a self-financing basis through local government budgets and this led to hospital closures (especially of makeshift civil war hospitals) and a reduction in beds by 30% in the RSFSR (Russian Soviet Federative Socialist Republic) (the Russian part of the Soviet Union) alone.[74] However necessary the shift to the NEP was, it is therefore not hard to see why it was viewed as something of a poisoned chalice.

Worse, the 1921 harvest was subject to major failure and in the winter of 1921–22 and the spring and early summer of 1922 massive famine developed. Although the famine was a product of the traditional drought cycle, its depth was also a product of the civil war. The worst affected area was in the Volga region. One contemporary estimate of its relative scale is set out in Table 2.7.

Table 2.7   The Historical Extent of Famine According to the 1921–22 Famine Commission

	Area Affected (acres)	No. of Provinces Affected	Population	% of Population	No. of Provinces Seriously Affected
1891	41,151,000	9	16,750,000	19	3
1906	48,578,000	10	21,143,000	22	5
1911	59,142,000	11	24,951,000	23	6
1921	49,944,000	13	25,081,000	25	12

Source: Anon., 'Statistics' 1922, p. 202.

Typhoid rates rose by 140%, relapsing fever by 125% and malaria by 61%. Epidemic disease swept into towns and other regions carried by huge refugee flows from the famine areas to the north, to the east towards Tashkent and to the south and the Ukraine.[75] Still largely isolated from the West, the government appealed for outside help but got little direct response. Western governments tried to use the famine as a bargaining counter to enforce the payment of Tsarist debts.

Aid came from private organisations like the Quakers, Save the Children Fund, and indirectly from the US government through the American Relief Administration under Herbert Hoover, an otherwise undistinguished politician and President. The former Norwegian explorer Fridtjof Nansen won a Nobel Peace Prize for his efforts in helping famine victims. Their efforts and those within the country saved a huge number of lives but could not stop the famine and related disease carrying away some 5 million people.[76]

This was the only major famine in Russia in which there were not major grain exports. But the government was caught in a trap. Without foreign exchange it could not import vital resources and equipment to help rebuild the economy. This was the context for its controversial decision to ask the Church to give up many of its valuables and then when too little was forthcoming to confiscate them. The Church's opposition has since been portrayed as a saintly struggle against incipient totalitarianism. But the Church had prostrated itself before the state before 1917 and it would do so again under Stalin. The identification of the Church's spiritual role with its worldly goods in a starving land hardly speaks well of the motives of those who led it and anathematised the Bolsheviks.

THE WANING DREAM

In physical terms Russia was now 800,000 square kilometres (4%) smaller than in 1914. But the territorial losses were nearer 15% of the area west of the Urals.[77] Divided in 1922 into six republics, Russia began to rebuild its infrastructure from the summer of that year. But the scale of the problems had increased enormously. At this point it was a land of 'broken families, homeless children and debilitated individuals' as well as a wrecked infrastructure.[78] But there was a clear commitment to widespread social improvement focused especially on the situation of workers and peasants. Demographers and health specialists produced a mass of studies: information not only poured out within Russia, but was also supplied to the Health

Section of the League of Nations. Local censuses were held to improve the basic data, but the crowning glory came on 17 December 1926 with Russia's second nationwide census. Public health planners and doctors worked to bring social improvement, though in the first instance far less pleasant tasks had to be undertaken.

Because capitalism was being broken, the belief was that it should be possible to avoid the most negative features characteristic of the past in Russia and of other contemporary societies. The best could be emulated and where possible surpassed in ways that reinforced the movement towards socialism, albeit constrained by the internal situation in Russia in the 1920s and its relative external isolation.

In practice the pressure of these constraints was enormous and it often needed heroic commitments just to avoid the worst elements, let alone emulate and improve. But the constraints also had an undermining impact on the commitment to deliver something different. Semashko had expressed the common idea of the revolution when he said that 'the health of the working masses must be in the hands of the working man'. The destruction of the mass base of the revolution during the civil war and the continuing day-to-day difficulties of the 1920s meant that it was difficult to engage the mass of the population and especially workers in a cooperative bottom-up programme of social reform. This accentuated the tension between the professional inclination to push for reform and the desire for it to incorporate a mass commitment. But the biggest problem was that as the revolution degenerated so the balance of conflicting pressures on the state began to push the leadership in the direction of creating a new set of priorities which would overturn the faltering attempts of the 1920s to create the beginnings of a significantly different system.

Before that happened though, something of a great leap forward took place with significant falls in the death rate and the infant mortality rate and a concentrated increase in life expectancy, as the data in Table 2.8 show.

There is some controversy over the precise falls and the table presents the middle estimates of a leading group of Russian demographers. The registration process had been made a civil one, but before 1922 it had no chance of developing. Lorimer described its rapid development after 1922 as 'stupendous', but even so there were significant and recognised problems with the registration of deaths and diseases. But the recovery is still clear and impressive.[79] Wheatcroft and Davis note that although a fall in the death rate was common across Europe, 'the improvement in the USSR was remarkable in view of the turmoil in the intervening years'.[80]

Table 2.8   Population Recovery in Russia of the New Economic Policy

| | Total Population | Birth Rate per 1,000 | Death Rate per 1,000 | Life Expectancy Years | | | Infant Mortality per 1,000 Live Births |
				Total	Male	Female	
1920	137.7	39.3	45.4	20.5	19.5	21.5	251
1921	137.7	40.6	39.8	23.8	22.5	25.1	238
1922	136.9	43.7	38.8	24.7	23.4	26.1	232
1923	137.5	47.0	29.1	33.6	31.5	35.8	229
1924	140.0	49.6	27.6	36.1	33.8	38.5	221
1925	143.0	47.3	28.7	35.2	33.0	37.5	219
1926	145.7	45.6	25.5	38.4	36.0	41.0	197
1927	148.7	46.3	26.5	37.5	35.5	39.7	182
1928	151.6	45.3	25.3	38.9	36.5	41.4	182
1929	154.7	44.1	26.5	37.4	36.2	38.7	190

Source: Andreev et al. 1993.

Given the widespread social dislocation (there were millions of orphaned children, for example) it is necessary to be realistic about what could be achieved. But it is also necessary to recognise that in this period priorities changed and were different from those before and after. Military spending was cut back and health spending was increased, as shown in Table 2.9.

Table 2.9   Health Expenditure as a Percentage of Output in the USSR in the 1920s

	Health Expenditure (%)
1923–24	1.8
1924–25	n.a.
1925–26	2.3
1926–27	n.a.
1927–28	2.4
1928–29	2.3
1929–30	2.3

Source: Davis 1983, pp. 348–9, as adjusted by note in section C of Davis's discussion.

One of the big advances, and symbolic of the difference between Russia and the rest of the advanced world in the 1920s, was the availability of abortion. Free abortion on demand was not available as is sometimes mistakenly thought. But abortion was more widely available than in any other advanced country and was used especially by married women to terminate later pregnancies. For obvious reasons it was much more easily available in the towns and the abortion rate varied between them. But abortion did help to bring down the level of maternal mortality and perhaps bring down the infant mortality rate, not only through its direct effect on the birth rate, but also through the way it gave families greater opportunity to have wanted children.

But as the 1920s progressed the revolution was drifting from the ideals of 1917. In Europe the revolutionary wave at the end of the First World War receded with the existing regimes still in place and Russia isolated. Within Russia the catastrophic social collapse had pushed power upward towards the Bolshevik party and leading groups within it. Lenin, incapacitated from 1922, finally died in January 1924, by which time the process was already well advanced. The funeral rites reflected this. Lenin's body lay in state for several days and was seen by huge numbers. Then it was taken to Red Square on 27 January to a makeshift mausoleum. The decision to preserve the corpse would have horrified Lenin himself; it horrified his wife and many others. The fact that the leadership looked to draw legitimacy from an embalmed corpse preserved like the body of an ancient pharaoh was a testament to its weakness and isolation. A revolution that was intended to empower the ordinary person was turning into something different under the strain and pressures of the time. No less disturbing was Stalin's mystical funeral oration vowing to honour Lenin's behest. Yet this was nothing compared to the cult that would develop after Stalin destroyed what was left of democracy in the party after 1928. Then his cult would take the form of him appearing as Lenin's 'only begotten son on earth'.

Stalin's rise to power involved what Boris Souvarine once called 'a molecular coup d'etat'.[81] The political process by which this happened is relatively well understood, its wider socio-economic dynamics and consequences remain controversial. The power of Stalin and the group around him depended on the support that they got from the middle orders of the bureaucracy. The strength of the bureaucracy was in part a reflection of the weakness of the party in which new members, attracted to power, swamped the revolutionary generation. Victor Serge told of a branch he knew (his own?) where 95% of the members had joined after 1921.[82] But behind the weakness of the party was the weakness of the working class itself which recovered slowly in the 1920s in a social sense but in an environment where it had diminishing political influence.[83]

What this meant was that the leadership was increasingly able to manipulate the party and state to achieve its ends. But what were these? Too little attention has been paid in most accounts to the broader dynamics of change. In the first instance the interaction between the leadership and the bureaucracy layer below it was primarily about stability and the security of a certain amount (not necessarily a large amount) of privilege. One aspect of this was the development of a privileged Kremlin medical service which took off especially in the first years of the NEP.[84] But this growth of privilege did not exist in a vacuum. The external economic and military weakness of the USSR posed a threat to its long-term survival. This was all the more so when Stalin and his supporters refined the aim of change as 'socialism in one country' so accommodating to the effective isolation of the revolution and breaking the link with permanent revolution that Trotsky advocated. Conflict over this issue was to be the political and economic battleground between Stalin and the bureaucracy and the left opposition. Internal tensions also created pressures that pulled the regime away from the earlier ideals. Over time the leadership was pushed and partly groped its way towards a solution to the dilemmas of the NEP. This involved both an industrialisation drive which would create the basis of a strong economy and a strong military and internal stabilisation through the increasingly repressive assertion of political control and the consolidation of power of a new social group at the top of society. This was Stalin's 'revolution from above' that began in 1928–29. It now changed the social nature of the regime by creating a society driven by accumulation and reinforced the basic class relationships associated with capitalism that had been partially dismantled between 1917 and 1928. Stalin carried with him some old Bolsheviks in this 'revolution' or better 'counter-revolution' from above but most were its victims. 'He will strangle us all', Lev Kamenev had warned Nikolai Bukharin in the late 1920s.[85] But it was not only the revolutionary generation that would fall victim to Stalin. His policies led directly in the 1930s to the second great population catastrophe and then, in the Second World War, to the third and greatest twentieth-century population catastrophe that Russia experienced.

3 Stalin, Mass Repression and Death 1929–53

In the years after 1928–29 the USSR was driven forward in a massive drive to industrialise. When Stalin died in 1953, this was far from complete. But a mass urban base was created and with it a heavy industrial base supporting a more modern army. This was what Stalin's propaganda called a 'revolution from above'. Its price was enormous coercion and loss of life. 'Build, build, export, shoot, build ... industrialisation is directed like a march through a conquered territory ...', wrote Victor Serge in the mid-1930s.[1] But the pattern of 'normal death' also reveals a society where, despite the propaganda claims to have eliminated class, its reality was etched in the gradients of death and the social mechanisms which produced and reproduced it.

Official propaganda recognised some difficulties but it insisted that by the mid-1930s 'life has become better, life has become gayer'. To sustain this myth obsessive secrecy was needed. Russia shifted from being one of the most open societies in the world in matters of self-examination in the 1920s to probably the most closed in the 1930s. Some of the problems this created were discussed in Chapter 1. But social turmoil and especially collectivisation (1929–32), the famine (1932–33), the Second World War (1941–45) and the postwar famine of 1946–47 also caused registration systems in some areas to collapse. Although many of these gaps can now be filled, others still exist – most obviously in terms of linking the detailed pattern of death to more precise social contours. Nevertheless, as we shall see, the indications are clear.

THE PRESSURE OF ACCUMULATION

During the 1930s and the postwar years it was claimed that the economy was growing at a rate as high as 16–17% per year. The real (though uneven) rate averaged nearer 5–6% but this was still impressive and it enabled, even with wartime destruction, overall output to grow from perhaps 20% or less of the US level in 1928 to between a third and two-fifths at the time of Stalin's death. But this achievement was driven forward by piling in resources of land, labour and above all capital to fuel accumulation and growth. In the 1930s capital investment grew on average at 9% per year. For the years from 1928 to the 1980s (if the war years are excluded) it averaged 7–8%, a figure 'almost without precedent for such long periods'.[2] Setting out to compete with the other major capitalist powers on their own terms, Stalin's regime outdid them all in its commitment to accumulation. But pushing up the rate of accumulation meant squeezing the workers at work and pushing down consumption. In any year consumption always took a residual third place to military expenditure and the heavy industrial base (hence the later defined 'residual principle'). This can be seen in the economic structure that emerged in the 1930s. Military spending rose from 2% of output in 1928 to 6% in 1937 and 15% in 1940.[3] After the war it fell to around 9% in 1950 but then rose to 15% in the 1970s and 1980s. Gross fixed investment ran at some 20% of output in the 1930s rising to nearly 30% in some postwar years. This is also sometimes portrayed as a sacrifice of current consumption for the future. If the economy grows faster, the more will become available later for collective and personal consumption. Economists can even play around with models that predict the 'gain' that will be available. But the pay-off never really came. Although consumption grew it continued to be squeezed by a system over which workers and peasants had no control. Investment was especially squeezed in areas like housing and infrastructure. The consumption share fell from 73% in 1928 to 64% in 1950 and as low as 55% in the 1970s and 1980s. 'Very few countries have sustained such a burden for so long', said one commentator.[4] Above all, the cost was to be enormous in terms of lives destroyed by violence and shortened by hunger and disease.

THE TOTAL NUMBER

The question of how many excess deaths can be attributed to Stalin's policies in the 1930s is still controversial. Table 3.1 sets out one set of estimates constructed by three leading Russian demographers who have tried to correct the official data for the under-registration of births and deaths. Taking the 1930s as a whole there was a slight overall fall in the crude death and infant mortality rates and therefore a modest increase in life expectancy.

This limited decline in deaths bore no relation to what was promised or claimed. It was much slower than that of the 1920s. It was poor in relation to the record of many other states. All this speaks to the way in which significant improvements in the normal death rate were hampered by other priorities.[5] But 'abnormal deaths' within these years also took away millions of lives and discouraged births so further slowing the rate of population growth. In the late 1920s Gosplan predicted a population by 1937 of some 181 million. As we saw in Chapter 1 the 1937 census recorded a population of 162 million – a deficit of 18–19 million. On 25 September 1937 the census was suppressed. The population was said to be 168.5 million, the statisticians were shot or sent to the camps. The new census was held in early 1939 and showed a population of 167 million, but 170 million was the figure announced by Stalin.[6]

Table 3.1   Andreev, Darskii and Kharkova Estimates of Main Population Data for the 1930s

	Birth Rate per 1,000	Death Rate per 1,000	Life Expectancy at Birth in Years[*]			Infant Mortality per 1,000 Live Births
			Average	Male	Female	
1928	45.3	25.3	38.9	36.5	41.4	182
1929	44.1	26.5	37.4	36.2	38.7	190
1930	42.2	27.0	36.5	33.7	39.5	196
1931	40.5	28.0	35.0	33.2	36.8	210
1932[**]	35.9	29.5	32.8	31.1	34.5	213
1933[**]	34.7	71.6	11.6	10.3	13.0	317
1934[**]	30.4	21.7	38.2	35.6	41.0	204
1935	33.0	20.6	39.6	36.9	42.4	198
1936	34.6	20.0	41.1	37.7	44.7	186
1937[**]	39.9	21.7	39.9	35.2	44.8	184
1938	39.0	20.9	41.4	37.2	45.7	174
1939[**]	40.0	20.1	43.6	40.5	46.8	168
1940[**]	36.1	21.7	41.2	38.6	43.9	184

[*] The very low figures for life expectancy in 1933 are a consequence of the high levels of infant mortality.
[**] Data for these years are most sensitive to demographic assumptions made.

Source: Andreev et al. 1993.

As in the case of the crisis between 1914 and 1922, three elements can explain the population deficit,

$$\text{Population deficit} = \text{net emigration} + \text{decrease in births} + \text{increase in deaths}$$

Migration can largely be ignored save in one instance, several hundred thousand peasants, mainly in Kazakhstan but also

Turkmenistan and Tajikistan, fled across the southern border of the USSR to escape collectivisation. What of births? If fewer people were born than predicted then there would be a population deficit. The greater the birth rate fall the more the deficit can be explained in this way. Conversely, the lower the birth rate fall, the more the deficit becomes a matter of excess real deaths.[7] But tracking both the birth and death rates in these years is difficult because 'during certain periods in various regions there was no longer anyone to carry out registration'.[8] Much of the controversy over the exact number of deaths depends on how much adjustment is made for under-registration. The years marked with a double asterisk in Table 3.1 are those when the adjustments are most difficult. 1932–33 saw famine, 1937 mass repression and 1940–41 new borders. The figures here, therefore, have the greatest margin of error. The most problematic are the years 1932–34 which were a time of deepening famine and the recovery from it. The worst year was 1933 when adult and infant mortality shot up and, because of this, life expectancy at birth collapsed. If the corrections in the table are right they lead to an estimate of a total of 11.5 million deaths in 1933 compared to 4.8 million in 1932 (when the trend was already rising). Some have taken this 6.7 million increase as the death toll of the famine in that year.[9] But we must be careful. Whereas births fell by 10.3% in 1931–32 these estimates have them falling only by 5% in 1932–33 and 1933–34. Given the way famine affects births by reducing conceptions this seems unlikely. Alternative accounts therefore point to a much sharper fall in the birth rate in these years and perhaps 5 million additional deaths. Taking the period 1928–36 as a whole, this lower estimate for 1933 gives a total of some 8.5 million excess deaths, to which we then need to add a further million for the years 1937–38 which were also probably undercounted. This gives a total of around 10 million additional deaths to those which might have been expected if earlier death rates had been maintained.[10]

A moment's reflection will show that if the estimate of the number of excess deaths depends so heavily on the level of the birth rate then most of the dispute over the overall level of excess deaths must derive from how many infants were dying and not how many adult deaths there were. We can in fact separate out adult mortality in a different way. This was pioneered by Lorimer on the basis of analysing age group data from the 1926 census and then looking at survival rates. He suggested that there were 4.8 million excess adult deaths. Biraben and Maksudov did the same type of calculation and put the figure at 5.7 million adult deaths.[11] This figure of 5–6 million adult deaths is important not because we want to diminish the significance of child deaths. The pain of failing to nurse a sick child back to health must be enormous. Rather, focusing on adult death allows us to set limits to the deaths that can be attributed directly to state terror on adults in the 1930s.[12]

DEATH AND REPRESSION

Stalin's Russia was built on mass repression. This was also no less true of many twentieth-century regimes than it is of many regimes today. But, for its time, the scale of repression was comparable only with that of Hitler's Germany and in some respects it exceeded it. Two questions stand out about this repression – its causes and its scale.

The dominant approach in the West before 1991 was to see it as a logical and necessary outcome of the revolution. Totalitarianism flowed from revolution. In the French Revolution St Just had said that 'the revolution devours its children' and then he had also fallen victim. In Russia it was the same with the process magnified by the influence of ideology. Stalinism did not 'betray' the revolution as Trotsky claimed – it was its logical culmination. As the USSR collapsed these arguments were then taken up by erstwhile supporters of the old regime with an alacrity that sometimes put into the shade the most conservative accounts previously offered in the West.

There are many things wrong with this view. Its all-encompassing claims about the dangers of revolutionary change need to be contested. It crassly merges different and opposing ideas into a seamless flow from Marx and Lenin to Stalin. It fails to distinguish between the limited and war-related violence of the 1918–21 period and the widescale use of violence in the 1930s. It fails too to deal adequately with the period of the NEP and the degeneration of the revolution. But most fundamentally it is unable to address the social basis and direction of Stalin's consolidation of power in 1928–29 and the way that it was this 'revolution from above' that laid the basis for even more extreme terror later. Stalin's counter-revolution was not simply an ideological and political one, it involved a social revolution which created a new set of exploitative class relationships.[13] These class relationships underpinned both the huge numbers of 'abnormal deaths' and the pattern of 'normal' death, which has rarely been examined by historians of this era. Whereas the new ruling class in command of the state increasingly thrived, the mass of workers and peasants experienced a very different kind of Russia.

The ruthless stress on accumulation made it necessary to attack what was left of the heritage of the revolution. But because Stalin's counter-revolution came from within, it also had to lay claim to a false continuity and had to change 'history' to match this. In the first instance, therefore, the repression was directed against the Old Bolsheviks who stood – some in a more corrupt way; some less – for the ideals of 1917. Repression had also to be directed against those specialists, workers and peasants (which we will treat separately) who might stand in the way of the restructuring of society.

This counter-revolution was unleashed in 1928–29. Tens of thousands were arrested. Sentences for those jailed lengthened and the numbers under secret police control began to rise sharply. In 1930 the OGPU (the United State Political Administration for struggle against espionage and counter-revolution) and within it the main camp administration, or Gulag, was given control of prisoners with sentences of over three years while others stayed under the control of the Commissariat of Justice. Then in 1934 they were all merged under the Commissariat of the Interior.[14] In the first instance the general level of repression rose as many aspects of everyday life were criminalised and politicised. Terror was directed against specific groups seen as real and imagined enemies of the 'revolution from above' and its new priorities. But in December 1934, Kirov, the most popular of the younger Stalinists who some saw as an alternative, was assassinated, whether on Stalin's instructions is still debated. Kirov's death suggested that there was resistance within the regime. Under the guise of an attack on Trotskyism and links with external enemies, terror and repression were jacked up, leading, in 1937–38, to mass arrests and executions. These got so out of hand (albeit encouraged from the top) that they consumed two heads of the secret police, Yagoda and Yezhov, and many others in the secret police itself. Then in November 1938 the leadership called a halt and dissolved the special administrative *troikas* of the secret police (then the NKVD) which had judged many of those arrested. But although repression moderated, it remained at a high level and would rise to a new peak before Stalin's death in 1953.

This terror was not indiscriminate but it became more so – the action to halt it was a sign of that. People could become victims simply as a result of denunciation by erstwhile friends, workmates and neighbours. This has led some commentators to stress the bottom-up character of the purge. But caution is necessary here in several respects. First, to the extent that mass denunciation occurred it was not unique to the USSR or the Eastern bloc. It was common in occupied France during the war and even in the US in the 1950s and 1960s. Secondly, the majority of people did not inform on one another. Thirdly, informing took place within structures which were created from the top down and was willed on by a leadership that had hands-on control.[15]

Let us try to clarify the different elements involved and how they led to death. Firstly we need to distinguish repression from party 'purges' or cleansing. The latter occurred on a significant scale in the 1930s and were formally similar to those of the 1920s. They were not part of the formal process of repression but resulted in it if the person excluded from the party was then arrested. The formal starting point of repression was arrest. The police dealt largely, but not exclusively, with loosely defined 'criminal acts'. The secret police dealt with most alleged 'political' acts but also made 30% or so of their arrests for 'criminal' reasons. Opposition to the political and personal consequences of what was happening, the climate of fear, the powerlessness to collectively resist, all produced individual despair and led to a number of prominent suicides.[16]

Arrest could lead to a person being remanded either under the control of the police or the NKVD. Between 1928 and 1945 some 3.5 million were arrested by the secret police.[17] Conditions for those remanded in custody grew worse in the 1930s and interrogations were increasingly brutal involving both physical and mental torture. Some prisoners succumbed directly to excessive violence, stress, prisoner-on-prisoner violence and bad conditions.[18] A 'trial' then followed. The most prominent were the show trials of the remaining leaders of the revolution which ended in the infamous call of the chief prosecutor Andrei Vyshinsky 'that the mad dogs be shot, one and all'. These trials were designed to send a clear message. Stalin was wiping out the remainder of the revolutionary generation who might carry a memory of something different. They were, said Victor Serge, 'the trial(s) of a generation and an epoch'.[19] The trials were also a public declaration that absolutely no opposition would be brooked in the present whether in politics or ideas. The trials of the mass of prisoners arrested for criminal offences and not under the jurisdiction of the NKVD went through the normal courts where some defence was possible. Those in the hands of the NKVD went before administrative *troikas* in which there was little pretence of any judicial process.

Some 'normal' prisoners were found innocent and released.[20] Few NKVD prisoners were. If the prisoner was found guilty and the offence judged minor then a non-custodial sentence could be imposed in the form of either a fine or what was effectively probation at work on reduced wages. More serious offences led to the prisoner being sent back to prison, or more usually from there to a labour colony (there were 425 in 1940) if the sentence was less than three years.[21] If the sentence was more than three years then the punishment was a labour camp and it was here that most of the serious criminals (widely defined) went, along with the politicals. In 1940 there were 53 camp complexes with the biggest, Bamlag, holding 260,000 and Sevvostlag (Kolyma) 138,000.[22] The worst case was that the prisoner might be found guilty of the most serious offences and given the death penalty. The courts did apply some death penalties but most were in the form of immediate executions following the decision of the NKVD.[23] Death, however, could also come in the prisons, colonies and especially the camps during the sentence. Transport to them was a nightmare with limited concerns for the welfare of prisoners. Conditions varied over time but once there prisoners had to work in situations that led directly to injuries and death, they had diets that were rarely adequate. They experienced basic sanitary problems and had to cope with the violence of guards on a day-to-day basis, in trying to escape and in suppression of the occasional revolts. Violence could also come from fellow prisoners and by their own hand through despair. In the years 1928–53, there were possibly 1 million camp deaths (most in the war years) to which must then be added several hundred thousand in the colonies and some 86,582 prison deaths between 1935 and 1951.[24]

The key statistical series that have been found in the archives are set out in the appendix. This shows the different dimensions of the system as well as most of the deaths involved. Since there is no single list of those repressed, further research will fill in the gaps and perhaps change some detailed figures but it is unlikely to involve major changes. However in individual terms the differences might measure much human suffering. Most historians for example now quote a general figure of around 1 million direct executions before 1941 to allow for 'error' and deaths yet to be properly accounted for.

People flowed continually through the camps as some escaped, some were released and some died. The total numbers passing through is therefore significantly more than an addition of the columns of camp numbers in the appendix would suggest. There is also some suspicion that camp mortality, which cannot be precisely estimated anyway, may have been held down by releasing some sick prisoners, though whether this was significant remains to be established. If it was, their deaths would be hidden in the 'normal' death patterns of the rest of society.[25] Thirdly, when prisoners were released they were often restricted as to where they could live and therefore had to survive in poorer conditions. This also may have had an impact on their life expectancy.

The peak of repression came in 1937–38 when the secret police sentenced 1.6 million people – of whom 682,000 were shot.[26] The camps were made up overwhelmingly of adult males (and relatively better educated ones), as were the victims of executions. The archival data also includes information on ethnic background which shows that *before* 1939 there was no great variation in the ethnic distribution of the population at large. This is especially important as it works against the argument that the regime practised a targeted policy of genocide.[27]

But this was a level of repression far higher than that in Nazi Germany before 1939 although the racist dynamics of that regime would lead it to directly murder many more people after 1939 than did Stalin. Wheatcroft suggests that in the 1930s there were approximately 1 million purposive killings but some 9 million avoidable excess deaths that arose from the deteriorating social conditions in society at large and in the camps and prison complex.[28]

Collectivisation and mass famine

Rapid industrialisation required the control of the countryside to ensure unencumbered food supplies to the towns and this was achieved by the collectivisation of agriculture. In 1928–29 temporary difficulties in maintaining the grain supply interacted with heightened hopes for industrialisation and external fears. This encouraged the leadership to launch a *de facto* war against the majority of the population. Collectivisation was effectively an enclosure movement compressed into a few years. Individual peasant holdings were forced into giant farms and traditional ways of life were broken up. It was a crucial part of the consolidation of the new regime of accumulation. Although the chaos it produced meant that fewer resources flowed to the towns than was hoped for, it did ensure the control of the countryside and control of the grain supply. It encouraged a mass of peasants to flee to the towns to work in the new factories. Those who resisted were repressed and the countryside devastated leaving it in even deeper poverty for more than a generation. Late 1920s levels of production would not be exceeded until the 1950s.

Collectivisation was said to be opposed by rich peasants or '*kulaks*' and their supporters. No one has ever satisfactorily defined who was or was not a *kulak*. Collectivisation was not selective, it was, as the platform of one party opposition group put it, 'directed against all the inhabitants of the countryside'.[29] The overall number dying at this stage remains unclear but some died fighting, whilst others were executed by the OGPU or by other armed groups from the towns (their right to do this was confirmed by an order of 2 February 1930 allowing the execution of 'malicious and stubborn activists'). These deaths are thought to be included in the 20,000 executions in 1930 and 11,000 in 1931. Most peasants did go into the collective farms. Some peasants went immediately to the towns while others migrated later. Those who resisted or were seen as potential enemies, *kulaks* and 'sub-*kulaks*' were dispossessed of their land and deported either within the regions in which they lived or eastwards as 'special settlers'.[30] Between 2.1 and 2.2 million suffered this latter fate. The conditions of their transport were terrible and on arrival they lived on the edge of starvation. 'The deserts of the vast Russias are going to swarm with little white crosses', wrote Serge.[31] A partial revolt of deported peasants was suppressed in Siberia in 1931. The death toll at this stage also remains unclear. The data we have on special settlers starts from 1932 when they are recorded as 1.3 million, but how many of the missing hundreds of thousands were dead, transferred, returned or fled is not clear.[32] In more backward areas like Central Asia, collectivisation involved the forced sedentarisation of nomadic peasants, and the shock and proportional impact in areas like Kazakhstan was much greater with large numbers dying even before the famine of 1932–33 developed to its greatest extent. Even contemporary figures recorded an 88% decline in the number of horses, 97% of sheep and 73% of cattle.[33]

The famine of 1932–33

Much of the dispute about the number of Stalin's victims in the 1930s revolves around the famine of 1932–33. Attributing 'blame' ought to be simple and all the more so since we have argued that famines should not be considered as 'acts of God' but man-made. But the precise process by which the famine of 1932–33 came about remains disputed. Some have claimed that the famine was entirely artificial, a direct product of state policy. It has also been suggested that this policy was targeted specifically on the Ukrainian countryside as an act of 'genocide' against the Ukrainian people.

The destruction and disruption created by collectivisation inevitably affected the level of planting and harvesting. But beyond this there was also a serious harvest failure from the drought cycle. The 1930 and 1931 harvests had not been good but things were especially bad in 1932. Famine in this sense was not intended policy.[34] Nor was it restricted to the Ukraine. The 22 million in the Ukrainian countryside were hit especially hard, but the famine spread far beyond these areas. What is certain is that little was done to alleviate the mass suffering. The overriding priority was to continue to push capital accumulation in heavy industry at all costs.

Problems began to intensify in late 1932 pushing up the seasonal cycle of death. But monthly death rates peaked in May–July 1933, reaching astronomical levels. The 1933 harvest was better and from August recorded death rates began to fall. The famine also affected the birth rate with lows in late 1933 and early 1934, nine months after the severest problems of hunger, diseases and death. For the USSR as a whole the uncorrected official annual death rate rose by over 80% (the recalculations of Table 3.1 have a 140% increase). However, some areas were little affected. In Belorussia the recorded increase was only 23% over 1932. In the RSFSR the recorded death rate rose by over 50%, but in the Ukraine it rose three times over the 1932 level which was itself affected by the impact of the famine in the latter part of that year. Annual recorded urban mortality in the Ukraine rose from 20.0 to 32.2 per 1,000 while the recorded rural death rate rose from 21.3 to 67.8 per 1,000. In the RSFSR in that year the recorded rural death rate rose to 33.3 per 1,000, slightly above the urban rate which was 32.1 per 1,000. This confirms that the Ukraine was the major centre of the famine and within it the death rate rose even higher. But the Ukraine was far from being the exclusive site of the famine. The annual recorded death rate in the Lower Volga Krai rose to 59.4 per 1,000. In the Moldavian ASSR (Autonomous Soviet Socialist Republic) it was 59.6 per 1,000 and in the North Caucasus Krai it was 55 per 1,000. The heights it reached overall in Kazakhstan are not known but must have been considerable.[35] In these terms to isolate 'the Ukrainian people' as victims seems more an affectation of latter-day Ukrainian nationalism which distorts history and does a disservice to the others who suffered and died in the famine.[36]

But showing how the famine had some complex immediate causes in the traditional agricultural cycle does not absolve the Stalin regime of blame. The roots of modern famine lie in the failure to address the socio-economic structures that keep the countryside poor. This was the argument made by socialists before 1917 and after that date they imagined that they were moving towards a regime that would mitigate and then eliminate famine in the near future. But Stalin's 'revolution from above' reinstated a society committed to ruthless accumulation, a society that pursued goals of national power at all cost. This necessarily led to it reproducing patterns of uneven development. Collectivisation to secure the countryside for the regime and resources for growth, as well as the resistance it created, then added more to the process of crisis. We can allow that significant elements of the rural crisis in the early 1930s may have been less unique to Stalin's Russia than is sometimes claimed without it leading to a 'normalisation' of our understanding of the famine.[37] The fact that there may have been elements that link the mechanisms of Stalin's famines to, for example, famines in Ireland in 1845–48 or Bengal in 1943 rather points to the need to integrate any critique of what happened in Russia at this time to a wider understanding of the roots of mass starvation in class systems across the globe and through time.

THE DETERMINANTS OF THE 'NORMAL' DEATH RATE

We suggested earlier that Stalin's counter-revolution 'from above' should be seen as a social revolution that began to systematically reproduce basic social divisions, albeit now refracted through the medium of a state controlled economy, rather than one based largely on private property. Those who controlled the process of accumulation were not only 'masters of men', they were also able to use their position to increasingly enjoy a different lifestyle and social conditions that came also to be reflected in the extended reproduction of inequality in death.

This was not just a question of the consolidation of a narrow elite but of a wider social class. It was not a smooth process – the repression is an indication of this. But it was marked by an ideological change in which ideas of equality were condemned, and widening differentials celebrated. The contrast that this produced in life then led on to contrasts in death. It even began to be reflected in underlying attitudes where, despite the rhetoric of equality, the practice of inequality began to tell in the condescension with which the rest of society was often viewed.

> I have heard the elegant in the literary salons praise the enthusiasm of the Donets miners and the political wisdom of the leader. I have seen others, fat and dressed in transparent silks, leaning on the arms of aviation officers, walking past children with bellies swollen from famine who moaned softly as they lay stretched out in the dust. The ladies turned their heads away. After all, they were only little Kazaks or Kirghiz ...[38]

Industrialisation was at the expense of the standard of living of both workers and peasants.[39] Conditions in the countryside – where the livelihood of the collective farm peasants came last – remained dire. 'Millions lived in wretched huts, feeding themselves from the products of their tiny plots of land (on which they grew potatoes, cabbage, cucumber, beets, turnips and onions) and their cow.'[40] In the towns things were not quite as bad but still nevertheless were very serious. The share of investment going into housing was cut from 17.4% in the first plan and, after a small rise in the second, to 8.1% in the third. The urban population more than doubled. What construction there was combined better-quality and larger apartments for the few with a mass of poor-quality housing for the many. This included barrack-style housing, especially in the new cities, though this was at least an improvement on the *zemliiankas* (holes covered by planks) in which some of those involved in construction lived. Living space per urban inhabitant fell from 6.4 square yards in 1926 to 5.6 square yards in 1932 and to 4.3 square yards by 1940. This was less than half the sanitary norm and, as with any average, masked considerable variations. Water supplies, sewage systems etc were expensive and their coverage expanded only to the most important towns and even there not to all parts. At the end of the 1930s, 460 cities had piped water supplies and only 160 had sewage systems. In many parts of towns sewage was collected in traditional ways through shovelling out cesspits and carting the contents away.[41]

In Moscow real wages in 1932 fell to some 58% of the 1928 level and although they rose again by 1937 they were still only 63.5% of the 1928 level.[42] They then fell again to a low during the war and did not recover their 1928 levels until the 1950s. *This means that for two and a half decades, in both war and peace, they were below Tsarist levels.* Household consumption fell less than this because, with the increase in the proportion of the population working, the ratio of dependants to wage earners fell – from 2.26 in 1927, for example, to 1.59 in 1935. This was largely due to the increased number of women workers. Trotsky suggested that the ruling class (although he refused to apply this term himself) comprised perhaps 12–15% of the population.[43] 'The rest of the population,' wrote Serge, '85 to 88 per cent lives in primitive conditions, in discomfort, in want, in misery, or else it benefits from a well-being that is illicit and concealed, and therefore mingled with insecurity.'[44]

The rationing of bread and other basic foodstuffs, especially in the years 1928–35, probably created a floor for those with ration cards which prevented outright starvation. But it did little to encourage good health as contemporary accounts of the lack of real sustenance in the food suggests. The unhealthy lives people lived continued to be reflected in the contrasts in their physical well-being. Serge contrasted the tan of well-fed wives and girlfriends of those at the top with the majority of women who, as of old, became disfigured and aged at 35.[45]

The strain of daily life was also reflected in other measures of social failing which directly or indirectly led to deaths in the home such as accidents, crime, suicide, murder, etc. Alcohol continued to be implicated in failings inside and outside the home. Yet Serge argued that people should not be quick to criticise workers for taking solace in drink:

> The alcoholism of the Russian people derives from its indigent condition, no home, no well being, few distractions, – life is joyless … Having lived with the poor of the country, I would not dream of reproaching them for getting drunk. I know too well the immense sadness of a life without escape and without joy.[46]

Within the new factories workers were largely on piece-work and then encouraged to compete with one another through 'shock work', 'socialist competition' and the Stakhanovite movement named after the Donbass miner Alexsei Stakhanov who smashed the production records in a carefully staged demonstration. Much less attention has been paid to the cost of this in terms of maimed bodies and lost lives as accident rates soared and workplace disease spread. Agriculture, construction, factories and mines were the scenes of numerous accidents. So far we have only been shown glimpses of the scale of death that resulted, but these do reveal problems comparable with the most ruthless phase of the Industrial Revolution in Western Europe a century before. In 1938–39 workplace deaths amounted to 4–5% of all deaths in Moscow. Beyond Moscow conditions in new towns and plants were worse. 'In the Cheliabinsk tractor factory, the Saratov Combine Factory, the Luberetskii agricultural machinery factory, accidents grew in the second half of the 1930s by 1.5 to 2 times', suggests V.B. Zhiromskaia.[47]

In the 1930s there was a rapid expansion of social provision and medical care but the scale of the problems was enormous. Much of this expansion was narrowly focused. The aim was to use both social security and medical care to keep the process of industrialisation going and to keep workers in work. Access to benefits was closely tied to performance. Withdrawal of benefits was a considerable stick and a doctor's failure to legitimate absenteeism with a medical certificate could lead to dismissal and eventually prison, as labour legislation became more repressive. To achieve this, it was necessary to uproot the system created by the revolution. In 1929 Semashko was replaced as Health Commissar by Vladimirsky who promised to gear health directly to production. He was replaced in 1935 by Kaminsky who had been appointed health commissar of the RSFSR in 1934. The Commissariat of Labour was disbanded and many of its functions transferred to the trade unions which had the task of acting 'as a good manager [to] achieve order and discipline'.[48] Above all policies were changed, narrowed and focused heavily on the urban workforce. The character of social insurance was set out by Shervnik, the new trade union leader, who told the Trade Union Congress in 1932,

> Bureaucracy and egalitarianism must be eradicated from social insurance. We must reconstruct the whole social insurance practice in order to give the most privileged treatment to shock workers and those with long service. The fight against labour turnover must be put into the forefront. We shall handle social insurance as a weapon in the struggle to attach workers to their enterprises and strike hard at loafers, malingerers and disorganisers of work.[49]

In health the focus was shifted to an ostensibly more 'scientific' approach concerned with medical cures. Preventative medicine became essentially a battle for cleanliness rather than the control of the socio-economic process. Eventually the USSR would have more doctors (including female ones) and more hospital beds per head than any other country in the world. But the doctors were also poorly trained and poorly paid and less well-equipped, unless they served those at the top. One doctor explained medical low pay this way: '[E]ngineers work with equipment purchased abroad with gold. We doctors work with poor slobs ... whose worth is obviously reflected in our pay.'[50]

Although the state claimed to be 'planning', much of what happened was a product of crude central direction that was often not even consistent. In 1936, for example, abortion was banned under the influence of growing pro-natalist concerns to push up the birth rate. The policy worked in the short term but the price was more maternal death in botched unofficial abortions. Mothers were also rewarded with more generous family allowances. But women were also needed as workers, so at the same time maternity leave was reduced from 16 to 9 weeks.

WARS

Stalin's Russia developed under the threat of war in the 1930s but, by its pursuit of national and great power objectives, it also contributed to it. 'Internationalism' was defined as 'unreservedly, unhesitatingly and unconditionally' defending the USSR.[51] Between 1928 and 1933 Moscow advised the German KPD to follow policies which made Hitler's coming to power easier and resulted in the deaths of thousands of German Communists. Thereafter international revolution was seen as a positive hindrance to Russian foreign policy, and NKVD agents were operational abroad, most notably in Spain, in 1936–39, to ensure that it did not happen.[52]

As tensions rose the leadership worried about the loyalty of discontented populations in the border areas. This led to the forcible removal of 36,000 'Poles' from the eastern regions in 1936–37 and 175,000 'Koreans' from the Far East to Central Asia amongst others. The limited concern for the people being moved inevitably brought more death. But armed conflict in which the army was involved came first in the Far East. Smaller clashes occurred in China in 1929 where the army lost 281 soldiers. The bigger clashes were with Japan in July 1938 at Lake Khasin when 960 soldiers died as the Red Army won back territory taken by the Japanese. The following year, after numerous border incidents, major conflict erupted at Khalkin-Gol in August 1939. The Japanese lost 18,500 dead and wounded and the Russians 9,203.[53]

But by this point diplomatic negotiations were taking place in Europe, which led to the Nazi-Soviet Pact being signed on 23 August 1939. Stalin calculated that by this point there was no possibility of an alliance stopping Hitler and this led him to further calculate that he could do a separate deal. The pact effectively established a Soviet sphere of interest allowing expansion into Poland and the Baltic at the price of 'neutrality' and exports of raw materials to feed the growing Nazi war economy. Table 3.2 sets out the territories and populations gained and some of the population movements. It would seem that this led to a mid-1941 population of the USSR of 190–193 million.

On 17 September 1939, following the earlier Nazi advance, the Red Army crossed into Poland. Some limited fighting took place, but by 31 October 1939 Molotov could tell the Supreme Soviet that 'a short strike at Poland, first by the German Army and, then, by the Red Army was enough for nothing to be left from this ugly offspring of the Treaty of Versailles'. Krivosheev's data suggest that it cost the Red Army 1,475 dead. Civilian losses have yet to be clearly established.[54] In June 1940 Russian troops entered the Baltic states and fixed elections took place for new national assemblies. On 14 and 21 July there was a vote for union with the USSR. While this was happening, Romania ceded Bessarabia and northern Bukovina to the USSR at the end of June, though here clashes did occur. Krivosheev suggests that there were no Russian losses, which stretches credulity and conflicts with the contemporary evidence.[55]

It was war with Finland to establish a more secure defence line around Leningrad that brought the greater casualties. When the Finnish government rejected Stalin's demands, a border incident was staged and on 30 November, Helsinki and other towns were bombed. A peace treaty was finally signed on 12 March 1940 with 19,576 Finns reported killed, 43,557 wounded and 3,273 missing.[56] But although Stalin secured major concessions, the war did not go well for Russia. At the time Soviet authorities said their casualties were 48,700, but it was later found that there were really 126,875 dead.[57]

As borders changed, however, mass movements of refugees took place. Some fled east from Hitler, others fled west from Stalin. The establishment of power then resulted in sweeping arrests and some shootings. In occupied Poland, for example, some 250,000 were arrested. Some were freed, others sent to camps and then officers and other leaders sent to special camps Kozelsk, Starobelsk and Ostashkov.

Table 3.2 Expansion, Population Gains and Movements 1939–41

	Date	Area	Population	Migration East–West	Migration West–East	Deportation East	Losses in Deportation
Poland	Sept.–Oct. 1939	69,000	11,000,000	145,000 (O)	30–40,000 (O)	139,000	300,000
						66,000	
					200,000 (R)	78,000	
Finland	March 1940	17,400	570,000				
Estonia	June 1940	18,300	1,130,000				
Latvia	June 1940	25,400	2,000,000	13,000 repatriated to Germany			
Lithuania*	June 1940	23,000	2,800,000	300,000	21,000	70,000	
Romania	June 1940	21,000	3,500,000	35–40,000 (R)	420–470,000 (R)		
Total		174,000	21,000,000				

O = official transfer; R = estimate of refugee flow.
* In 1939 there was a wave of refugees from Poland to Lithuania.

Sources: Lorimer 1946, pp. 186, 194–5; *Naselenie Rossii* 2001, pp. 9–10, gives estimates of the population of the incorporated areas by the area of the USSR which they became or were integrated into.

Fearing that these might be a source of leadership to further opposition, on 5 March Beria proposed to the Politburo that the officers be killed without trial and Stalin signed the minutes and the leadership signed the letter of instructions. In the spring of 1941, 21,857 were recorded as being shot in the Katyn forests which had long been under the control of the OGPU/NKVD.[58] In the Baltic states a similar wave of arrests occurred with 40,178 Balts being deported within a year of the takeover. But none of this brought security.

The Second World War

On 22 June 1941 Stalin's miscalculations about his capacity to manipulate Hitler were finally exposed as the Nazi Wehrmacht crossed the Soviet border. Four years later, on 7 May 1945, the Nazi regime surrendered with the Red Army in Berlin. As the victorious Allies began to fall out and war turned to Cold War, Stalin was anxious that Russia's weakness not be fully revealed. 'The USSR was the only country among the belligerents which did not proceed to have a census after the war. The powers-that-be wanted to hide the enormous war losses.'[59] The figure that was first announced was 7 million. Following the 1959 census, in 1961, Khrushchev quoted a figure of 20 million, but today we know that *excess* deaths numbered 26.6 million, to say nothing of the birth deficit. Excess deaths of men are put at 19–20 million and of women at 7 million. But excess deaths are a demographic concept. Overall 42.7 million in Russia died in the war years. The fact that many of these would have died in normal circumstances does not mean that their death was not hastened directly or indirectly by the war.[60]

The complexity of war deaths in and around Russia in these years can be simplified if we think in terms of those in the Nazi zone and those in the Russian zone. On the Nazi side it was a war of extermination against the Jews and death and enslavement of the *untermenschen* ('sub-human') Slavs. The rules which applied in the West did not apply in the East. The Nazi armies and their allies took some 5.7 million Russian prisoners of war, of whom 3.2 million or nearly 60% died. Perhaps 0.6 million were executed on capture or by the Einsatzgruppen extermination squads and the rest died in captivity or on forced marches to captivity. One was Stalin's son, Yakov, captured in July 1941 and who was shot in 1943 on an electrified camp fence either in a foolhardy attempt to escape or driven to suicide. It is hardly surprising that one German unit reported in February 1942 that 'Red Army soldiers ... are more afraid of falling prisoner than the possibility of dying on the battlefield.'[61] A second source of death came from Nazi atrocities. The standard estimates suggest that 2.2 million Jews from within the USSR's 1941 borders were killed. Possibly as many as 1.4 million Jews and others died at the hands of the Einsatzgruppen with the biggest single killing the 33,771 at the ravine of Babi Yar near Kiev in the Ukraine.[62] Others were taken to ghettos and then to the concentration camps or, more usually, were taken directly there. But the atrocities went wider. Hitler's 'Commissar Order' of 6 June 1941 encouraged the killing of anyone suspected of being a Communist. Atrocities were also visited on populations suspected of opposition or helping the various partisan groups – possibly a quarter of a million died in reprisals against villages held to have supported the partisans. A third source of death came as a result of the forced labour that 2.8 million civilians in the occupied zone were pressed into in Germany and elsewhere. The area of the USSR occupied by the Nazis at any one time had held a prewar population of 82 million (42% of the population) with 21–22 million in the recently acquired areas and the rest in pre-1939 territories.[63] Allowing for those who fled east, and subtracting those areas only briefly occupied, then perhaps 70 million suffered a more extended occupation and their standard of living fell drastically and hunger and disease spread as the Nazis lived off the land.

Deaths on the Soviet side are more complex. Red Army combat deaths and deaths from wounds seem to have been 8.7–9.2 million.[64] Questionable strategic decisions made by Stalin and lesser ones by his generals perhaps raised the death toll unnecessarily. Those that have given rise to angry debate range from the refusal to retreat in Kiev in 1941, to the lives wasted so that a Red Army soldier could symbolically raise the Soviet flag in Berlin in May 1945. Order 270 issued in August 1941 said that anyone who surrendered was a traitor. Order 227, following the loss of Rostov in July 1942, established units that would be 'placed directly behind unreliable divisions … to shoot the panic mongers and cowards on the spot in the event of a disorderly retreat'.[65] The price of failure was also high for those in command. In 1941 the commander of the Western front, D.G. Pavlov, and his immediate subordinates were shot along with some 50 other generals as the war progressed, while some others committed suicide. But a leadership and an army was created and supplied so as to be able to defeat Hitler and his allies.[66] Some 30.6 million were mobilised during the war including nearly 1 million women. Nearly 1 million were also released from the camp system to serve in the army – many in 'penal units' which undertook the most dangerous jobs, but including some officers who went straight from the Gulag back to command positions.

Civilian deaths derived partly from death in the battle-zones or in the various sieges of which the most important was the Siege of Leningrad which lasted 872 days from the autumn of 1941 to 1943.[67] Only some 600,000 of the 3.2 million in the city managed to flee before the siege closed. The Smolenskoye cemetery on Vasilievskii Island was used for mass burials, as was the Serafimoskoye cemetery on the Petrograd side. But the mass of victims, 470,000 according to the official figures, were buried in 186 mass graves at the former village of Piskaryovska. It was here in 1960 that the city's main memorial complex was opened. Overseen by a huge statue is a long commemorative wall inscribed with a verse by Olga Berggol who survived the blockade but whose husband did not.

Here lie Leningraders
Here are townspeople – men, women and children,
Beside them are the soldiers of the Red Army. With their whole lives
They defended thee, Leningrad,
Cradle of the Revolution.
We cannot give each of their noble names,
There are so many under the granite.
But we know as you look on these stones,
That no-one has been forgotten and nothing has been forgotten

The words are moving and so is the monument. The human tragedy involved is immense. But the regime would now use the war as its legitimating myth and in the process much was forgotten and so were many – victims not of the Nazis but of Stalin's regime and the system on which it rested.

But the larger number of civilians died because of deteriorating conditions away from the front line. Medical measures appear to have stopped mass epidemics breaking out but they could not avert the effects of the general deterioration in standards.[68] But the suffering was far from equal and the class divisions that had been established in peacetime continued during the war. Indeed, the fleeing of many at the top in Moscow, with their families, in 1941 as the Nazi armies neared the city provoked bitter resentment.

During the war repression continued though many camp inmates were mobilised. Within the camps, colonies and prisons the deterioration of conditions was even more marked and NKVD statistics suggest that there were 1.01 million deaths between 1941 and 1945.[69] The death rate rose to its highest levels in the camps in the worst years of the war. A quite different source of death came in the form of the orders to deport various national groups over fears of their disloyalty. Table 3.3 sets out the main waves of deportation under Stalin. It can be seen that the war deportations were as large as those of collectivisation though smaller than in the 1930s as a whole. In 1941 the Volga Germans were the main victims; in 1943 the Kalmyks and the Karachai and then in 1944, the Chechens and Ingushi, Crimean Tartars, Balkirs and Mesketians. They were forced to move largely to Central Asia and parts of Siberia.

Table 3.3   Main Waves of Internal Deportation under Stalin by Major Phase

	Number Deported (000)
Collectivisation	
1930–31	2,050
1932–34	535
'Border Security'	
1935–38	260
Western Expansion	
1939–41	395
War Deportation of Nations	
1941–42	1,200
1943–44	870
1944–45	260
Post-war	
1947–52	400
Total	5,970

Source: Polian 2001, p. 239. Polian's appendix 1 lists details of the basic movements within groups and years.

As with the earlier deportation of the *kulaks*, some died resisting, others died on the long journeys and marches into deportation and still others died from the conditions they found on arrival and the struggle to survive in the next years.

Finally we need to note the controversy over what happened when the Red Army rolled forward. Many of the horrors perpetrated by the Nazis in Russia were repaid in kind as the Red Army advanced.

The exact dimensions of this has been the subject of bitter controversy with claims of mass rape and mass killings contributing to the movement of millions of refugees. This was hotly denied in the USSR. Today it is accepted that 'wild actions' did occur but there is still much debate about how widespread these were. What is more difficult to contest is the political indifference at the highest levels. Those in the way of the Red Army got their 'just desserts'. It was also believed that the army had to be given its head. Stalin asked of the ordinary soldier 'How can such a man act normally? And what is so awful in his amusing himself with a woman, after such horrors?' When he heard of the shelling of refugees in East Prussia he said: '[W]e lecture our soldiers too much; let them have some initiative.'[70]

THE END OF THE STALIN ERA

Victory over Hitler led to the consolidation of the USSR's 1941 borders and to the addition of a small amount of other territory.[71] Overall, on its postwar territory, the USSR had an estimated population of 170.5 million in 1946, some 20 million less than in 1941. Whereas US industrial production had grown by 50% during the war, in the USSR, even on its own distorted statistics, industrial production in 1946 was only three-quarters of the 1940 level and output per head fell back to some 20% of the US level. Rapid recovery would therefore require continued pressure on the population. The expansion into Eastern Europe initially allowed a considerable amount of plunder and exploitation which partially relieved some of the burden of reconstruction at the expense of the local population. In February 1946 Stalin recognised that catching up with the US was now a long way off. 'Perhaps three new five year plans if not more' would be needed, he said, to obtain a basic economic security. This meant reinforcing the prewar priorities. The end of the war saw a return to a more 'civilian' economy. As the Cold War developed and Russia's grip tightened over its empire, then 'defence' became more necessary and the pattern of global and local competition was consolidated by the Korean War. In 1950 the direct military effort had been cut to 9% of output. This was less than 1940 but still 50% higher than in 1937.[72] In the next year it was ratcheted up as relations with the West deteriorated even further. New resources had also to be found to support a creation of a nuclear deterrent to compete on equal terms with the US.

The satellites

It was in Eastern Europe that a new empire was created over a territory of 1 million square kilometres and a population of 92 million. The crude and disorganised exploitation of the liberated areas of Eastern Europe in 1944–46 suggests that Stalin was uncertain how close a control Russia would have in the postwar years. But as the Cold War developed, Stalin's grip was consolidated. It is striking that in the most authoritative account of Soviet military losses, there is no discussion of those in Eastern Europe between 1945 and 1953.[73] Yet in most cases the creation of Moscow-style regimes owed nothing to genuine mass movements and even where they might be argued to have had a role, this was secondary. Instead the new regimes were imposed and manipulated from the top down and built on the already extensive state control that existed in the region after the war. But the aim became to create regimes that were not only loyal to Moscow but which copied its system and supplied resources and production for reconstruction there. Repression, which began against local fascists, shifted to the non-Communist Party left and then within the Communist Parties to those who might be thought disloyal. The Russian secret police were there to direct operations. Bela Szasz, a Hungarian Communist, briefly had a special interrogator in the form of Major-General Belkin. Another Russian secret police official told him, this man was 'not only Governor of Hungary like Horthy was, but he is Governor of Austria, of Romania and of Yugoslavia, and of Czechoslovakia and of Albania. Because you know Comrade Belkin is the Chief of the Secret Police for Eastern Europe.'[74] And behind the secret police and their local stooges stood the Red Army. This repression intensified after Tito in Yugoslavia spurned Stalin and revealed some of the exploitation involved in relations with Moscow. The direct and indirect loss of lives that these policies caused in the satellites was considerable. The casualties suffered by the army of occupation that ultimately enforced them still need to be properly established.

Repression at home

In Russia itself the hopes for a postwar political relaxation quickly disappeared. War had brutalised the regime even more. The Cold War only encouraged more suspicion of 'the enemy within' and it helped to fuel, and was in turn fed by, more extreme nationalism and a celebration of 'Russian' achievements. The dynamics of political dictatorship narrowed the basis of power even more on the dictator and, growing paranoia and suspiciousness fed back down the chain of command. Stalin's cult was intensified to provide a focus for a population traumatised by the recent past and its current fears. It was in this phase that the Gulag reached its greatest extent although the direct killings were less than in 1937–38. Some of the detailed figures involved are set out in the postwar data in the appendix.

Those suffering from repression in the years between 1945 and 1953 fall into five main groups. One was returning prisoners of war whose loyalties were doubted.[75] A second group was repatriated civilians including those accused of collaboration. Between 1944 and 1952, 5.46 million were repatriated, many forcibly.[76]

The third group came from internal populations that were deemed to be insufficiently loyal. There was some basis for this in as much as resistance to the reimposition of Stalin's rule took place in some areas. In Lithuania, for example, 40,000 are said to have been killed between 1944 and 1953 with most in the years 1944–45. There was also a near-guerrilla war in parts of the Ukraine. Krivosheev's account gives 6,223 Soviet military deaths for national uprisings in the Baltic and Western Ukraine for the years 1940–56, but most were postwar. Many went to the camps but there was also a continuation of the wartime policies of deporting peoples. Polian gives a figure of 400,000 deportees to the East, mainly from the Baltic states and the Ukraine, and there were also significant deportations from Moldavia and other places.[77] Even Jehovah's Witnesses were deported *en masse*. As in the prewar years the deaths of those in special settlements appear to have been captured by the wider mortality figures though given the poor circumstances, the death rate was almost certainly higher than that of the population at large. For those in the colonies and camps the postwar years were paradoxical in as much as hunger was widespread – some even spoke of 'the great hunger'. But the death rate did fall in the camps in these years, though this may have involved some falsification.[78] In the West, some 4.3 million German soldiers and their allies were taken prisoner. Then the August 1945 Manchurian campaign added 0.6 million Japanese troops and their allies.[79] In a half-starving and half-destroyed society such prisoners were not a high priority and over 1 million died, though how deliberate the neglect was is a matter of controversy.

But the repression also focused on groups close to the regime and individuals at the heart of it. The worsening atmosphere came to a head after 1948. This new terror re-inforced a campaign against 'cosmopolitanism' and focused it on Leningrad where people were perhaps seen as less loyal than in Moscow. The most prominent victim was N.A. Voznesensky, the head of Gosplan in 1938–49, and a group of 200 others who were shot in 1950 after a secret trial. But with Stalin's morbid suspicions growing, the repression swept up many in the families of his closest supporters. The wife of Kalinin was arrested. And in 1949 Molotov's wife was arrested, it having been suggested to him earlier that he divorce her.[80] Stalin also watched impassively as members of his own family were arrested and sent to camps.

'Cosmopolitanism' also became a code word for 'Jewishness'. In January 1949 Soloman Mikhoels, a leading actor, who had headed the wartime Jewish Anti-Fascist Committee was reportedly killed in a car crash but was most likely murdered by Stalin's agents. In 1951, arrests of Jewish doctors began which led to the arrest of doctors in Stalin's entourage who were said to be plotting to poison him. This 'doctors plot' was announced on 13 January 1951 so that when Stalin was taken ill his senior doctor, Vinogradov, was not at hand since he was in the Lubyanka (secret police headquarters). In 1953, 13 out of 14 members of the Jewish Anti-Fascist Committee were executed and by 1953 plans were afoot to shift the entire Jewish population to Eastern Siberia. Had this occurred many would have died. This has led to speculation that Stalin was planning his own 'final solution' in the Nazi sense. But this view is not supported by the evidence of the plans or by an analysis of the dynamics of the regime.[81] Racism played a role in this society which should not be neglected but it did not have the genocidal character that developed in Nazi Germany.

The wider population

Social conditions in the immediate postwar years for most Russians were possibly worse than in 1932–33. The pressure on the standard of living of the mass of the population was intense. It was not helped by the reimposition of rigid controls in agriculture and industry and the crude re-enforcement of labour discipline. The stick was far more evident than the carrot not simply because there were few carrots but because everything was being driven from the top down.

Rural standards of living were very low and drought in 1946 led to famine in 1946–47 in the traditional famine areas. Overall it is estimated that perhaps 1–1.5 million died in this famine. Its cause clearly lay in the destructiveness of the war and the earlier legacies but it was also accentuated by the continuing indifference to the situation of the collective farm peasants. Certain of control at home, but uncertain in Eastern Europe, the regime even exported some grain there in an attempt to build support.[82] The destruction of the housing stock in the occupied areas was estimated at 50% but people continued to move to the towns – 10.6 million in the RSFSR alone between 1946 and 1953.[83] The immediate postwar building had a limited effect and there was a further fall in housing space per person and growth of overcrowding. Apart from rebuilding the infrastructure of the big cities, some attempts were made to extend it in others. The Fourth Plan (1946–50) named cities like Archangel with a population of 280,000 and Tomsk and Irkutsk with populations of 200,000, for sewage systems.[84] But the resources devoted to these areas were compromised by the way that Stalin wanted to ornament his regime. The skyscrapers that were built in Moscow in the postwar years symbolised the gulf between the few who had access to them, and the mass of the population that they towered over.

The death rate remained high in the first years after 1945 but then began to fall sharply and by 1950 it was below that of 1940. Several factors explain this. One was the fall in the birth rate after a postwar birth boom. With fewer children being born, there were fewer to die and keep up the death rate. Those who were born also benefited from a sharp decline in recorded infant mortality. By 1950 infant mortality was down to 104 per 1,000 (Table 3.4). This reflected a concerted effort to do something about this problem. Adult mortality also began to benefit from attempts to apply some of the lessons learned in the war and the beginning of the use of new drugs and mass vaccination. Finally the demographic effect of the changing age structure of the population also contributed to a fall in the crude death rate but this meant that the fall in the standardised rate was much less than the crude figures suggest. Nevertheless the improvement that did begin, and which was to continue into the 1950s, marked the second great decline in the death rate after that begun before 1914 and continued in the 1920s.

'Lenin is John the Baptist and Stalin the Messiah', Beria is reported to have advised a screenwriter working on a film in which Stalin's character would appear.[85] But the 'Messiah' died in 1953 and hopefully descended into hell, or imagined that this was his destination in his last moments. Following a stroke his doctors struggled in panic to keep him alive (including bleeding him with leeches). At 9.50 p.m. on 5 March 1953 one of the greatest mass murderers in history was certified dead. 'The death agony was horrible,' his daughter Svetlana later said, 'he literally choked to death as we watched. At what seemed like the very last moment he suddenly opened his eyes and cast a glance over everyone in the room. It was a terrible glance, insane or perhaps angry and full of fear and death ... .'[86]

Table 3.4   Population Change in the Last Years of Stalin's Rule

	Population (m)	*Birth Rate per 1,000*	*Death Rate per 1,000*	*Life Expectancy in Years*			*Infant Mortality per 1,000 Live Births*
				Average	*Male*	*Female*	
1946	170.5	28.5	15.8	46.1	41.5	51.0	167
1947	172.1	29.6	20.3	40.4	34.8	46.4	190
1948	173.7	26.4	13.6	52.2	47.6	56.9	115
1949	175.9	31.0	12.6	55.0	51.3	58.9	113
1950	179.2	28.8	11.7	57.3	53.1	61.7	104
1951	182.3	29.1	11.6	57.8	53.7	62.0	107
1952	185.5	28.3	11.4	58.2	54.8	61.7	104
1953	188.7	26.4	11.0	59.0	55.4	62.8	92

Source: Andreev et al. 1993.

4 Policy, Inequalities and Death in the USSR 1953–85

The years between Stalin's death and the collapse of the USSR in 1991 saw a succession of less extreme regimes under which conditions improved for the mass of the population. 'Destalinisation' led to a huge reduction in the level of state violence – but not its disappearance. Some of the benefits of modernisation were now allowed to filter down to the mass of the population and there were dramatic falls in the death rate and the infant mortality rate. But this relaxation and improvement was constrained by the self-interest of the wider social group on which the system rested. This helps to account for the peculiar history of the death rate in the USSR after the mid-1960s.

The attempt to 'normalise' or 'routinise' political life required some confrontation with the excesses of the past. In 1956, at a secret session of the 20th Party Congress, Khrushchev denounced Stalin and the 'cult of personality'. But since the leadership itself had bloody hands, there were limits as to how far this confrontation with the past could go. It was only during the 22nd Party Congress that, after a much fuller discussion of Stalin's crimes, the decision was taken on 30 October 1961 to remove his body from the Lenin Mausoleum.

The poet Yevgenii Yevtushenko imagined breath seeping through the chinks of the coffin as it was carried out with Stalin scheming his return. In fact that night the body was reburied in a deep pit behind the Lenin Mausoleum and covered with several truckloads of concrete. The grave was finished with a granite slab inscribed 'J.V. Stalin'.[1] Yevtushenko asked 'how to remove Stalin's heirs from Stalin!' but his poem 'The Heirs of Stalin' still echoed the official line that 'the cult of personality' had sullied a past 'so healthy and glorious/ of Turksib/ and Magnita/ and the flag raised over Berlin ... We sowed our crops honestly/ Honestly we melted metal/ and honestly we marched ... .'[2] It would take another generation and more before the real past could be confronted. When the system did begin to open up after 1985 the new spirit was symbolised by another story of the corpse that would not rest. This was the Georgian director Tengiz Abuladze's 1987 film *Repentance*. Georgia, Stalin's birthplace, was where his statutes could still be found. Abuladze's film starts with the mystery of why the body of Varlam Aravidze, a local 1930s boss clearly modelled on Stalin, keeps being dug up and left in the family garden. While Varlam's son knew of his father's crimes, his grandson, Tornike, was ignorant but curious. Then a local woman is arrested for digging up the corpse. At her trial she declares that, 'you may bury him seven by seven times and I will dig him up seven by seven times. Such a man isn't worthy of resting peaceful in his native earth.' Her story allows the full horror of Varlam's past to be revealed but the son condones it. The allegory expressed the essence of the failure to confront the past. Only when the grandson commits suicide does the son himself dig up the body and throw it over a cliff, saying: 'Damn you, Satan.'[3]

JUDICIAL DEATH AND REPRESSION

Ironically it was Beria, the former secret police chief, who led the process of reform in the weeks immediately after Stalin's death but it was also Beria who presented the greatest threat to the other leaders. This sealed his fate. On 26 July 1953 he was arrested, tried later in the year, and ignominiously shot with six other officials in December 1953.[4] Thereafter change at the top no longer involved bloodletting. Khrushchev overcame the opposition of his rivals to become leader and in 1957 he defeated a group led by Molotov, Malenkov and Kaganovich. Molotov went to Mongolia as ambassador, Malenkov and Kaganovich were demoted to industrial managers in Kazakhstan and the Urals. When more revelations about their 'plot against the state' emerged in early 1961 Khrushchev made it clear to the Party Conference how much had changed. Kaganovich, he said, had begged not to be dealt with 'as they dealt with people under Stalin' and he had replied that Kaganovich could 'work and live tranquilly if you work honestly'.[5] When Khrushchev himself was deposed in 1964 he too was allowed to live out his disgrace in pleasant obscurity recording his memories for posterity.

On 27 March 1953 Beria proposed a decree by which 1.2 million prisoners (largely criminal) were released from the camps. Then camp revolts in 1953 and 1954 further encouraged the process of releases although many former inmates still had restricted residence rights. By 1959 less than 1 million were in camps and colonies with only 11,000 sentenced for more explicitly political reasons. In 1954 restrictions were lifted on where the children of special settlers could live and in 1955–56 on the deported nationalities, though only the Chechens and Ingush were allowed back to their traditional lands.[6]

The detailed story of the final camp revolts can be found elsewhere.[7] The exact number killed in repressing them depends on whether we believe the lower secret figures recorded in the archives or the unofficial estimates. But it seems that once order was restored the full brutality of the state was now restrained. In September 1953 the special boards of the secret police were abolished and in 1959 the right of the secret police to summary execution was also abolished. This meant that execution, capital punishment, now came more or less wholly within the sphere of the judicial system. But the legal basis for it was widened. On 30 April 1954 the death penalty was restored for murder. This seems to have been related to a moral panic about the threat of ordinary criminals after their release from the camps in 1953. Something of the way this was perceived by ordinary Russians is portrayed in the film *The Cold Summer of 53*. In 1961–62 the list of capital crimes was then extended for economic and other specified offences and in 1973 hijacking was added. In the Brezhnev era the case against the death penalty was allowed to be put on isolated occasions but the general line remained that which was set out in 1964 by N.R. Mironov, a leading apparatchik. Justice in the USSR should combine 'a humane approach to minor offences' with 'decisive measures … against that insignificant group of dangerous criminals which inflicts great harm upon society …, such criminal elements should of necessity even more decisively feel the retributive force of the all-people's state'.[8] The death penalty came to focus largely on murder and rape though in the late Khrushchev years it was more widely given for economic crimes. Exposure could also lead to others anticipating punishment. In the Uzbek cotton scandal of the 1980s which involved major fraud both Sharaf Rashidov, the head of the Uzbek Party, and Nikolai Shchelokov, the USSR Minister of the Interior, committed suicide.[9]

The authoritarian state did suppress crime levels but crime continued to be reproduced through similar social mechanisms to those in the West. Open discussion of this was censored and this helped to create a mystique about the underworld and 'big' crime.[10] But most crime was a function of direct material want or indirectly of the wider alienation, some other crime linked to the black market even had a degree of functionality within the system and was tolerated so long as it did not become too scandalous. Crime levels were higher in urban areas and especially in areas where immigration was most recent and life less stable. Although some murders were undertaken as part of other crimes, most were home based and in Moscow at the end of the 1960s some 70% were said to involve alcohol as a contributing cause. 'Capital rape' can also be related to the nature of socialisation, sexual repression and the reinforcement of a degree of male machismo beneath the false aura of equality. How many of those convicted were genuinely guilty remains unclear. For 'ordinary' crimes there was the possibility of defence but the authoritarian nature of the system no doubt lent the police the benefit of the doubt even more often than in the West.[11] Between 1962 and 1990 in the USSR, 24,500 people received the death penalty and some 21,000 were executed. The number fell from around 2,000 a year in the early 1960s to several hundred in the late 1970s and early 1980s. The fall was welcome but this was still a disreputable record in a world where the death penalty was gradually being given up.[12]

Much reduced in size and overwhelmingly the product of 'normal' criminal procedures, albeit authoritarian ones, the size of the prison and the camp population fluctuated around a million until *perestroika* caused a degree of re-examination of penal practice. The reduced prison-industrial complex was therefore still the largest of any industrialised country *at this time* and if conditions improved they still remained bad. What of more political crimes? The memory of the repression of the past remained just below the surface but the changed atmosphere by the early 1960s was reflected in a semi public exchange between Khrushchev and the poet Yevtushenko who defended contemporary art saying that its deficiencies would be 'straightened out over time'. Khrushchev then said 'The grave straightens out the hunchback', but Yevtushenko, unbowed, said: 'Nikita Sergeyevich, we have come a long way since the time when in our country only the grave straightened out hunchbacks.' But Khrushchev did not push his own proposal in 1961 for a monument to 'the memory of our comrades who fell victim to tyranny'.[13] And these limits to the discussion of past and present became more evident after his fall in 1964. Dissent tended to produce imprisonment and exile though conditions in the prisons and camps remained brutal and some, like the dissident Anatolii Marchenko, did not live to see out their sentences.[14]

Public order

In this new situation outbursts of civil unrest did occur, and were sometimes brutally put down. The grievances of the local population and deported peoples led to a continuation of what might be considered a low-level war of attrition in parts of the USSR like Kazakhstan in the 1950s, as attacks on local officials had a political edge. Open collective protests across the USSR were rarer. One account lists over 400 between 1953 and 1983 but over half involved less than 100 participants. However, the number of protests grew from 32 between 1953 and 1964 to 174 in the years 1965–74 and 203 between 1975 and 1983. The few big protests usually had a national focus and were dispersed by the militia with occasional help from the army. In 1965, for example, some 100,000 demonstrated in Yerevan. There was another notorious clash in Uzbekistan prompted by a football match, which left many dead.[15] Clashes also occasionally arose from protests against economic oppression – the most notably was in Novocherkassk in 1962 – an incident that became infamous and which led to 24 workers being shot.[16] Deaths in mass protest have been common in the West too. The overall numbers killed in the USSR between 1953 and 1985 have yet to be properly tabulated but they seem comparable to some Western countries. The difference is that there were fewer collective actions because the state and the forces of order used their powers and the memory of the past to 'dissuade' people from organising protest.

IMPERIALISM AND WAR

The rivalry between Russia and the US continued to structure global conflict and competition until the late 1980s. The centre of the 'Cold War' fortunately stayed 'cold' because between them the two superpowers controlled 97% of all nuclear bombs and could have destroyed humanity many times over. The world came closest to such mass destruction in the Cuban missile crisis of October 1962 before a degree of détente brought about a more moderate phase of the 'Cold' War. The armed side of the Cold War was fought more on the Soviet side through its support for proxy forces against US backed regimes or US forces deployed in the field. In 1987, as the Cold War neared its end, there were some 2 million troops stationed abroad. Of these, 730,000 came from the USSR alone and 492,500 from the US, with an additional 244,800 personnel afloat. The biggest US and Soviet deployments were either side of the 'Iron Curtain' in Europe. Elsewhere the USSR, with the exception of Afghanistan, had fewer and smaller deployments. In 1987 the biggest were in Cuba (7,700) and Syria (4,000).[17]

The driving force of development in the Eastern European satellites continued to be competitive global pressures and military security. This was translated into continual pressure on their living standards and the need to support Moscow. Over time control did loosen. The rulers of the satellite regimes gradually developed a significant degree of autonomy and were even able to articulate their own interests on occasion. But there were limits as to how far the Russian leadership in Moscow was prepared to see power slip from its grasp especially in the areas of greatest strategic concern. After the events of 1968 in Czechoslovakia, people talked of this as 'the Brezhnev doctrine' but the idea of limited sovereignty long predated Brezhnev himself.

The stationing of Russian troops in many parts of Eastern Europe meant that Russian soldiers were occasionally involved in individual acts of violence or were themselves subject to them. While these acts were not usually overtly 'political' they reflected the frictions of power no less than similar incidents involving say US or British troops abroad. But the big explosions had a more dramatic character which brought into stark relief the claims that these were societies which did not oppress the population at large and workers in particular.

Unlike in Russia, open revolt broke out on a number of occasions. In three of them – the workers' strikes in East Germany in June 1953, the Hungarian Revolution of 1956 and the Czechoslovak 'Spring' of 1968, Soviet troops were deployed against protesters who, especially in the first two cases – were drawn largely from the working classes. A detailed history of these events would take us too far into the history of these countries and not least because, as in Poland in 1956 and again in the early 1980s, Moscow preferred to allow the local ruling classes to solve the problems. But Table 4.1 sets out what is known about the direct Russian involvement.

Table 4.1   Death and Repression in Confrontations in Eastern Europe

	Russians Killed or Missing in Action	Local Civilian Deaths	Subsequent Emigration	Imprisoned	Executed
GDR 1953	n.k.	*c.* 50			200
Hungary 1956	720	2,700	200,000	22,000	350
Czechoslovakia 1968	98	94			

Sources: Krivosheev 2001, pp. 532–4; Ratkovskii and Khodiakov 2001, p. 366; Granville 1997; Dennis 2000, p. 68.

Another area of conflict was China where the Sino-Soviet dispute brought out underlying tensions in the 1960s and 1970s. By 1966 China had identified the USSR as its major military adversary. As with the US much of this conflict was 'cold' but border disputes flared up and, after minor incidents, more serious fighting broke out in 1969 for the control of Damansky Island (Zhenbao to the Chinese) on the Ussuri River. The Russian side lost several score of soldiers and Chinese casualties were higher both as a result of the direct fighting and bombing behind the Chinese lines.

The politics of the Cold War were built on an ideological trap. You had to be either for Washington or for Moscow. Today the similarities look clearer. There was the same attempt at the projection of power, the same attempt to sow ideological confusion, the same drive to sell arms. There was also the same insouciance of power that allowed each side to unleash death on hapless victims in incidents and actions that sometimes uncannily paralleled each other. As Russia invaded Hungary in 1956, for example, Britain and France were invading Egypt prompting the US cold warrior John Foster Dulles in a moment of private candour to say of Britain and France that, 'it is a mockery for them to come with bombs falling all over Egypt and denounce the Soviet Union for perhaps doing something that is not quite as bad'.[18] Yet, of course, he did not view US actions the same way and in public he could also be found denouncing death at the hands of Russia while excusing it at the hands of US and Western forces, often in the name of 'anti-Communism'. America destroyed much of Vietnam and Cambodia with little compunction, Russia much of Afghanistan. There were even parallels in more 'minor' incidents. In 1983, for example, the Russian military shot down a Korean jumbo jet which had flown off course into Soviet airspace killing all 269 abroad. It was, said Ronald Reagan, 'a crime against humanity', an embodiment of 'the evil empire'. Then, in July 1988, the US military shot down an Iranian airbus with the loss of all 290 lives. It is perhaps time therefore to take more seriously the argument that this parallelism was rooted in essentially similar drives and structures on each side.

The actions of the two sides were more distinguished by degree than kind. The US as the greatest superpower had greater reach, more military muscle and could support its military might with economic leverage – a set of powers that have become even more obvious since the collapse of the USSR. 'The Soviet Stalinists were never in this (American) league, they were lousy imperialists beyond the sphere of influence that Churchill and Roosevelt granted Stalin at Yalta. The West and Japan, on the other hand, have capital and debt as their levers of control.'[19] A measure of the difference in scale is reflected in the contrast between the CIA estimates that between 1955 and 1985, Russia trained some 70,000 military personnel from the Third World compared to the US Department of Defense's estimate that the US trained 457,675 in the period 1950–86 and that the annual operating cost of US foreign bases alone was $8.4 billion in the mid-1980s.[20] The Guatemalan journalist Julio Godoy even suggested that people in the Soviet Empire were luckier than Central Americans: ' ... while the Moscow-imposed government in Prague would degrade and humiliate reformers, the Washington-made government in Guatemala would kill them. It still does [and] has taken more than 150,000 victims.'[21]

But in the right circumstances, even after 1953, Soviet power could be deployed with the same brutality as US power. This was demonstrated in Afghanistan between 1979 and 1989 – a country whose unhappy history reflects the effects of one superpower's action in the 1980s and another at the turn of the new century. The major Soviet deployment came in December 1979. When the pro-Soviet Kabul regime faltered in the face of rebel attacks, the Soviet leadership ordered troops in. They stayed for nearly a decade with the last soldier leaving Kabul airport on 14 February 1989. Far from resolving the local problems, the invasion intensified them. Although less than 100,000 Soviet troops served in Afghanistan at any one time (with others serving on the Soviet side of the border) in total some 750,000 were posted there – mainly conscripts. Some 15,000 were killed and 50,000 wounded, of whom 11,500 suffered some kind of permanent disability; 80% of the casualties occurred in search-and-destroy operations.[22] Bodies came back in zinc coffins and veterans returned, often traumatised, to a society that found it hard to understand their plight – all the more so when, from the start of 1989, the invasion began to be spoken of openly as a crime.[23] But, like Vietnam, while the sufferings of the soldiers of the imperial power got some attention, those of the local population were hardly noticed. One Afghan government source quoted a figure of 243,900 Afghan soldiers and civilians killed, but other estimates put the figure anywhere up to 1 million. Counting the dead was difficult not simply because few counted direct Afghan casualties but because with social dislocation and large-scale refugee movements the wider demographic consequences in a backward society were difficult to estimate.[24]

THE PATTERN OF NORMAL DEATH

The stabilisation of the regime meant that most people could now look forward to a 'peaceful death'. But the wider distribution of death and the manner of a person's passing remained profoundly unequal. At the top some did die young but most lived long lives and now had honourable deaths. To the plot behind the Lenin Mausoleum after 1953 went Kliment Voroshilov, the head of state in 1953–60 and Commissar of Defence 1925–40 who was interred in 1969, as was the Civil War General S.M. Budyonny in 1973; M.A. Suslov, the official ideologist in 1981, and the last three leaders of the USSR who died in post – Leonid Brezhnev (1982), Yuri Andropov (1984) and Konstantin Chernenko (1985). The ashes of other regime figures and heroes continued to be given a place of honour in the Kremlin Wall. Beyond the Kremlin the Novodevichy cemetery, closed to the general public, welcomed other figures. More problematic figures could also find a place of honour. The poet, singer and actor Valdimir Vysotsky, not a dissident figure but tolerated uncomfortably by the regime, died of heart problems at the age of 42 (somewhat embarrassingly in the midst of the 1980 Olympics). The darling of the intelligentsia, his body was allowed to lie in state at the Taganka Theatre and the queues were said to be 15 kilometres long. His funeral and burial in the Vaganovskoe cemetery produced the biggest spontaneous demonstration in Moscow since that of October 1927 when the Left Opposition had made a final public gesture on the tenth anniversary of the revolution.[25]

For the mass of the population the extreme inequalities of the Stalin era were reduced but the class gradient in life and death remained. Living standards greatly improved but people continued to take second place to rockets and machines. It is here that we find a large part of the explanation for the peculiar trajectory of the death rate in Russia in the years between 1945 and 1991. Table 4.2 shows the fall in the death rate and the rise in life expectancy in the 1950s and early 1960s. This was a time of enormous optimism in the USSR, as in the West. The economy boomed in 1961 – Khrushchev told people that the USSR was growing so fast that 'by 1980 our country will leave the United States far behind in industrial and agricultural output per head of the population'. Using the rhetoric of 'socialism' and 'Communism' even as day-to-day realities belied it, he said that 'socialism has more than doubled life expectancy. Communism will yield a further rise in life expectancy and make a reality of the poet's dream: "We'll live to longevity, never reaching senility."'[26]

Table 4.2   Changing Death Rates and Life Expectancy in the USSR 1946–58

| | Total (m) | Birth Rate per 1,000 | Death Rate per 1,000 | Life Expectancy at Birth in Years | | | Infant Mortality per Live 1,000 Births |
				Average	Male	Female	
1946	170.5	28.5	15.8	46.1	41.5	51.0	167
1950	179.2	28.8	11.7	57.3	53.1	61.7	104
1951	182.3	29.1	11.6	57.8	53.7	62.0	107
1952	185.5	28.3	11.4	58.2	54.8	61.7	104
1953	188.7	26.4	11.0	59.0	55.4	62.8	92
1954	191.6	27.7	10.3	61.0	57.3	64.8	81
1955	195.0	26.6	9.3	63.4	59.6	67.3	73
1956	198.5	26.0	8.7	64.9	61.0	68.9	62
1957	201.9	26.2	9.1	64.0	60.0	68.1	64
1958	205.3	25.9	8.0	66.9	63.1	70.8	55

Source: Andreev et al., 1993, pp. 118–36.

Strong economic growth enabled the Soviet leadership to allow real wage levels to rise (albeit too modestly and unevenly) and to build and reconstruct many towns and cities on a scale that could not be imagined before 1941 or in the later years of the regime when growth slowed and budgets became much tighter. But these trends were also supplemented by a wider role for medicine in the prevention of infectious diseases through vaccination and immunisation. Figure 4.1 shows the dramatic decline in the levels of the major infectious diseases. To take one example, in 1934, at the peak of the malaria epidemic, there were over 9 million cases. In 1945, 3.9 million cases were recorded and in 1965 a mere 392.[27] Whatever the deficiencies of the statistics, this was a major change.

These successes were claimed as a triumph for 'the socialist system' and grandiose claims were made about what could be cured.[28] But the real logic of policies in the USSR was no different from those in the West, or increasingly in the Third World, where death rates also began to be brought down. Scientific medicine had to an extent created a 'magic bullet' that brought about the destruction of mass killer

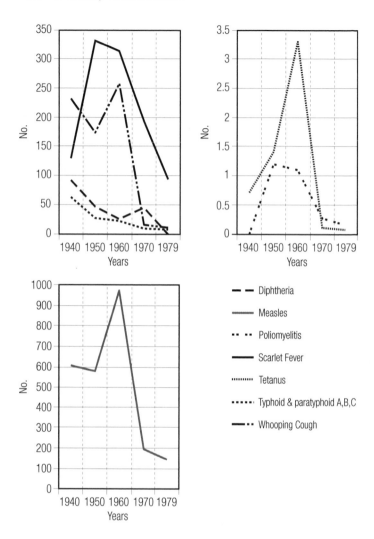

Figure 4.1   Selected Infectious Disease Rates per 100,000 in the USSR 1940–79

Source: Fesbach 1983, pp. 222–3.

diseases. This had a perceptible impact on the death rate with a lesser role for change in the wider social conditions. But the capacity of medicine to transcend social conditions was not, and is not, unlimited. Once the major reductions in deaths from infectious diseases had worked through, the pressure of levels of development and social inequality continued to be reflected in the difficulties of achieving further improvements in life expectancy.[29]

The curves of late Soviet mortality

The change that took place in the late 1960s is shown in Figure 4.2 which shows one set of estimates of comparative life expectancy. The impressive increases between 1938 and 1965 stand in stark contrast to the situation after that date. It is true that there is variation in the

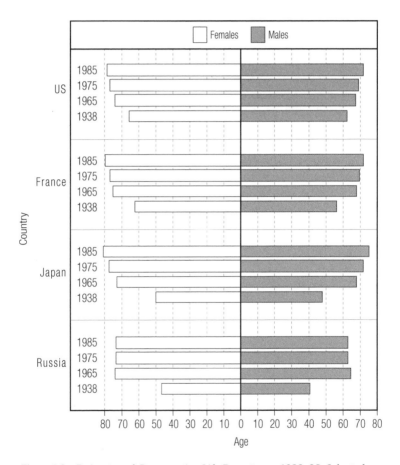

Figure 4.2   Estimates of Comparative Life Expectancy 1938–85, Selected Countries

Source: Shkolnikov et al. 1996, pp. 174–5.

West and, given its wealth, the record of the US hardly looks creditable, especially for men. But what happened in the former Soviet Union in these years demonstrated an even deeper malaise.

Whereas in Western Europe, for example, from the mid-1960s to 1989, the age-standardised death rate fell by some 25%, in the USSR (and the Soviet bloc more widely) it rose largely because of increased male deaths in the middle years of life. By the end of the 1980s the USSR (and Eastern Europe) had the worst age-standardised mortality rates for any industrialised states anywhere in the world and their situation did not look good when compared to many developing societies either. In the USSR the age-standardised death rate in 1988 was 15.6 per 1,000 for men compared to an unweighted average of 10.4 per 1,000 for 18 West European states. For women the USSR figure was 9 per 1,000 while the West European average was 6.3 per 1,000, and the overall age-standardised death rate was 11.6 per 1,000 for the USSR and 8 per 1,000 for Western Europe.[30] Table 4.3 shows the specifics of the shift in the USSR between the mid-1960s and the end of the 1980s by disaggregating the extent to which the death rate increased for different age cohorts in this period. The rise in the death rate in the adult male group is especially obvious.

Table 4.3   Percentage Change in Age-Specific Death Rates per 1,000 in the USSR for Cohorts Aged 20–69 between 1965/66 and 1989

	30–34	35–49	40–44	45–49	50–54	55–59	60–64	65–69
Male	−5	0	21	25	24	25	20	25
Female	−21	−17	−4	−3	2	11	4	19

Source: Eberstadt 1994, p. 202.

The patterns of death now became dominated by heart disease, cerebrovascular disease, cancer and respiratory diseases like bronchitis, emphysema, asthma, etc. It is often imagined that these are all diseases of longevity. Degenerative diseases have long gestation periods. Smoking-related deaths, for example, in any year are a function of smoking patterns of some two decades before. But the majority of degenerative disease is preventable. This was well put a generation ago by Cairns in an elegant statement of the role of environmental factors in cancer, but his argument has much wider application:

[M]ost of the common kinds of cancer seem to be caused in large part by environmental factors; because we can act to alter the environment ... these cancers are potentially avoidable ... if by appropriate public health measures the incidence of each kind of cancer could be reduced to the lowest level observed anywhere in the world, the overall incidence of cancer would be reduced at least tenfold. That is roughly equivalent to the reduction in mortality from infectious diseases that has been achieved in the past 50 years.[31]

The problem is not longevity but longevity in an environment that is not adapted to capitalising on the biological and psychological potential for human life.

Analysing class effects

We have seen that life expectancy is a function of both the overall level of development and class differentials within any country. In an important extension of this argument R.G. Wilkinson argued that beyond a certain point the various correlations of mortality and output per head weaken. However, a strong relationship does appear to exist in advanced countries between mortality patterns and levels of inequality. As Wilkinson puts it: 'if health differences within the developed countries are principally a function of income inequality itself, this would explain why social class differences in health have not narrowed despite growing affluence and the fall of absolute poverty'.[32] In fact his wider analysis goes beyond a narrow focus on income inequality but the essential insight that class determines the rate of death remains fundamental and it is supported by a mass of material from other countries including the Black Report in Britain.

In the case of the USSR the real level of development at the end of the 1980s was not so high as to mean that improvements in the overall standard of living were not an important aspect of the wider improvement in mortality (or that declines in output per head would not be devastating). But Wilkinson's analysis points to the vital need to integrate a wider concern with class reproduction and death into any discussion of mortality. Intriguingly, one commentator suggested that Wilkinson's argument about the central role of class in mortality might be refuted because Eastern Europe and the USSR had 'ostensibly egalitarian income policies' but still high mortality levels before 1991. He did allow that the subsequent transition might be an important test and, as we shall see in the next chapters, it does indeed offer support for Wilkinson's arguments. But what of the situation before 1991?[33] It did not seem to occur to Wilkinson's critic that the USSR might indeed be a class society. Perhaps the high levels of mortality and wide class differentials within them pointed to the real causative inequalities not simply of income but of power and control, of exploitation and alienation. As two British observers have put it, 'the finding in central and eastern Europe of a social gradient in mortality similar to that observed consistently in Western countries suggests the operation of powerful social and economic forces determining the unfavourable mortality in the East. The question is how these operate.'[34]

Discussion of this class effect continued to be suppressed though indirect evidence of aspects of it, like spatial variation in death rates, did occasionally surface. We do have one powerful indicator in retrospective estimates of mortality and life expectancy in relation to levels of education. Education continued to be both a means of social mobility into the upper sections of society and a central mechanism by which these groups were reproduced. As the social system matured, this latter element in the reproduction of inequality became more important.[35]

Let us look first at an example from the Ukrainian part of the USSR. Table 4.4 shows how the death rate of the 20–69 age group varied in 1979 in relation to the level of education. The average death rate was nearly twice as high for those with the lowest level of education compared with those in the highest group and for men it was more than twice as high.

Table 4.4   Relationship of Death Rate to Educational Level for Age Group 20–69 in the Ukraine in 1979 (Average Death Rate for All Groups = 100)

Educational Level	All	Male	Female
Higher education	73	66	77
Middle specialist	84	83	84
Middle general	99	103	97
Incomplete middle	144	147	141

Source: Geller 1989, pp. 101–8.

These gaps are quite comparable with those found in the West and mark out the way in which a sharp social gradient of death continued to exist. Yet although by the late Soviet era few outside commentators accepted the rhetoric of equality and classlessness, they were nonetheless reluctant to consider that the USSR might be a class society with class reproduction mechanisms.

That this was so can also be seen from other examples. In Moscow between 1960 and 1985 sample surveys were undertaken of those dying and the causes of their deaths. Unfortunately the factors included in the surveys changed over time but they included, at one point or another, sex, nationality, place of birth, job, length of time in Moscow, family situation and education. For the moment we have only the report of a 'qualitative analysis' of it. But this points also to the way in which not only was the overall rate of death socially unequal but so also was the reason for death. A broader quantitative analysis of the 1979 and 1989 census data for Russia alongside data from another local study has, however been undertaken. This showed gaps quite comparable to those in the West for additional life expectancy in the adult years after the age of 20. Those males with higher education could hope for 44.37 years, with those with middle specialist, 42.65; those with middle general, 39.14, and those with incomplete general, 38.99 – a gap of 5.38 years. The gap for women was more compressed but, at 1.04 years, still significant. Gaps depending on employment were only analysed in the broadest terms but also pointed to real inequalities. The authors of the commentary on the Moscow data were forced to recognise that policies designed to bring down the death rate must consider 'the social-demographic specifics of different groups of the population'.[36] What they did not ask, writing in 1991–92, was whether those who had presided over the past inequality and who, their own statistics suggested, had benefited from it, had any interest in doing this. As we shall see in later chapters, they did not.

There is another related factor to consider here. The degree to which death is premature varies by causes of death. Degenerative diseases *on average* shorten life by a few years. Deaths from accidents, suicide, murder and the like shorten it by a much larger number. If we measure not the loss of life itself but the lost years of life, then these causes weigh more heavily. And because these causes of death lay more heavily on those at the bottom than those at the top, so here too class becomes a major factor in the lost years of life in Russia, as in the West.[37]

EXPLAINING THE PATTERNS OF DEATH

What still conditioned the pattern of death was the continuing push of resources into arms competition and accumulation for heavy industry and the distribution of the rest of society's effort in profoundly unequal ways. On the eve of the Cuban missile crisis, Khrushchev said:

> We shall see to it that our armed forces possess the most up-to-date means of defence of our homeland – atomic and thermonuclear weapons and rockets of every range – and that all types of war material are maintained at the proper level. The strengthening of the USSR's defences and of the might of the Soviet armed forces – that is the paramount task of the Soviet people.[38]

The same line was echoed by Brezhnev and his successors until the contradictions of *perestroika* forced a partial rethink in priorities and orientation. This militarisation of competition within the global economy drained resources everywhere. But the Russian leadership faced a West where the US economy was at least twice as large as the Soviet economy and where the burden of arms spending could be shared more easily amongst NATO. The drain on the USSR was therefore proportionally much greater. In this military competition, said one writer,

> There were no 'battlefield casualties' but the commitment of huge amounts of human and material resources to the building of armaments led to ... 'buying death with taxes'. Weapons killed before they were ever used. They drained by their existence resources that could have been used to increase the welfare and the health of the population, decrease mortality and increase life expectancy.[39]

Nor did the post-1953 integration into the wider economic mechanisms of the global economy change priorities much. The USSR remained a weak player depending largely on oil and other raw material exports in its trade with the West, though this still generated considerable revenues. But imports reflected attempts to maintain the core system. The consumer goods imports that were allowed were partly used to buy popularity, as with the exchange of vodka for Pepsi-Cola in the 1970s. They also looked to meet the needs of the better off and more powerful sections of society. In the *glasnost* era, for example, the then Health Minister, Chazov, attacked Gosplan's priorities for imports: 'I would like to ask ... what is more important to buy from abroad – labels for the food industry, plastic bags, cigarette filters and cosmetics, or medicines to save the lives of sick people?'[40] The list is interesting because it emphasises the trade-off between medicine and consumer goods (rather than domestically manufactured producer goods) and because these imports were clearly not being undertaken to improve the consumption of the mass of the population.

But when it comes to analysing the more specific determinants of death, the analysis becomes more complicated. Epidemiological studies try to correlate disease, death and particular aspects of social life such as income, diet, behaviour, etc, but factors like income, diet and 'lifestyle' are all related in complex ways. However, when these are taken into account, premature death remains a product of society and its divisions. As Gorbachev would later put it, 'health is conditioned, first and foremost, by working and living conditions, the state of well-being'.[41]

The underpinnings of unequal death

Low standards of living, material deprivation, housing problems, lack of more general control over daily life can directly contribute to ill health and premature death and indirectly through the stresses that they create. They can lead to behaviours – 'lifestyle factors' – that undermine health and these are often used to berate people for their individual failings. But a generation ago Eyer and Sterling suggested that stress-related mortality had its roots in class society in general, and capitalism in particular. One aspect of this, external to the individual and a product of the wider social processes of alienation and exploitation, are the insecurities of daily life – the fear of unemployment, the division of labour, pressure in the workplace, etc. The other, internal to the individual, arises from socialisation into habits of individualism, competitiveness, acquisitiveness, etc.[42] In the case of the USSR the drive for growth meant that there was less insecurity in terms of unemployment (though dismissal could be a serious threat) but Soviet society seemed to exhibit the rest of these features in abundance.

Some Western studies too have drawn attention to the way in which material circumstance can limit our choices directly and force us to choose between unpalatable alternatives. The parent who struggles to provide a decent life for their children and smokes to cope with the burden is not necessarily acting reprehensibly once their situation is understood. Will is always easier to demonstrate when you do not share a person's problems. Indeed, one of the strengths of the Black Report in Britain was precisely that it tried to show in some detail how such choices were constrained and made.[43] In the USSR, where formal organisation was not allowed to counter demands from above, the pressure on the individual became all the greater. Most workers experienced 'shortages of food and other daily needs, unfulfilling work, little or no reward for effort at work, low control over lifestyle and feelings of disadvantage ...'.[44] One important piece of evidence reflecting this more general level of alienation can be found in evidence that self-rated health was much lower in the Soviet bloc than in the West, with self-rated health also varying between social group.

Culture will reflect the socially structured 'injuries of class'. Some of these will be open but others will be hidden, an internal response to the frustration of lives embittered and hopes unrealised. In the 1920s Trotsky made a further point that is still relevant, that culture and behaviour is also an accumulation of past social traits. The more subservient, alienated, repressed and exploited a group, the deeper will be the imprint of this on behaviour.[45]

Class relationships arise from production and extend into society at large. In the USSR workers continued to have no control over the process of production. The physical conditions of work were a direct source of ill health and death themselves but they also throw light on the wider way in which society was structured and the pressures it created.

In the post-Stalin era, work conditions saw substantial improvements but they remained poor.

> We are without working tools. We have no means of transporting them to the site where the new station will soon be established. We have to move heavy blocks but have no means of doing so. We have to put up the frames by hand. We carry cement in shovels. We still use the pickaxe. This is not modern work, this work is from the stone age.[46]

This was how the manager of an extension project to the Moscow Metro described working conditions to a *Moscow News* journalist in late 1987. The numbers of accidents and deaths at work remained a secret until the late 1980s, but even though they fell (especially in the 1980s) they remained high across the economy. A narrower range of industrial diseases was recognised and recorded. With no right to independent organisation workers were dependent on the sensitivity of their bosses to their situation. Rules existed and might be enforced but there was no guarantee of this. How insensitive the situation could be is illustrated by the situation of the miners. When they struck in 1989 it was revealed that their soap ration had not changed since 1923.[47]

The instrumental view of the worker was reflected in the process by which workers were paid bonuses, given supplementary foods and allowed earlier retirement if they worked in hazardous or demanding conditions. What this actually meant was workers were expected to tolerate dangerous conditions, poorly designed safety equipment or the lack of it in return for financial compensation for risking their health and lives – a strategy which any serious trade unionists would fiercely oppose. When figures finally became available it appeared that in 1986 nearly 15 million workers were employed in unfavourable working conditions.[48] Those who worked in unhealthy conditions could also unwittingly carry harmful dusts and materials into their own homes at the end of each day.

The improvement in the standard of living evident in the 1950s and 1960s continued until the early 1980s when it was overcome by the slowdown in the economy. But standards remained low for most people. Families acquired more and a better variety of consumer goods but even the official statistics suggested a large minority still living in or close to the poverty level. Diets also improved. The 'dumpy' citizen of the past gave way to a slimmer and taller adult. Women especially moulded their bodies to avoid the look of their parents and grandparents.[49] But the extent, variety and stability of the food supply left much to be desired even in some of the bigger cities. Vitaliev suggested a rule, only half jokingly, that the quantity and quality of food available to the mass of the population in any place was inversely proportional to the quantity and quality of food available in the top restaurant of the party officials. Shortages of key foodstuffs would suddenly emerge. Fruit was always a problem in areas to which it had to be imported. In some places items like milk could be sold only on prescription.[50]

Housing too improved. The average housing space per person rose above the sanitary minimum set by the state in the 1960s and by 1985 there were nearly 14 square metres per person. But problems were still serious. In the mid-1980s, 9 million families remained in communal housing and many young workers were still housed in barracks and hostels. Moreover a significant minority of people still lived in housing without running water and proper sanitation.[51]

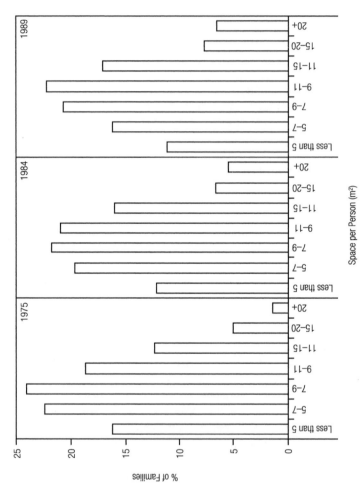

Figure 4.3　Percentage of Urban Families Living in Housing Units by Space per Person

Source: *Ekonimika i zhizn*, no. 33, August 1991, p. 14.

Given the historical squeeze on resources for housing this was an area where, at least in terms of area per person, there was less inequality. But when the statistics became available they showed how misleading simple averages were as can be seen in Figure 4.3.

Even in areas where expansion was rapid and there was need to attract new workers housing resources were squeezed. In the oil-rich Tyumen *oblast* (administrative region) to which large numbers flowed there were some 405,000 people on the housing waiting list in 1990 with some 160,000 workers living in makeshift accommodation and converted railway wagons.

> The main causes of so depressing a situation was that attempts to change the tradition of the 1930s–1950s – first production, then everything else including the people with their needs and concerns – were inconsistent ... Most destructive of all was the policy of the authorities who preferred to produce temporary homes instead of buildings requiring capital investment.[52]

The consequences of all this were twofold. While infectious disease now explained a minority of deaths it still played a more significant role than in other industrialised states. But more importantly high levels of death from degenerative disease and deaths from different forms of 'violence' (in the widest sense) now became a distinguishing mark of Russian society and especially for Russian men. By the 1980s smoking was implicated in up to 40% of adult male deaths with alcohol making another huge direct and indirect contribution. The continued consumption of high levels of legal and illegal alcohol meant that death rates from 'alcoholism' were as much as ten times as high as in France at the end of the regime. The state's response to this continued to be top-down pressure. Huge numbers passed through sobering-up stations.[53] But alcohol remained an important source of revenue and what one dissident called 'Commodity No. 1'. It was both part of the official culture and the counter-culture.[54] These pressures also spilled over into high levels of despair and violence in daily life. In 1984, on the eve of *perestroika*, there were 81,000 suicides in the USSR, a rate of 30 per 100,000, compared to rates of 22 per 100,000 in France, 21 per 100,000 in West Germany and only 9 per 100,000 in Britain. The murder rate was similarly high with 24,000 murders, a rate of 9 per 100,000. Indeed 'the standard-ised death rate by homicide was almost eight times as high as the European average'.[55] Men were much more likely to kill themselves and they were also much more likely to be the victim or the perpetrator of murder. But rates varied between republics in relation to patterns of development and tended to be highest in the Baltic states and the Russian Federation. Alcohol was implicated here too but the key question is what lay behind this and how it related to the wider problems that people had.

Death also came from the external world – air and water pollution, traffic accidents and other accidents, so-called 'natural disasters', etc. Pollution was one of the few areas where more open discussion could take place in the 1970s and early 1980s provided that problems were not seen as having systemic causes. But of course they had. Industry spewed out filth and plundered resources across the USSR with little regard for the environment or the pollution. Raw sewage and solid waste, for example, continued to be dumped in many areas. Plumes of smoke over the bigger industrial centres were visible reminders of the problems which the use of unleaded petrol compounded.

We have stressed that 'natural disasters' and accidents often have a man-made element to them. One obvious and high-profile area where this was so was in the civilian and military nuclear programme. The most notorious nuclear disaster before Chernobyl occurred in the Urals in 1957.[56] But earlier nuclear testing was cavalier. One later correspondent to the newspaper *Argumenty i fakty* told of how as a child she was part of a group of schoolchildren who were marched into a local ravine and told not to look up as a nuclear test was held nearby. In another test at the same place the top floor of the school was destroyed along with much local housing. 'Clearly,' she said, 'we were not considered humans then – or now, for that matter.'[57]

These conflicts of interest remained rooted in the trade offs imposed by competing goals and the instrumental nature of 'planning'. Stalin's search for wreckers disappeared but, since the systemic failure in respect of safety was still ruled out, blame tended to be on lower levels. There was a widespread perception that, in the words of a Russian saying, 'when a train crashes the man who sets the points usually gets the blame'.

Social security and health

Reforms in the 1950s and 1960s gradually widened social security and health provision and began to address the problems of the countryside. With society under centralised direction it was easier to allocate a minimum level of subsistence and care than in a more market-based system, and there is no doubt that, as with the NHS in

Britain, this was popular. But the fact that this was no more under popular control than any other aspect of society meant that the gap between rhetoric and reality remained considerable.

Let us consider the elderly. In the 1920s and 1930s less than 7% of the population were over the age of 60 but by the 1980s this share had doubled. The USSR boasted some of the earliest retirement ages in the world – 60 for men and 55 for women. By the late 1980s there were some 55 million dependent on pensions, most from old age but 6 million due to invalidity and 6 million due to the loss of the family breadwinner (and therefore often younger). Old age pensions were far from generous, even allowing for the reduced costs of rent and travel, etc. When the system opened up after 1985 the faces of the aged, and even more the rural aged, stared back out of the newspapers in silent rebuke. One regime economist made a revealing calculation. To bring up a worker, he suggested, cost 15,000 roubles. A worker could then create 125,000–137,000 roubles of value. Approximately half of this would be surplus. Part of this could repay the costs of bringing him up. The rest could then be divided between the pension (13,000 roubles) and the surplus put 'at the disposal of society [sic] for further development of the productive forces'.[58] The logic of squeezing the conditions of the old is clear and not surprisingly in 1988 a quarter of old age pensioners worked – making up 4–6% of the labour force in many industries and as much as 10% in some areas, such as retailing. Most of these were men aged 60–70. 'In other words,' said one account, 'many are working while they still have the strength.' And this is to say nothing of the army of grandmothers who filled in the many deficiencies in the state childcare system for their working daughters. The popular view that '*starost – ne radost*' – 'old age is not pleasure' – was essentially right, said one commentator.[59]

Health spending rose from 5.17% of government expenditure in 1940 to 6.5% in 1960 but, as can be seen in Figure 4.4, it then began to fall.[60] As a percentage of GNP, health spending peaked in 1968–69 at 4.4%; in 1970 it was 4.1%, and by 1985 it had fallen to 3.9%.[61] In its last stages the USSR was the only industrialised country in the world to be reducing the share of resources devoted to health spending.

It is true that the Soviet system continued to depress the wages of medical staff and the price of drugs while in the West (and especially the US) they were inflated, so such figures do not necessarily reflect the real level of resources delivered by the sectors. But, as in Britain

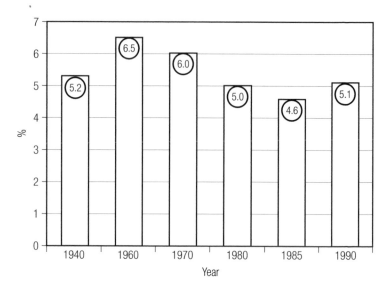

Figure 4.4   Government Expenditure on Health as a Percentage of GDP

Sources: *Narodnoe khoziastvo* 1987, p. 588, 1989, p. 612.

while there was widespread support for universal and equal healthcare, there was dismay at the inability to properly resource it.

In the 1980s one investigator suggested that 25% of the population had access to a high standard of facilities if they lived in the capital cities; 24% had decent facilities in industrial and provincial cities, and the remainder, just over half, had less than adequate facilities in small towns and rural areas.[62] This division was geographical but it was also partly social. But the social division becomes clearest of all if we consider the facilities that existed at the very top which were extended in this era and available perhaps to around 1 million people or 0.4% of the population. This was the so-called Fourth Directorate of the Ministry of Health. One anecdotal suggestion is that this special health service consumed almost half the resources going into health. This seems unlikely, but were it true it would even more clearly point to the enormous scale of inequality built into the system.[63] At the very top the doctors of the Politburo had a base in the Central Clinical Hospital – opposite the Kremlin. In the period from the early 1970s onwards they were increasingly called upon. Brezhnev began to show signs of degenerative illness in 1973 and had increasing problems with movement. Treating him was the responsibility of the chief doctor to the leadership, Yevgeny Chazov. Andropov as head of KGB told Chazov that even the Politburo should not know the full extent of Brezhnev's problems for fear of igniting a power struggle. To Chazov's frustration Brezhnev's nurse (with whom there were suspicions of sexual liaisons) gave him sleeping pills and tranquillisers. But the key task was to keep up appearances, first with Brezhnev and then with Andropov and Chernenko.

> We worked out a special system of televising the sessions and meetings in which Brezhnev and Andropov appeared. The producer and the cameraman knew concretely from which angles and points to shoot ... In the new facilities for the plenary sessions of the Central committee, special railings were installed to help the leaders to get to the tribune. Special ramps were devised to lift Brezhnev into his aeroplane, and on to the top of the mausoleum. But the height of hypocrisy came in the television speech of General Secretary Chernenko on the eve of the elections to the Supreme Soviet in 1985. In order to show people their boss, despite all our categorical objections the dying Chernenko was taken out of his bed and put before the television cameras ...[64]

The system looked after its own, but those who looked after the system also had a duty to it.

NATIONAL VARIATIONS WITHIN THE USSR

Rapid development after 1945 also led to significant improvements in the situation of the different national republics but there were difficulties in sustaining these as growth slowed in the 1970s and 1980s. Centralised direction enabled a degree of moderation of the level of uneven development that more market-oriented development created in the countries along the southern periphery of the USSR. This led some intellectuals in those countries to set aside doubts about other failings in the USSR, and to look to it as something of a model. But because the centre remained constrained by the wider imperatives of military competition and accumulation they were not able to properly confront the legacy of the past or avoid reproducing inequalities in the present. The Russian republic remained less developed than the Baltic states but the gaps between the Baltic states and Russia and the Central Asian states remained. Much was made too of the generalisation of medical care, rather less about the failure to deal with more costly infrastructure shortcomings and backwardness. Moreover, without detracting from the fact that positive progress did occur, it also needs to be recognised that the process of improvement had hidden elements of injustice within it. If levels of development between republics are compared this presents a more flattering picture of improvement than if the situation of the main ethnic groups by republic is compared. Then there is the issue of class in these regions. Stories are legion of the opulent lifestyle of those at the very top. But more systematic data of the link between education and life expectancy shows the contours of class were as real in the periphery as they were in the heartlands. Table 4.5 shows what happened in Kazakhstan based on an analysis of the 1979 census data.

Table 4.5   Social Differences in Life Expectancy in Kazakhstan by Educational Level

| | Life Expectancy in Years | | % of Group Reaching Pensionable Age | |
	Male	*Female*	*Male*	*Female*
Higher and incomplete higher	63.2	71.1	73.4	90.1
Middle special	60	68.8	65.4	88.5
Middle general	60.1	73.5	64.6	85.5
Middle incomplete	57.7	65.6	56.9	84.3
Elementary	52.1	63	45.7	72.2

Source: Borokhod 1990.

National variations within the USSR were important in another sense. In 1971–72 the infant mortality rate suddenly began to rise in the USSR and in 1974 the publication of the figures was stopped. The hidden debates this may have created have still to be explored. But in the West commentators were divided between those who saw this as an expression of a worsening situation in the 1970s and those who saw it as a product of the better registration of deaths. Instead of admitting earlier statistical weaknesses, they had used them for propaganda purposes. In the late 1950s, Tajikistan, for example, claimed the infant mortality rate of a developed country. If true this would have made Moscow the most benign imperialist ruler in history. When more reliable statistics began to be collected, they had therefore to be consigned to the secret archives. The problem was a past undercounting of infant deaths and the allocation of those that were registered between the stillbirth and infant-death category. But as the ideological Cold War intensified in the early 1980s, the idea that Moscow was hiding a massive deterioration in public health was attractive propaganda for the West. But most demographers saw the problem as one of registration, especially as the biggest increases in recorded infant mortality were occurring in the Central Asian republics. On the other hand, were the trend to be real, it would be an even more powerful indictment of the processes of uneven development within the internal Soviet Empire. The official data are set out in Table 4.6 along with comparative figures for Estonia as a more developed republic.

Table 4.6   Recorded Infant Mortality Rate per 1,000 Live Births, Selected Republics

	1972	1975	1980	1985
USSR	15.8	18.2	17.1	14.0
Estonia	24.7	30.6	27.3	26.0
Kazakhstan	27.0	38.8	32.7	30.1
Kyrgyzstan	40.4	42.5	43.3	41.9
Tajikistan	48.1	80.8	58.1	46.8
Turkmenistan	50.2	56.5	53.6	52.4
Uzbekistan	37.3	53.8	47.0	45.3

Source: Velkoff and Miller 1995.

The fact that there was a slight rise in developed areas suggested that the increase in infant mortality was not entirely spurious. But a significant demographic study has thrown more weight behind the real explanation by showing that much of the increase in infant deaths in central Asia occurred in babies aged one month to a year old and that it was the result of infectious disease and respiratory problems.[65] In Turkmenistan, for example, three-quarters of infant mortality was put down to infectious disease and respiratory problems, compared to only 16% in Lithuania.[66] Moreover, while the growth in infant mortality was apparent in both rural and urban areas, it was more so in the former. Yet serious doubts remain about this view. Although conditions were getting difficult in these republics the temporary intensity of the rise in infant mortality problems suggested by the data does not seem to fit the economic and social history. One explanation that has been offered is a restructuring of medical care away from the villages, but the chronology is not right and medical care is, as we have stressed, not a central explanation for major variations in death rates. All that we can say at the moment is that whether the increase was real or artificial it nevertheless speaks to the gap between the benevolent view that Moscow had of its relations with its republics and the reality. Like all imperial powers Russia was reluctant to give a proper account of its role lest a bigger set of issues be opened up. In the event the competing claims of benevolence versus exploitation would lay the basis for an increasingly sharp debate in the *glasnost* era. And out of this would come part of the logic of the breakup in 1991 of not only the USSR but also of Russia in its older, pre-1917 form.

5   The End of *Perestroika* and the Transition Crisis of the 1990s

PERESTROIKA AND THE COLLAPSE OF THE USSR 1985–91

The latter period of Brezhnev's reign became popularly designated as the 'years of stagnation'. Yet, after his death in 1982, the Soviet Union's economy continued to stagnate, first under the geriatric leaderships of Andropov (1982–84) and Chernenko (1984–85), and then, from March 1985, under the more youthful leadership of 54-year-old Mikhail Gorbachev. The deaths of three successive leaders in 1982–85 seemed to suggest that the failings of the system as a whole had become focused on the failing bodies of its leaders. Season tickets were to be issued to the laying-in-state in the Kremlin's Hall of Columns, said a joke of the time.

It was under Gorbachev that recognition was finally and unequivocally given to the fact that neither the economy nor society could be run along the old lines. The command economy set up in 1928/29 was not succeeding in generating sufficiently high growth levels to enable the Soviet Union to do to what Stalin primarily designed it for: to maintain a military-industrial complex that could militarily compete with the major Western powers. The consumer and service needs of the population could not perennially be relegated to the status of 'residual principle'. Given this pincer movement on the demands of the Soviet economy, changes needed to be made quickly – changes whose aim would be to increase productivity of all sectors of the economy so that, on the one hand, military needs could satisfactorily be met and, on the other, improvements in the living standards of the mass of the population – alongside the granting of more freedoms and democratic rights – could be provided.

When Gorbachev came to power in 1985 there was, therefore, a sense that the system needed shaking up. But he was initially firmly convinced that this would involve limited reform and more discipline. But this approach soon floundered and Gorbachev and his allies were forced to open up a wider debate to attempt to circumvent bureaucratic resistance. As this happened, a process of social, political and economic change began to develop, built around the ideas of two Russian words associated with Gorbachev's reforms that became famous the world over: *glasnost* and *perestroika*. The former meant 'voiceness' or 'openness'. Its gist was the granting of greater freedoms and the opening up of the deficiencies of society to public scrutiny. Related to this was *democratisatsia* – bringing the mass of the population into the political system in however timorous a fashion. *Perestroika* meant economic restructuring or improved efficiency of the economy.

The *glasnost* era saw the publication of an avalanche of detailed information about the past and present. The most traumatic was the story of those who had died in the famine, mass repression, the war, and the like. At first, much of the information did not go beyond what was available in the West; indeed it often drew uncritically on it. But soon archival revelations began to complement memoirs and revealed the picture we have analysed in Chapter 3. Organisations like Memorial (or Remembrance) were set up to record and preserve the memory of the past, but there was also a spontaneous process in which countless individuals for the first time talked through their own suppressed memories. 'Conscientious citizenship begins with the feeling of historical guilt. In saving the present by remembering the past, we save the future ...', said Yevtushenko.[1] But *glasnost* also allowed the indignities of the present to be unravelled too. Journalists like Vitali Vitaliev described for the first time in public how 'social injustice ... extends further into death. It was the tradition for the elite to be buried separately from those whom they ruled.' This extended down to some smaller cemeteries which had their 'avenues of fame'. But bribery could also enable your corpse to lie alongside the great as in the case of a Georgian mafia boss who managed to buy himself a burial place (temporarily) next to Valdimir Vysotsky. At the other end of the scale were the indignities that could befall the ordinary person – the bureaucratic processes by which a body had to be collected, the difficulty there might be in finding a coffin, the insensitivity of the price differentials for the cremation of children and adults, the perception of the indifference of crematory workers, the need to offer bribes to have graves dug properly. Not everyone experienced this, but enough did. For Vitaliev, it was summed up by the situation that arose in his home city of Kharkhov when a local factory making urns for funeral ashes was converted to make lavatory pans and a notice had to be posted in the local crematorium: '*Because of the absence of urns, ashes will be given out in polyethylene bags.*'[2]

Information also began to emerge about the detailed pattern of death, some of its social contours, accidents and death at work, disease patterns, the beginnings of AIDS and so on. In June 1988, Chazov, the Minister of Health, summed up the deficiencies of the system at the 19th Party Conference saying that in the mid-1980s, the Soviet Union ranked 32nd in the world for life expectancy, 50th in the world for its infant mortality level, and between 70th and 80th out of 126 countries in terms of percentage of GNP allocated to health spending.[3] But the deficiencies of the system were also exposed by contemporary disasters. The most infamous was at the Chernobyl nuclear power station in Ukraine where an explosion threw radio-activity high into the atmosphere and down on the surrounding countryside. The bravery of those who tried to contain the radioactive leaks contrasted with the bureaucratic indifference that had led to the explosion, and the speedy evacuation of the children of local top-ranking officials while the rest of the population was kept in darkness for 36 hours. In the event, the toll of premature death and injured lives from Chernobyl continues. Thirty-one were killed immediately, but thousands more have died since. Hundreds of thousands were displaced and 160,000 resettled. There has been a sharp increase in thyroid cancer and birth abnormalities, to say nothing of myriad other diseases.[4]

The Chernobyl tragedy, and the discussions and revelations it gave rise to, were the tip of the 'iceberg of hope' that a better society might be built. Pressure for change mounted. This was reflected in the development of spontaneous organisations and mass movements committed to democratic change, social justice, and an attack on the privileges of those above. But the argument that the old society was in some sense 'socialist' inevitably created enormous confusion. If this was 'socialism', many naturally thought that 'capitalism' might be preferable – though they had little sense of what this might mean, and the argument tended to narrow to one of state versus market.

One optimistic sign of the times was that the death rate began to fall in the mid-1980s, and life expectancy rose (male, from 61.7 in 1984 to 64.9 in 1987; female, from 73 in 1984 to 74.6 in 1989).[5] This was partly a positive effect of the otherwise resented campaign from the top to reduce alcohol consumption. But it perhaps also reflected the initially positive wider public scrutiny of life that began to develop. Certainly the suicide rate declined somewhat – a reflection perhaps of the excitement and more positive climate of the period. But, after 1987, the overall death indicators were beginning to turn up again as social dislocation rose (male life expectancy fell to 63.6 by 1991). Now also in the glare of publicity, more narrow indicators of crime, murder, social unrest and civil disaster also began to move upwards. But if this provoked some to more activity, the generalised confusion began to demobilise others or lead them to look towards more private solutions. As early as 1988, one commentator talked of 'our increasing "socio-political immune deficiency" to other peoples' misfortunes' in the context of the acceptance of the necessity of unemployment.[6]

The Gorbachev regime equivocated in the face of popular discontent – sometimes suppressing protests, especially national ones, violently. But more generally it lost its way in the face of competing pressures. In 1990, for example, Chazov resigned as Health Minister frustrated, he later said, by the 'hopelessness of fighting for a renewal of Soviet health care'. Politically these pressures came from three broad groups. Some sections of society and the leadership looked back to the stability of the past, others looked forward in however a confused way to developing change from below. A third group looked more to capitalise on the inconsistent yearning for change by seizing the opportunity to shift the organisation of society to a more market-based one – if necessary at the expense of the mass of society. In this they were assisted by advisers from the West who portrayed 'the market' as the cure-all to the problems of 'the state'.

The subsequent collapse of the USSR in December 1991 has been seen as an example of collective suicide by the old ruling groups. It was no such thing. Already before the failed coup of August 1991 there had been the beginnings of a shift in sections of the ruling class to 'privatise' some of its collective power. In the 1991 coup defeat, this movement became more rapid from below, and manipulated at the top, so that as the USSR broke up in 1991–92, across its fragments, and not least in Russia itself, there was a wholesale conversion of power which belied any claims about the 'death' of the old ruling class. Just because this was a process of survival and class restructur-ing, the benefits and costs of change were again to be unevenly distributed. This undercut claims that 'the market' could produce a 'fairer' situation, leaving home-grown enthusiasts for it, and their Western allies, not only looking foolish but also implicated in a new range of policies that once again helped spread death throughout the land. The US demographer Nicholas Eberstadt, for example, suggested that 'properly framed and implemented policies, pursued on realistic budgets, should be capable of eliciting steady improve-ments in general conditions through the region [of the former Soviet bloc]'. In fact, even as he wrote this, Eberstadt was also forced to admit that the early evidence was that policies were 'not adequate'.[7] This proved quite an understatement as it soon became apparent that the health impact of the transition was generally devastating.

Of the two central planks of reforms, it was *perestroika* that really interested Gorbachev. Put briefly, this was the attempt to induce an improvement in the incentive regime of the economy by incorporating elements of the market mechanism with the aim of launching the reforming economy into an accelerated (*uskorenie*) growth path. There were similarities between *perestroika* and Russia's shock therapy reforms of 1992. For Gorbachev's chief economic adviser, Abel Aganbegyan, *perestroika* implied revolutionary qualitative transformation – a term synonymous with 'radical reform, major reconstruction, radical change, transformation to new quality, and a breakthrough'.[8] In essence, this is precisely what shock therapy meant and was intended to achieve. Yet, for advocates of shock therapy, *perestroika* was half-hearted and far from truly radical. Lipton and Sachs, advisers to the Polish Solidarity government, had pointed to the dangers of such 'timidity' in Poland – the first former Eastern bloc country to implement shock therapy in January 1990. They had specifically wished to avoid the modest market reforms of Hungary's 'New Economic Mechanism (NEM)' of 1968 which quickly came to grief. Arguably, the *perestroika* reforms were a Russian version of NEM.

It quickly became clear that there was a chasm between the aims of *perestroika* (and Gorbachev) and reality as the real economy continued to deteriorate and the population continued to suffer. Though Gorbachev's popularity might have been soaring in the rest of the world, in the Soviet Union, it was heading for the rocks. What reforms he did introduce were hesitant and lacking in direction. Constrained by powerful party *nomenklatura* and bureaucratic vested interests (who were fearful of loss of power and control), and uncertain of the possible results, Gorbachev simply muddled along. During his reign, there were no less than twelve economic reform plans considered and rejected.[9] *Uskorenie* proved a chimera. What Gorbachev in fact did was to start dismantling the centralised planning mechanism without creating anything like the necessary framework for a market system that would compensate for the inevitable dislocation and chaos the former would entail. Hence the economic legacy of Gorbachev, which ultimately sealed his fate, was this: neither plan nor market – whereas he wanted both. Output therefore dropped even faster – caused not by shortage of demand because people still hoped to spend their savings, but by supply-side shortages which were accentuated by the fracturing of the planning system.[10]

If Gorbachev's label of the Soviet Union of mid-1980s as 'pre-crisis' was correct,[11] then what followed his departure can only be described as an overwhelming crisis. Aganbegyan's estimates for the Soviet Union's national income for the 1981–85 period were practically zero growth (compared to the official rate of 3.3% per annum); in other words, the economy had already been struggling when Gorbachev took over the reins in 1985. It was this that compelled Gorbachev to contemplate meaningful '*perestroika* reforms' – which Aganbegyan expected to yield a growth rate of 4% per annum for the 1986–90 period.[12] However, the actual performance was disastrous: official growth was given as 1.3% per annum but more accurate figures now show a growth rate of just 0.2% for this period.[13] The reforms had plainly failed to work.

The failed right-wing coup against Gorbachev in August 1991 sealed his fate, and that of the Soviet Union. In December 1991, the USSR was dissolved and split into 15 constituent republics, most of which then joined the loose association known as the Commonwealth of Independent States (CIS). With no country to rule over, Gorbachev's position became redundant and his powers largely passed over to Boris Yeltsin who had earlier been elected president (in June 1991) of the largest republic, the Russian Federation. Unlike Gorbachev, Yeltsin did not muddle in implementing reforms – indeed he had been assiduously putting together advisers to prepare a comprehensive reform programme for Russia. Initially, this was thought of as a relatively gradual transition with liberalisation and stabilisation implemented in one year. But, with urging from Western economic advisers, such a 'gradual' approach was spurned in favour of a 'big bang'. Similar advice, in fact, had earlier been proffered to Gorbachev in the autumn of 1990 by a joint report compiled by the big guns in international aid and finance, namely the IMF, the World Bank, the OECD, and the EBRD. Challenging Gorbachev's gradualist plans, they strongly advised radical reforms. It was acknowledged that this would lead to an immediate drop in output in combination with rapid inflation, but the expectation was of rising output within 'two years or so' and that 'growth in productivity and output would likely exceed that of most mature market economies'.[14] Such reasoning no doubt equally applied to Russia, but the reality, as we shall see, would be very different. Thus, in January 1992, Russia embarked on the path to a market economy by implementing 'shock therapy' reforms. Chief architect was the newly appointed Deputy Prime Minister and Finance Minister Yegor Gaidar, and the reform programme became known as the 'Gaidar Plan'. The aim was a rapid marketisation of the economy and a retreat of the state from economic life, meaning the destruction of the command economy and abandonment of the planning system.

SHOCK THERAPY REFORMS OF 1992

The drive to fully marketise the economy was a culmination of thinking within the Russian elite that centralised, bureaucratic, planning was giving rise to crippling rigidities, and that it was time to grasp the nettle that the command system lacked the flexibility and efficiency of the market mechanism. The ideological reasoning was clearly summed up in the introduction to the 500-Day Shatalin Plan for the USSR in 1990:

> Mankind has still not succeeded in finding anything more efficient than a market economy. The market creates a strong stimulant for mankind's self-fulfilment, for an increase in the economic activity and for rapid technological progress. Its self-regulating mechanisms guarantee the best co-ordination of all the activities of the economic actors, a rational use of the materials, financial, and work resources and a balance of the national economy.[15]

One factor that pushed the leaders towards this conclusion was that there was already in existence a very large 'informal', but largely illegal, economy – accounting for as much as 25% of the USSR's GDP[16] – run on the principles of supply and demand. In other words, illegal market activity was rife and was plugging the gaps in the central plan especially with respect to consumer goods and services. Though attempts had been made in many Stalinist economies to formally use elements of the market, in the attempt to buttress the command system, these had always been very limited given that this necessitated relinquishing control over large tracts of the economy which, in turn, threatened Communist Party/*nomenklatura* rule. Moreover, such efforts never succeeded. But all of this changed after the August 1991 attempted coup. It was felt by Yeltsin and his group of young Thatcherite economic advisers (both Russian and foreign) that 'there was no alternative'. The command economy was to be thrown into the dustbin of history and a viable replacement sought. The option of genuine democratic planning from below was something that had never registered on the radar screen of Russia's leaders since Stalin's consolidation of power in 1928. By curtailing mass activity, the leadership best ensured its survival.

The decision was quickly made to take the lead given by Poland when it launched shock therapy reforms in January 1990. Moreover, this accorded well with Western advisers and international financial institutions. The unwritten deal was that suitable assistance would follow the implementation of rapid reforms. However, this never came. But the reformers and their theorists thought they knew where they were headed, and they were convinced as to how to get there. Their theory indicated two broad courses of action. The first step was to scrap the planning mechanism that was already under severe strain, and quickly replace it with the price mechanism. The second was for the state to throw in the towel in regard to owning and running enterprises – it was time to let others (private agents) have a go, necessitating the largest privatisation of state-owned enterprises ever known. This was the foundation of Russia's 'shock therapy', launched in earnest on 2 January 1992.

Price shock, cutback in public expenditure, but no stabilisation

The 'shock' was essentially the immediate move to market clearing prices – in other words, the removal of administered prices and subsidies. Ostensibly, this was a reasonable move. The aim of creating a market economy had at least broad, passive, support from the population – though this did not imply that the shock therapy route was the most popular, nor that many knew of its implications. But there was certainly no significant pressure to retain the old, failed, command economy structures. The shift to a market economy implied that the central plank of the reform programme had to be the attainment of market prices. Shock therapy reformers argued that there was no other realistic option as hyperinflation was damaging the fabric of the economy and that, after Gorbachev's procrastinations, there was need for decisive measures. Politically, there was also the imperative of ensuring that the rule of reformers under Yeltsin was quickly cemented and any return to the old system blocked. Yeltsin took a very optimistic view of the prospects for the economy arguing in the autumn of 1991 that:

We must unreservedly embark on thoroughgoing reforms. The situation in Russia is difficult, but not hopeless ... There is a unique opportunity to stabilise the situation over several months and to begin improving that situation ... A one-time changeover to market prices is a difficult and forced measure, but a necessary one. For approximately six months things will be worse for everyone, but then prices will fall, the consumer market will be filled with goods, and by the autumn of 1992 there will be economic stabilisation and an improvement in people's lives.[17]

As we shall see, this was dangerously naive, faulty reasoning, filled with empty promises. Such naivety was clearly summed up by Gaidar who agreed that Russia lacked requisites for the creation of an effective market economy but argued that there was no time to sit around and wait till the preconditions were created.[18] By the same token, if one does not have the prerequisites to make a motor car, this is not a problem, just proceed with what you do have and not worry if the contraption crashes at the first instance (assuming it starts). But the result of such naivety for the mass of the population was a jump out of the frying pan of the defunct command economy and into the fire of the nascent, chaotic market economy. Many would not survive this transition, or their life expectancy would be curtailed, as we shall see in the next chapter.

The key element of the 'big bang' economic reforms was deregulation of most prices *at once* to market clearing levels. Inevitably this would lead to an initial burst of 'corrective inflation', but in the long term it was believed that prices should stabilise as supply and demand balanced. This would immediately put an end to that perennial phenomenon of Stalinist economies – the dreaded queues. To put it in more technical terms, repressed inflation (given expression by queues and lack of consumer choice leading to forced purchases) would give way to open inflation (rising prices) as those who could not afford to pay the market price for a purchase would obviously not bother queuing. But the neoclassical theory that underpinned shock therapy, predicted that there would also be a supply response, as new competitors to existing suppliers would arise. This would begin to pull prices down in the medium- to long-run. The reality, as will be seen, was the opposite – prices continued to rise vigorously.

The budget deficit in 1991 had reached an astonishing 31% of GDP which was fuelling inflation. Therefore, there would have to be a sharp cut-back in government expenditure and ending of subsidies to consumers in the form of fixed prices and to struggling enterprises (i.e. the abolition of what Janos Kornai had famously termed the 'soft budget constraint' and its replacement by the 'hard budget constraint') so as to drastically reduce the budget deficit and in the long run, achieve fiscal balance and the easing of inflationary pressures. Reduction of public expenditure was helped by the collapse of the Russian Empire. There was now a widespread acceptance that Russia was no longer such a great superpower; that the Cold War was over and, therefore, the outlay on the military, the single biggest component of the state budget, could be reduced. At the same time, the central bank would stop printing money. Interest rates would rise to real levels (above the inflation rate) to reduce the money supply and force enterprises to pay for loans. The aim of this was the efficient allocation of capital. The rouble would be set to market clearing (in effect, 'black market') levels and made convertible with hard currencies, above all the dollar. The economy would be opened to the outside world and barter-type CMEA (Council for Mutual Economic Assistance, or Comecon) trade would be replaced by foreign trade using international market prices. Thus, the foreign trade regime would be liberalised and non-discriminatory, that is, protectionism would be eschewed (importantly, this is invariably a key IMF loan conditionality).

A market economy requires the guaranteeing of property rights and the promise of the full liberalisation of the private sector. These were quickly implemented and indeed some assumed that this new, rapidly expanding, sector would prove to be the engine of growth of the new economy. The reality would, in fact, be different. The economy was dominated by very large enterprises and it is these that continue to dominate it. Given their size, they would naturally exercise very high levels of market power under free market conditions. To curb this, there would need to be de-monopolisation of the largest state-owned enterprises (SOEs) but this proved far easier in theory than in practice.

Finally, moves were quickly afoot to rapidly privatise the vast majority of SOEs. Theoretically, this was the key plank for the achievement of what was called 'effective corporate governance' (that is the efficient management of enterprises). In practice, it became the method by which the old *nomenklatura* became rich. The neo-classical view (indeed all proponents of free market theory and practice) sees state intervention as distortionary. Owing to information constraints, there is an inevitable misallocation of resources under economic activities that are under the state's ownership or control. The changed enterprise behaviour is intended to lead to improved productive efficiency: reduced costs of production, increased quality of output, increased variety of products and services, rational use and allocation of investment. It was essentially this reasoning that proved so appealing to the 'market Stalinists' who could readily point to the abject failure and inefficiencies of SOEs. Where once they had advocated and defended the command economy, the reformers (including Yeltsin) now argued for unbridled free enterprise.

The move towards price liberalisation was already underway in 1991 with the raising of production prices and retail prices, which rose by 70%.[19] Nonetheless, 70% of prices were still fixed or regulated by the state. The question, therefore arose as to what to do with these: gradually continue to free prices or liberalise all or most prices at once? The answer was the latter – shock therapy – option. The impact was widespread. It affected consumer and producer goods and services, though some items were excluded, including basic foods, medicines, public transport, rent, public utilities and energy. For the rest, prices rose very sharply: four-fold for food, 2.5 times for non-food products, 3.5 times for all retail prices, and five-fold for wholesale prices.[20] On average, prices in January rose by nearly 250% – this was the 'burst of corrective inflation'. Thereafter, the monthly rate dropped but did not stabilise to low levels as predicted, indeed it rose markedly from August (9%) to December (25%). By December 1992, prices were an astonishing 2,500% higher than in December 1991 (see Figure 5.1). The rapid increase in prices of inputs (particularly energy),[21] removal of subsidies, and devaluation of the currency, provoked Russian enterprises to utilise their market power and push up prices. Worst hit by the price shock were wage earners and pensioners, who did not obtain compensatory wage increases and pensions. The consequences for savings were devastating. They immediately became massively devalued, and so were virtually wiped out for the majority. On the other hand, non-wage earners who gained income from private business and those receiving interest payments on hard currency savings gained from the early reforms. Not surprisingly, income inequality rapidly increased (before stabilising in 1997) as seen from the continuing rise in the Gini coefficient of income (see Table 5.1, which tracks the movement of various economic indicators during the transition period).[22]

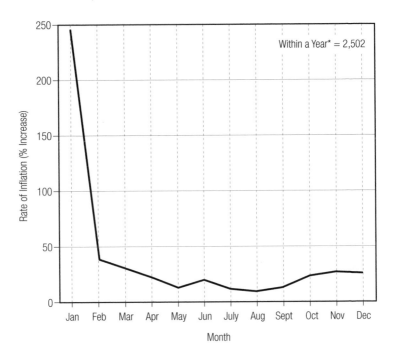

Figure 5.1   The Rate of Inflation (% Increase) Each Month during 1992

* Within a year refers to December 1992 over December 1991.

Source: UN ECE 1993, Table 3.2.14, p. 104.

However, the goal of achieving stabilisation and, ultimately, Western levels of inflation was never achieved. The annual average inflation rate has never reached single figures, though the decline from nearly 200% in 1995 to 15% in 1997 was dramatic. Nonetheless, inflationary pressures were persistent as enterprises continued to obtain credits and the large budget deficit was readily financed by the central bank. Even though the sharp cutbacks in public expenditure contributed to decline in the share of the government sector – from 58% of GDP in 1992 to 38% in 1999, in the context a shrinking GDP – the budget deficits remained very high owing to increased demands on expenditures under conditions of declining tax revenues. Consequently, the deficit was almost 19% of GDP in 1992; it fluctuated between 6% and 10% in later years before falling to just over 3% deficit in 1999. The authorities believed

Table 5.1 Various Economic Indicators for Russia 1991–2001

	1991	1992	1993	1994	1995	1996	1997	1998	1999	2000	2001
Inflation Rate*	160	1529	875	309	197	48	15	28	86	21	22
GDP Index	100	85.5	78.0	68.1	65.3	63.1	63.7	60.5	63.8	69.5	73.0
Industry Index	100	82.0	70.4	55.7	53.9	51.7	52.8	50.0	55.5	62.1	65.2
Government Balance†	−31.0	−18.9	−7.3	−10.4	−6.0	−8.9	−7.6	−8.0	−3.3	3.0	2.9
Government Expenditure†	n/a	58.4	43.6	45.1	39.1	42.4	44.4	41.4	38.4	35.8	35.8
Registered Unemployment‡	n/a	4.7	5.5	7.5	8.9	10.0	11.2	13.3	12.2	9.8	9.0
Index of Real Wages§	100	68	68	63	45	51	54	46	37	45	n/a
Gini Coefficient¶	n/a	0.289	n/a	n/a	0.381	0.387	0.401	0.399	0.400	0.399	0.396
Merchandise Exports ($bn)	n/a	53.6	59.6	67.5	81.1	88.6	88.3	74.7	75.7	105.6	103.2
Merchandise Imports ($bn)	n/a	43.0	44.3	50.5	60.9	68.8	73.5	57.8	39.5	44.9	53.8

* Annual average percentage increase in consumer prices (figures are rounded).
† % of GDP.
‡ Based on Goskomstat's monthly estimates according to the ILO definition, i.e. including all persons not having employment but actually seeking work.
§ 1991=100.
¶ Monthly earnings, with bonuses, for full time employees as reported by employers (excluding small-scale employers).

Sources: Inflation rate and GDP: UN ECE 2002, appendix tables B.1 and B.8; government balance and expenditure: EBRD 2000, p. 205 and 2001, p. 189; registered unemployment: UN ECE 2002, appendix table B.7; real wages: derived from UNICEF 2002, table 10.9, p. 87; Gini coefficient: Goskomstat 2002, table 7.11; exports and imports: EBRD 2001, p. 189; preliminary data: EBRD 2002.

there was a trade-off between gains in suppressing inflation, and lost output and overall living standards and so relaxed the policies towards the former in the hope of boosting the latter.[23] This, however, did not prove successful. Moreover, the ensuing financial crisis saw Russia default on its debts and this led to a collapse of the rouble in August 1998. This had a direct impact on inflation, as import prices rose, causing the rate to soar once more to 86% in 1999. In 2000 and 2001, the rate fell back again but still to a de-stabilisingly high 21% and 22% respectively.

As inflation rose, output levels fell drastically: by almost 15% in 1992, and a further 7.5% in 1993. GDP was just 60% of the 1991 level in 1998, the year of the financial crash, before recovering quite strongly during the 1999–2001 period. However, it was still only 73% of the 1991 level in 2001. Industrial output, responsible for the bulk of employment in this 'overindustrialised' economy, fell even more sharply – plummeting to just 50% of the 1991 level in 1998 before recovering to 65% in 2001. The evidence, therefore, points to a decisive failure of the reform programme – be it the initial shock or later gradual methods. The following summary for the 1992 reforms given in the *Economic Survey of Europe in 1992–1993* applies equally well for the whole decade of reforms:

> The attempt to solve the payments crisis through large-scale credit expansion clearly had failed: the only tangible result was runaway inflation, free fall of the rouble, and continuous recession in the production sector.[24]

Privatisation and corruption

A few months after the price shock, there followed a privatisation shock, under the tutelage of another Yeltsin Young Turk, Anatoly Chubais, who was appointed Minister of Privatisation in November 1991. In fact, privatisation had comprised a major plank of Gorbachev's economic reform programme for the USSR. He had signed a decree authorising it just before its dissolution. In Russia, the precursor to privatisation was the Law on Enterprises and Entrepreneurial Activity of December 1990 which had removed restrictions on private enterprise – though, in reality, local authorities demanded licences that were often obtained by bribery.[25] The first stage of privatising SOEs was via the passing of the decree on cor-poratisation in July 1992. This converted SOEs into commercial, market-oriented companies, with all shares initially under the state's ownership. The next stage was selling these into private ownership.

The Stalinist system was so discredited that workers at first overwhelmingly favoured the privatisation of state-owned enterprises. An opinion poll had shown a 5 to 1 majority in favour of the Shatalin Plan for the USSR in 1990, which included privatisation. Another poll in the summer of 1992, well into the Gaidar reforms, showed that more than 75% of workers thought privatisation was necessary.[26] Many workers felt that here at last was the chance to receive something from the state, a share of the enterprises in which they worked but which they had never considered 'their own'. The enterprise managers, the Communist Party, and its *nomenklatura* had long been acknowledged to be the real owners and controllers of state assets. Indeed, the subsequent passing of SOEs to erstwhile members of the *nomenklatura* via 'spontaneous privatisation' (where party officials and managers illegally transferred assets of SOEs into personal ownership) or 'voucher' privatisation represented the legalisation of a *de facto* control that had long existed.[27] But the corrupt nature of so much of the privatisation process caused support to plummet: opinion polls in September 1992 showed three-quarters of the public viewing privatisation either with indifference or negatively.[28]

The Privatisation Programme was passed in June 1992 with the aim of privatising most large SOEs by June 1994. A process of 'voucher privatisation' was begun for medium and large SOEs from December 1992. Every citizen was given a 10,000-rouble voucher that could be exchanged for cash or shares in enterprises. Many sold their vouchers for cash, and soon these became concentrated in the hands of those with large amounts of hard currency and connections, some of whom would quickly become the new oligarchs. Preference was given to management and employees of an SOE who received the majority of shares at low prices; a minority of shares were granted to others, with the remaining shares eligible to be sold at auction. In reality, employees' shares were locked in trusts controlled by managers who thereby also controlled the enterprises.[29]

Some 15,000 enterprises were to be privatised, including most industrial SOEs but excluding military and oil SOEs, and medical facilities. Very large SOEs (with more than 10,000 employees) required special permission to privatise. A former colleague of Gaidar, Tatyana Koryagina, made the frank admission that 'the privatisation process will be beneficial only to foreign business and domestic shadow business [the mafia]'.[30] This proved highly prescient.

Criminal activity spread like wildfire, feeding on the privatisation frenzy: the essence of what became known as 'corruptalism'. By the mid-1990s, there were an estimated 200,000 active criminal groups and 5,500 large criminal organisations involved in extortion, burglary, embezzlement, and misappropriation of public and private funds. Gangsters controlled retail markets, and smuggling was rife with one-fifth of petroleum and one-third of metal production being smuggled out of the country during 1992–94. Corruption became endemic: 70–80% of banks and state and private enterprises made payments to racketeers and corrupt officials. Much of Russia's wealth quickly became concentrated in the hands of a few billionaire oligarchs who, having acquired enterprises at knock-down prices, were more interested in asset-stripping than upgrading them.[31] They also systematically courted, supported and funded Yeltsin and, by so doing, began to wield great political power.[32] These were young (usually 30-something) men who, only a few years earlier, had been practically unknown but who had the connections to work the system to their advantage.[33]

The result of the privatisation process was dramatic – it was pretty much complete by mid-1994 with 14,000 SOEs privatised through voucher auctions. The private sector, from officially constituting 5% of the GDP in 1991, had shot up to 70% of GDP by 1997,[34] a level similar to advanced market economies. With the whole economy permeated with corruption, one is tempted a wry smile when remembering that the *raison d'être* of privatisation was improved corporate governance, leading to a massive boost in efficiency and output. Unsurprisingly, none of this materialised and the economy continued to languish throughout the 1990s.

THE IMPACT OF REFORMS: LOW PAY, POVERTY AND INEQUALITY

The impact of the reforms on living standards was absolutely punishing. Table 5.1 shows that in 1992, real wages fell by 42% and continued to decline thereafter. By 2000, real wages were just 46% of the 1991 level.[35] It has often been pointed out that the impact of the recession (meaning depression) has been greater than that in the US following the 1929 Wall Street crash. There has, however, been a debate as to how true a reflection of drop in living standards this is. The argument is that an array of mechanisms were developed by perhaps the majority of people to boost earnings. Because much of this is constituted in the 'black' or 'shadow' economy, the figures are not fully captured in the official data. Estimates of this were as high as 40% of GDP before 1998.[36] Indeed, income from work, that is, the formal sector, steadily declined after 1992, as shown in Figure 5.2.

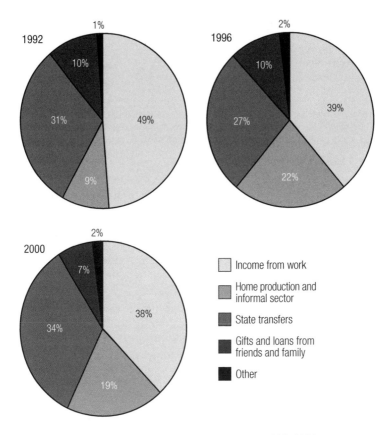

Figure 5.2   Sources of Household Income in Russia 1992–2000

Source: UNICEF 2001, table 2.2, p. 30.

Nonetheless, despite the existence of a huge black economy, this does not invalidate the fact of a massive deleterious impact on living standards and welfare. By 1995, it was estimated that 80% of Russians had experienced a substantial decline in their incomes.[37] Low pay is rife, as can be seen from Table 5.2.

In 2000, almost one-third of all workers were on 'low pay' and one-eighth on 'very low pay', though the figures vary significantly

Table 5.2   Low Pay in Russia 2000

	% All Employees[*]	% Low Paid[†]	% Very Low Paid[‡]	% With No Pay
Wholly government-owned	48.5	39.9	14.5	18.4
(Public service workers)	(13.3)	43.9	11.4	15.8
Private/joint venture	36.2	24.6	8.2	14.3
(Foreign-owned)	(4.1)	15.0	3.5	7.3
Not disclosed	15.3	29.4	10.5	18.8
All employees	100.0	32.6	11.6	17.0

[*] Data is restricted to employees in current job who have worked in the last 30 days.
[†] 'Low paid' is earnings of less than two-thirds median earnings.
[‡] 'Very low paid' is earnings of less than one-third median earnings.

Source: Klugman et al. 2002, table 4.2, p. 30.

according to sector. Pay is substantially lower in the state sector (40% on low pay) in comparison with the private sector (25% on low pay), with lowest pay occurring in public service jobs (44%). But even in the foreign-owned component of the private sector, 15% are on low pay and 3.5% on very low pay. These are, of course, relative levels, dependent on the level of the median itself as defined according the notes in Table 5.2.

Naturally, low levels of pay and declining real wages resulted in rising poverty so that the official poverty rate doubled in 1992, and continued to rise thereafter. Regional differences in poverty also became marked. Provinces whose economy is based on agriculture and food processing (such as Astrakhan and Orel *oblasts*) showed the highest levels of poverty (over 50% defined as poor with over 20% as very poor). Industrial or mixed regions (such as Krasnoiarskii Krai and Moscow *oblast* – which excludes Moscow City) registered medium levels of poverty (20–40% poor, with 10–20% very poor); and regions rich in mineral resources (such as Magnitogorsk City) having the least levels of poverty (17–30% poor, with 5–13% very poor). The 'poor' are defined by Goskomstat as those not having enough income to purchase the subsistence minimum consumer basket. The 'very poor' are defined as being unable to afford even the food component of the subsistence minimum (which, in reality, is tantamount to complete destitution).[38] These figures would be considerably worse if a rather more stringent requirement for poverty was adopted. Such a view seemed to have been taken by respondents to an opinion poll conducted in 1995 by the Russian Centre for

Public Opinion Research, 80% of whom reported living in conditions of poverty.[39]

Alongside rising levels of low pay and poverty was the sharp increase in inequality of income and earnings. Mikhalev's calculations of Russia's Gini coefficient are higher than those shown in Table 5.1: 0.27 in the period 1987–89, rapidly rising to 0.47 for the period 1997–99, a 74% increase. This was over half as much as the figure for the OECD nations (0.31 in 1994–95) and higher than that of the US (0.41), the most unequal OECD country. Such inequality is concretely reflected in the ratio of incomes of rich persons (on the 90th percentile of incomes) to incomes of poor persons (on the 10th percentile of incomes). This ratio rose from 3.1 in 1989 to 8.8 in 1999: in other words, whereas the rich earned three times as much as the poor in 1989,[40] they earned almost nine times as much in 1999. In fact Russia had become much more unequal than Central Europe: the respective ratios for Poland were 3.3 and 4.3, and for Hungary 2.5 and 3.0.[41]

Despite credits to enterprises and burgeoning inter-enterprise indebtedness that prevented widespread bankruptcies and redundancies, open, registered unemployment (based on ILO methodology) quickly reached almost 5% in 1992 and continued to rise – reaching 13.3% in 1998, the year of the financial crisis. Since then, it has steadily declined to 9% in 2001. Evidence suggests that enterprises are often reluctant to shed labour not so much because of threat of industrial unrest, but because of the costs involved: three months' redundancy pay plus all the wages in arrears and benefits. The cost difference, therefore, between retaining or firing workers becomes highly significant – estimates of between five and ten times over a six-month period for the latter in comparison with the former.[42] Also, the government might well prefer enterprises to retain workers so as to avoid demands for universal, liveable unemployment benefits. From this point of view, we could view the retention of poorly paid workers without meaningful jobs as the *de facto* 'working unemployed' where wages are tantamount to unemployment benefits. If so, then this situation is similar to the existence of 'hidden unemployment' in the USSR where the illegality of open unemployment, combined with the pressure to hoard labour in the endeavour to fulfil plan targets, meant that a significant proportion of workers were without any real work. Nonetheless, with a minimal social security system where total expenditure on unemployment benefits was just 0.3% of GDP in 1999, and where only one-eighth of the unemployed reported receiving unemployment benefit in 2000, rising unemployment indubitably translated into rising poverty and insecurity with attendant health risks, as is examined in the following chapter.[43]

Alongside price liberalisation came the freedom to trade and with it arose myriads of hawkers and street markets in large towns and cities. Often, people undertaking this were doing it as second or even third jobs in a desperate attempt to maintain living standards. One consequence, as we shall see in the next chapter, was a decline in public hygiene caused by poor controls on traders, particularly on food and drink outlets.

In terms of international trade, enterprises were free to trade globally and, with the collapse of the CMEA, there was a rapid shift away from the former Soviet Republics so that by 1999, over 80% of exports were to, and 75% of imports were from, non-CIS countries. Exports steadily increased from $54 billion in 1992 to $89 billion in 1996, a 65% increase in four years. However, they declined sharply to $76 billion in 1999 – ostensibly surprising given that the financial crisis and devaluation of the rouble implied increased competitiveness and potentially stronger export performance. However, this was offset by a fall in commodity prices (especially of natural gas) which led to the decline in the dollar value of exports.[44] But increasing volume and prices led to a surging ahead of exports to $106 billion in 1999. The composition of exports is indicative of where Russia's economic strength now lies. The bulk of commodity exports are concentrated in the primary sector, the norm for developing countries, with manufacturing accounting for a small proportion. Thus, to a significant extent, Russia's post-1992 development strategy is natural-resource exporting. Consequently, this represents a downward shift in the international division of labour as the 1999 figures for exports by sector show: raw materials (27%) and fuel (42%) dominate. Other primary products such as food and agricultural products account for only 3%. In contrast, more sophisticated products, including manufacturing, were: chemical products and intermediates (15%), machinery and equipment (11%) and other manufacturing (2%).[45] Imports have always been less than exports leading to a perennial trade surplus. There was a sharp dip in 1999 following the dollar devaluation that resulted in reduced purchasing power and lower imports from non-CIS countries. But the high level of the trade surplus has positive and negative aspects: it generates foreign exchange reserves but is also counterproductive owing to the fact

that imports of capital and intermediary goods are essential for tech-
nological upgrading yet these declined sharply in 1999. With overall
foreign direct investment low,[46] and concentrated heavily around
Moscow, this has not been sufficient to plug the domestic savings
gap and generate the type of multiplier effects which could swing
the economy round. Indeed, the problem of lack of investment is
compounded by the fact that between 1993 and 1998, Russia
experienced a net capital *outflow* of 2.1% of GDP,[47] strikingly under-
scoring the lack of confidence that the new private owners had in
Russia's liberalised market economy.

MISTAKEN ASSUMPTIONS UNDERLYING THE REFORM PROGRAMME

Under conditions of severe market failures as prevailing in Russia,
the assumptions of rational, predictable responses to shock therapy
measures proved illusory and elusive.[48] A society largely run on
bureaucratic commands with little experience of internal, formalised
market relations cannot be expected to perform as if it had been a
market economy with a plethora of institutions and behavioural
patterns therein. Indeed, it has long been known that even in
advanced market economies, responses to economic policy
frequently fail because of market failures, though, as defenders of
the market mechanism hasten to add, under 'pure conditions' there
is no superior alternative. Such theorising, however, proved cold
comfort to those subjected to the whims of the theorists.

There was a sharp contradiction in the assumptions of the
reformers, and not just in Russia, but also throughout the former
Eastern bloc. Collapsing living standards were deemed necessary, on
the one hand, for macroeconomic stabilisation via the removal of
the demand overhang and consequent wage inflation but, on the
other, sucked demand away from the domestic enterprises – who was
to buy their products in the context of plummeting real wages? This
also affects the producer goods sector which supply the consumer
goods sector, albeit at one remove. One crucial exception may
potentially be the military sector but this also cannot escape under
conditions of civilian rule and rapidly falling state revenues. The
most obvious option to pick up the domestic slack would be exports
which the military sector can perhaps best utilise given its long
history of producing and exporting competitive, state-of-the-art
hardware. However, given the invariably low quality by international

standards, this was not feasible for consumer goods manufacturers. Moreover, trade liberalisation and removal of protectionist barriers further squeezed domestic producers from better-quality imports. This inevitably led to a decline in production and rising unit costs, which, as we have seen, resulted in enterprises simply pushing up prices to offset this. Thus the objective of choking off inflation necessarily floundered.

Mainstream theory would suggest that loss-making enterprises should be forced to exit the market, that is, be bankrupted. The trouble with this is that a large proportion of the tradable sector would simply go under, with resultant effects of a massive increase in unemployment, an increase in the burden on the state budget for social security provisions and, importantly, the loss of an array of skills which could, potentially, be upgraded. Hence, rather than Schumpeter's 'creative destruction' of capital there would be just plain destruction with little guarantee of a phoenix of rapid modernisation and development arising from the ashes of shattering industrial decline. Indeed, shock therapy reformers wished this scenario to materialise arguing that the skills and capabilities of loss-making enterprises were 'dedicated' for the command economy and so were pretty much useless for the new market economy. To use a term popularised by Williamson,[49] the 'asset specificity' of many Russian enterprises gave rise to what could be termed 'skills specificity'; hence neither are readily transferable and the solution is to massively restructure and re-skill the workforce, in other words, invoke widespread closures and redundancies. Any 'interference' by the state to halt this process was denounced, as Bogomolov's comments of 1994 make clear:

> The radical liberals are indignant at the idea of intensifying state intervention to stop the crumbling of production, to prevent social cataclysm, chaos and further criminalization of the economy, and to support entrepreneurship. This idea instantly raises complaints about a return to the command system and provokes an outcry about making concessions to conservative directors in industry and 'red Barons' in agriculture.[50]

But this theoretical madness was not going to be tolerated on a never-never basis by those at the receiving end. Indeed, with strong protests from workers' organisations, Yeltsin soon came to realise that a fierce political reaction would sooner or later be generated should the shock continue unabated. Gimpelson argues that the Russian government implicitly agreed to restrain the rise in unemployment as the price to be paid for reduced social and political conflict.[51] Given this, complaints by supporters of Russian shock therapy of a subsequent loosening of fiscal and monetary policies, and the removal of Gaidar before the end of 1992, are disingenuous and avoid fully confronting the reality that it was the ferocity and callousness of the reforms, and resistance to them, that brought about a slowing down of the pace of reform – akin to Polanyi's 'countermovement' against the market economy in the nineteenth century.[52] It needs emphasising, however, that although there was continuous resistance by workers (especially strike waves in the spring of 1992 and between November 1993 and the spring of 1994),[53] several of the key unions continued to support Yeltsin and dampened down demands for strike action.[54] However, after Yeltsin's presidential victory in 1996, strike activity again increased in 1997 involving almost 900,000 workers and leading to 6 million unworked days. Thereafter, especially after the 1998 crisis, the number of days lost through strikes rapidly declined to reach negligible levels in 2001 which involved a mere 13,000 strikers (see Figure 5.3).

Unemployment inexorably rose and quickly reached double figures. With no tradition of independent trade unions and weak, compliant, ex-official unions, the economic hurricane dealt a powerful blow. Almost from the earliest beginnings, enterprises began witholding payment of wages so that in the period May–July 1992, arrears in cash wage payments were one-fifth of total monthly income.[55] Approximately 60% of workers are not paid on time (the lag is typically between two and six months) and where, on average, wages paid each month are only two-thirds of wages earned.[56] The phenomenon of wage arrears is almost unknown in the West, yet persists in Russia with each passing year, and so graphically illustrates the weakness of workers' organisations. At most, therefore, it was the *threat* of major social and political upheaval that had more of an impact on Yeltsin's government rather than widespread, militant action by workers.

The UN Economic Commission for Europe (UN ECE) provides explanations for the failure of the reforms, especially in regard to stabilisation, in three key areas.[57] First, deficiencies of the programme itself, including the assumption that standard macroeconomic policies work under fundamental structural imbalances. This is quite correct, but then great stress is laid on the role of lack of wage controls

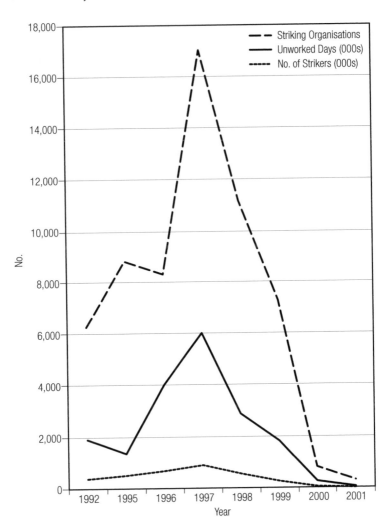

Figure 5.3   Strike Statistics for Russia 1992–2001

Source: Goskomstat 2002, table 6.13.

as a key factor in the failure to stabilise, even whilst acknowledging that real wages had fallen by 40%. Clearly, not only is this erroneous reasoning, but it also lacks credibility. Second, lack of political support, and constant opposition to reforms. Again, this is true, but the authoritarian manner in which the reform process was planned and conducted was hardly conducive to receiving much support within and without parliament. Moreover, the continuing deterioration of the economy was bound to stiffen the resolve of the opposition. And third, lack of external assistance, namely at the outset, the absence of aid and loans from the West (notably the IMF) in the manner of a stabilisation fund, similar to that granted to the Polish government when it launched its shock therapy reforms in January 1990. However, if the latter was deemed so crucial, then forceful arguments should have been made *against* the shock therapy reforms on this ground – but they were not. Obviously, the ideological appeal of the rapid switch to a market economy muted such criticisms and concerns.[58]

So, undeniably, the post-reform decade had been a most torrid one for ordinary Russians. Inevitably, this took its toll in the form of a massive decline in health and the highest levels of normal mortality seen in peace time. Alongside these were also extraordinarily high levels of abnormal mortality, as shall see in the next two chapters.

6 'Normal' Deaths During the First Decade of Transition

Very rarely has a sense of triumphalism turned so quickly to despair and demoralisation as it did in Russia during the first years of transition. When the transition began, perhaps the vast majority of the population were swept along with a genuine sense of optimism, and supported the system change that would see the casting aside of the authoritarian command economy and its replacement with the market system. But once the severity of the new system was exposed, a degree of resistance followed. Nonetheless, detestation of the previous regime and system did not lead to (and has not led to) any significant pressure to revert to it. In a haphazard way, the implicit common refrain has been 'there is no alternative'. The portents for a swift turnaround in the economic and social conditions of the majority of Russians are not promising.

The World Health Organisation stresses the link between poverty and health, noting that it is a key determinant of poor health and a potential consequence of it. The associations are elaborated upon clearly:

[w]hether defined by income, socio-economic status, living conditions or educational level, poverty is the single largest determinant of ill health. Living in poverty is associated with lower life expectancy, high infant mortality, poor reproductive health, a higher risk of contracting infectious diseases, higher rates of tobacco, alcohol and drug abuse, a higher prevalence of non-communicable diseases, depression, suicide, antisocial behaviour and violence, and increased exposure to environmental risks.[1]

Given the decline in real incomes and real living standards, and rapidly rising poverty, we should expect to see a rise in these health-related phenomena during the transition period. This indeed is precisely what has happened but the scale was beyond what anyone expected. The transition produced the last of Russia's four great mortality crises of the twentieth century and one that would continue into the twenty-first century. In this chapter we shall focus on 'normal' deaths emanating from the economic reforms of 1992. Normal deaths, as defined in Chapter 1, are those ordinarily arising in the vast majority of instances (and exclude deaths directly due to the state) under 'normal' circumstances (i.e. without war, repression, famine or 'natural' disasters).

UNPRECEDENTED PEACETIME MORTALITY

Figure 6.1 shows changes in crude death rate and crude birth rate since 1980. Russia has the second highest death rate in Europe after Moldova, and one which is twice the rate of the EU average.[2] The most striking aspect is the widening gulf between the death and birth rates. Up until 1991, the birth rate was greater than the death rate implying that the population was being replaced without recourse to migration. In 1992, however, there was a sudden reversal as the death rate rose from 11.4 to 12.2 whilst the birth rate fell from 12.1 to 10.7 (all per 1,000). By 1994, the death rate was 64% higher than the birth rate. During 1995–98, it declined by a greater proportion than the birth rate, though it was still 55% higher. However, in 1999, the death rate rose once more and the birth rate fell, and in 2000

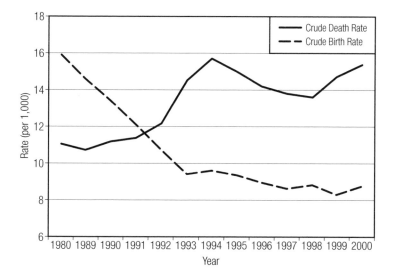

Figure 6.1   Crude Death Rates and Birth Rates for Russia 1989–2000

Source: Goskomstat 2001a, table 2.1.

the death rate rose again, resulting in it being 76% higher than the birth rate. Inevitably, this has led to a population decline, as shown in Figure 6.2.

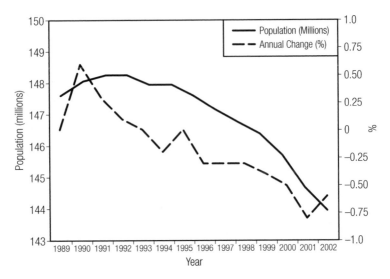

Figure 6.2   Total Beginning-of-Year Population for Russia 1989–2000

Sources: Goskomstat 2001a, table 1.2, and 2002, table 5.1.

Allowing for the unreliability of population figures (the new census was delayed until 2002), the nominal population appeared to be fairly constant until 1995 before falling steeply (by 4.4 million between 1995 and 2002 (3% of the total). This, however, most likely underestimates the true population as there have been substantial levels of unregistered immigration – probably much more so than unregistered emigration[3] – with significant numbers of ethnic Russians moving to Russia from former non-Russian Republics of the Soviet Union. The true effects of the gap between crude death and crude birth rates are given by the figures for 'excess mortality' (the difference between predicted and actual levels of mortality). By 1999, Russian excess mortality was 2,566,000 which represented almost 80% of the total for transition countries (see Table 6.1). Excess mortality is the difference between the actual number of deaths during 1990–99 and the number that would have occurred in this period had death rates in each country been at the same level as those prevailing in 1989.[4] Given that there were no significant levels of death by famine, environmental catastrophe, or epidemic of infectious diseases, *this is unprecedented in modern peacetime history.*[5]

Table 6.1   'Excess Mortality' in the Former Eastern Bloc 1990–99[*]

	Excess Mortality[†]
Central Europe	(488,000)
South-Eastern Europe	22,000
Baltic States	47,000
Western CIS	3,680,000
Russia	*2,566,000*
Ukraine	896,000
Belarus	156,000
Moldova	62,000
Caucasus	(125,000)
Central Asia	217,000
Net Total	*3,353,000*

[*] Excess Mortality = difference between the actual number of deaths during 1990–99 and the number that would have occurred in this period had death rates in each country been at the same level as those prevailing in 1989.
[†] Only positive figures indicate excess mortality; brackets indicate negative figures (i.e. reductions).

Source: UNICEF 2001, table 3.1, p. 49; personal correspondence.

The rise in the crude death rate naturally led to a decline in life expectancy though there was a significant variation between males and females. Figure 6.3 provides life expectancy data. Female life expectancy declined from 74.3 to 71.2 between 1991 and 1994 before slowly rising to 72.9 in 1998. However, there was a fall to 72.1 in 2001 – an overall decline of 2.2 years (3%) since 1991. In contrast, male life expectancy experienced a truly catastrophic fall: from 63.5 in 1991 to 57.6 in 1994, a fall of 5.9 years (9.3%). It rose to 61.3 years in 1998 before falling back to 58.6 in 2001, still 4.9 years below the 1991 level (almost 8%). It is this that indicates unprecedented peacetime excess mortality. Russia's male life expectancy is one of the lowest in the former Eastern bloc – only Kazakhstan (62.6) and Turkmenistan (62.3) had lower life expectancy in 1991. And the only country to experience a comparable fall is Ukraine – from 66.0 in 1991 to 61.0 in 1996. Russia's gender life expectancy gap (the difference between female and male life expectancy) of 13.5 years in 2001 is one of the highest in the world, contrasting with an average of 7.6 years for Central European countries and 6.3 years for the EU.[6]

Figure 6.3   Life Expectancy at Birth 1989–2001

Sources: Goskomstat 2001a, table 2.6, 2002, table 5.8.

Table 6.2 gives a breakdown of mortality rates by gender and age from 1989. Generally, in line with decreasing life expectancy figures, the overall mortality rate rose sharply between 1991 and 1994, and fell back between 1995 and 1998 before rising again in 1999 when the rate was still higher than for 1991. In regard to age groups, infant and under-five mortality rates showed a modest overall decline, female aged 5–14 remained constant, whilst male aged 5–14 showed a significant improvement. It is important to stress that though the infant mortality rate fell after 1993, and is now *lower* than that predicted by Russia's GDP, this does not imply that overall medical care has improved.[7] On the contrary, as we have seen in the previous chapters with regard to rapidly declining fertility rates, a rapidly declining infant mortality rate should also follow. This is because the avoided births tend to be in the high-risk and high-mortality categories (e.g. older mothers from poorer, working-class backgrounds having fewer children) and also because greater scarce and specialised resources per mother and child become available (such as pregnancy screening in problematic cases, care of premature newborns, and neonatal services).[8] From this consideration,

Table 6.2 Breakdown of Mortality Rates by Gender and Age (Deaths per 100,000)

	1989	1990	1991	1992	1993	1994	1995	1996	1997	1998	1999	2000
Infant mortality	17.8	17.4	17.8	18.0	19.9	18.6	17.6	17.4	17.2	16.5	16.9	15.3
Under-5	22.8	22.3	23.2	23.7	26.4	23.9	23.4	22.0	21.7	20.4	21.5	19.2
Female age 5–14	35.8	33.2	36.8	36.4	39.1	37.5	39.1	35.1	30.9	33.7	34.1	32.5
Male age 5–14	65.4	64.2	73.1	69.6	70.0	64.5	68.2	59.4	57.0	57.0	60.6	58.0
Female age 15–19	64.2	62.8	66.2	72.0	78.5	80.8	84.5	80.5	75.2	79.7	80.8	
Male age 15–19	154.0	161.9	166.4	180.4	209.7	212.0	239.6	214.8	188.2	189.8	201.4	
Female age 20–24	70.4	71.4	74.1	84.1	96.9	100.1	103.8	98.6	99.4	100.6	112.5	114.4
Male age 20–24	260.4	259.9	272.5	317.5	372.9	400.6	428.2	412.7	384.5	402.7	448.5	496.1
Female age 25–39	110.1	112.6	120.3	139.0	174.6	194.9	191.7	173.2	160.8	157.4	174.8	184.8
Male age 25–39	416.5	438.4	468.6	564.7	724.5	808.4	776.4	687.9	614.0	602.9	673.6	734.7
Female age 40–59	498.9	504.4	506.3	551.0	682.4	770.6	716.7	640.9	578.5	545.7	582.6	606.2
Male age 40–59	1,387.0	1,434.6	1,441.9	1,649.5	2,109.2	2,410.3	2,235.4	1,969.3	1,736.1	1,645.5	1,806.2	1,937.9
Female age 60+	43.3	44.3	44.1	45.0	50.1	52.8	51.0	49.5	49.0	47.6	49.4	
Male age 60+	57.2	58.2	58.1	59.9	70.1	75.3	71.1	67.5	65.6	63.5	67.7	
Total	3,203.8	3,285.6	3,369.4	3,810.8	4,724.3	5,250.3	5,046.7	4,528.8	4,078.1	3,963.1	4,330.6	

Sources: TransMONEE 2001 database, UNICEF 2001, UNICEF 2002, statistical annex.

therefore, there is no cause for satisfaction or complacency in regard to the infant mortality rate.

For all other age groups, and for both sexes, the mortality rate increased. In terms of gender, for all age categories over five, the mortality rate is higher for males than females with the male rate varying from two to over four times the female rate. By far the highest rate is for the middle-aged male group (aged 40–59) which comprises more than 40% of the total. Reasons as to why this group has inordinately suffered are explored in the next section. Over 60% of the gender gap is due to two broad sets of causes: cardiovascular disease and external causes.[9]

Even though the situation of women is much better than men in regard to mortality rates, their lot is not generally a happy one. Women continue to carry the 'double burden' of working and caring for the family, as Russia remains a deeply sexist society. Consequently women are prone to exhaustion, illness and disease – and have a life expectancy that is considerably lower than that of their Western counterparts. Also, a combination of lack of education, economic pressures and a shortage of means of effective contraception has led to abortion continuing to be the commonest method of birth control.[10] Though hard data is not available, inadequate clinics and facilities implies that abortion can give rise to an array of medical problems such as inflammation, haemorrhages and gynaecological diseases. Consequently, there must necessarily be a high incidence of morbidity and mortality from botched or problematic abortions. In 1992, for example, there were 3.3 million legal abortions in Russia, suggesting that thousands of women must die annually from the operation.[11]

WHY SO MANY DEATHS?

We noted, in Chapter 4, Wilkinson's argument that beyond a certain level of development, the correlation between mortality rate and output per capita weakens. Cornia provides support for this and estimates that this weakening starts at GDP per capita of over $5,000. Hence, even large increases in GDP per capita beyond this will result in relatively small increases in life expectancy.[12] Cornia further argues that a 'recession model' of mortality (where the mortality rate rises following a decline in living standards) is only useful for those at the margins of society such as vagrants and those living in extreme poverty. Paniccia has also shown that in Russia the increase in deaths directly from malnutrition was negligible. Male Russians may now have Third World levels of life expectancy but not its level of hunger. In contrast to so many in the Third World without land, many Russians are able to grow their own food in plots, and approximately half of the poorest 10% did so in 1994.[13] Similarly, the number of deaths directly from 'diseases of poverty' is low – though in percentage terms, these did show a large increase: a rise of 80% from 1991 to 1995 for males, and 47% for females.

Does this, therefore, imply that the fall in Russia's living standards should be considered as largely irrelevant to mortality, because at over $7,000 per capita in 1995, it was still well above Cornia's threshold? We think not and adhere to our theorisation of the determinants of mortality in Chapter 1 that per capita income and its change remain of central importance. Let us assume that Russia's income per capita rose three-fold to average Western levels. We should expect that, in turn, average life expectancy would also rise to Western levels – male life expectancy would increase from 59 to 74. At 25%, this is obviously much less a proportional increase than that of income level, but it is still highly significant. Cornia's 'threshold argument', however, is more appropriate for women where a three-fold increase in income should lead to average female life expectancy rising from 72 to 79. Though less than a 10% increase, we argue this is still a substantial improvement and worth striving for.

But Cornia also shows that Russian life expectancy was well below the predicted level for 1990–94,[14] that is, that it should approximate more to those of countries with a similar level of GDP per capita, such as Poland and Malaysia (see Table 6.3). Part of the reason for this is that the very high prevalence of circulatory diseases and cancers (especially in middle-aged and elderly men) require resource-intensive technologies for effective treatment but which have never been properly funded in Russia. Moreover, since 1992, even less resources have become available for such purposes. Russian medicine, particularly outside the large urban centres, remains at a level of the provision of basic primary healthcare. This certainly makes it better than that of developing countries but prevents it from treating in large numbers people with disorders and diseases that are readily manageable in developed countries.

Table 6.3 shows life expectancy figures at different ages for a selection of countries and their per capita GDP. Three of the countries (Poland, Malaysia and Lithuania) have GDP levels similar to Russia's but all have life expectancy at birth for both male and female that are

Table 6.3 Life Expectancy at Various Years, Selected Countries

Country	GDP per Capita (1999 in PPP$)	At Birth	Age 5	Age 20	Age 40	Age 60	Probability at Birth of Reaching 65 (1995–2000) (%)	Year of Data
Russia male	7,473	58	60	61	65	73	47	1995
Russia female		72	73	74	75	79	77	
Poland male	8,450	68	69	70	71	76	66	1997
Poland female		77	78	78	79	81	85	
Malaysia male	8,209	70	71	71	73	77	71	1998
Malaysia female		75	76	76	77	79	82	
Lithuania male	6,656	67	67	68	70	76	60	1998
Lithuania female		77	78	78	79	81	84	
USA male	31,872	74	74	75	76	79	77	1997
USA female		79	80	80	81	83	86	
Japan male	24,898	77	78	78	79	81	84	1998
Japan female		84	84	85	85	86	92	
India male	2,248	60	67	69	71	75	60	1992–1996
India female		61	69	71	74	78	65	
Malawi male	586	44	57	62	68	74	28	1992–1997
Malawi female		47	60	64	70	75	30	

Sources: UN 2001, table 22; UNDP 2001, pp. 141–4, 166–9.

higher. In comparison with developed economies such as the US and Japan, the life expectancy gap is even larger. It is only in comparison with a poor developing country such as Malawi that a significant life expectancy gap opens up. Malawi's life expectancy at birth is 44 for males and 47 for females. However, these figures are so low partly because of the extremely high infant mortality rates. By the time Malawi children reach the age of 5, life expectancy jumps to 57 for males and 60 for females, though still significantly less than Russia's.

In Russia, between birth and the age of 20, male life expectancy is fairly constant at just under and just over 60. But those Russian males who survive past the age of 40 see a jump in life expectancy to 65, and those who survive till the age of 60 can expect to live for another 13 years. In contrast, developed countries such as Japan and the US show life expectancy to be fairly constant until the age of 60. Russia's male life expectancy is lower than India's – a country with a per capita GDP of only 30% that of Russia – and considerably less than countries such as Malaysia (a newly industrialising 'tiger cub') and Poland, considered a relatively successful transition country, both of whom have similar per capita GDPs.

Russian females in comparison live considerably longer but on average five to ten years less than their Western counterparts. This is similar to life expectancy for Western males for all ages. It is higher than India's female life expectancy and almost equal to Malaysia's but, less than Poland's and that of developed countries. In terms of the probability of surviving to the age of 65, Russian males have less than a 50% chance – which is much less than Indian males' chances of 60% and in stark contrast to a survival probability of 66% and 71% respectively for Poland and Malaysia and much lower than 80% for developed countries. For women, the probability of surviving to 65 is far higher at 77%, which is similar to countries with a similar GDP per capita but significantly lower than the approximately 90% probability of women from developed countries. This provides evidence for the argument that Russian male life expectancy is much lower than expected but that female life expectancy is only marginally lower than expected.

Table 6.4 sets out the major causes of 'normal' deaths for 1991, 1994 and 1998 at ages 15–74.

Three sets of causes are by far the most important: 'diseases of circulatory system', 'external causes' and 'all neoplasms' (cancers) – together accounting for 84% of the total. For male and female, both these sets of causes increased sharply between 1991 and 1994; and

Table 6.4 Male and Female Age-Standardised Death Rates per 100,000 at Ages 15–74 for Selected Causes of Death[*]

Causes	Male Mortality Rates			Female Mortality Rates			Male Ratio 1998:1991	Female Ratio 1998:1991
	1991	1994	1998	1991	1994	1998		
Infectious diseases	24.1	43.8	41.7	3.9	6.9	6.2	1.73	1.59
All neoplasms (cancers)	343.6	345.7	314.5	151.5	154.1	147.2	0.97	0.97
Diseases of circulatory system	612.8	927.6	742.9	289.2	399.4	331.5	1.21	1.15
Diseases of respiratory system	86.0	146.8	95.5	20.7	28.5	19.1	1.11	0.92
Diseases of digestive system	45.4	75.1	61.0	19.9	31.7	25.4	1.34	1.28
External causes[†]	294.1	527.7	382.8	62.3	114.9	84.0	1.30	1.35
All Causes	1,463.1	2,181.1	1,716.7	587.1	791.8	656.1	1.17	1.12

[*] There is a problem with the data. The broad headings combined do not add up to the total given in 'All Causes', implying that there is a missing element.
[†] See Table 6.5.

Source: Shkolnikov et al. (2001).

markedly declined between 1994 and 1998. There was, however, little change in the incidence of neoplasms, suggesting that mortality from cancers had stabilised in the early years of transition (but cancers do require a considerable time-lag to manifest themselves and so are not immediately responsive to economic crises).[15] For all causes, for both male and female with the exception of neoplasms, and excepting diseases of the respiratory system for females, despite the decline after 1994, the 1998 levels were still higher in comparison with 1991. Though low in absolute terms, the greatest percentage increase was that for infectious diseases. Tichonova et al. note that '[m]ajor economic and social changes in the Russian Federation have coincided with epidemics of previously controlled infectious diseases'.[16] These include syphilis (which they report on), cholera and diphtheria, which are 'diseases of poverty'. The incidence of tuberculosis is nine times higher for men than women mainly due to its transmission in prisons, which overwhelmingly have male inmates (we shall explore this further in Chapter 7).

The incidence of the HIV virus is rapidly increasing at present, and this can lead to other infectious diseases emanating from a deficiency in the immune system that it induces. In 2002, there were 201,000 cases of persons registered as HIV positive but actual numbers may be four to six times this level. Most of those infected are drug-abusing unemployed young men between the ages of 15 and 30 injecting heroin with dirty needles. According to Vadim Pokrovsky, director of the Federal AIDS Centre, if half of the HIV-infected population spreads the virus to one sexual partner (a conservative scenario as the young tend to have sex with multiple partners in relatively short periods) there may be at least 5 million HIV cases by 2010. The potential impact of this could be profound. First, since almost no one is receiving modern anti-retroviral treatment, *about 1 million could die* according to the UNAIDS representative in Russia.[17] Second, the demographic impact might be severe, as those with AIDS will not have children, thereby accentuating the population decline and concomitant adverse affect on the economy as the able-bodied-to-sick ratio will inevitably deteriorate. The AIDS timebomb should provoke a response from the government to attempt to tackle it. But with limited budgets, the channelling of resources to healthcare might reduce funds for investment in social spending, infrastructure and industry, and so intensify the downward spiral of economic malaise, deteriorating health and increasing levels of death. However this crisis actually develops, the increase of diseases such as TB and AIDS clearly indicates a weakening of the healthcare, sanitary and social assistance systems.[18] Those who have suffered the most in deteriorating health and rising mortality, and will continue to do so, will be the poor and working-class people.

KEY FACTORS OF MORTALITY DECLINE

Decline in healthcare expenditure

Past underfunding in health meant that Russia was unable to satisfactorily shift from a 'health-extensive' approach (i.e. provision of basic healthcare via large staffing levels with basic training) to the 'health-intensive' approach (utilising highly-trained specialists and sophisticated equipment) which has increasingly become the norm in the West. Ostensibly, however, as Figure 6.4 shows, the number of health professionals per capita is still impressive. Russia has more physicians per capita than Western countries such as France and Germany, and more than twice the UK's. The numbers are also higher in comparison with other former Eastern bloc countries. In regard to nurses, the per capita rate is also very high, with only Germany having more. However, the numbers of dentists are relatively low, whilst the rate for pharmacists is far lower than that of any other country for the sample of countries given. But one needs to treat these figures with caution because although the *quantity* of health professionals may appear high, the same cannot be said for their *quality*. Thus, in the latter years of the Soviet Union, the quality of physicians was well below world standards, and corruption was rife in the health service 'including bribery in the admission and graduation of physicians, [a] shocking proportion of whom could not perform the simplest medical procedures ...'.[19] As we shall now see, the decline in healthcare expenditure must necessarily mean that, at best, the situation has remained the same since 1991.

But for those at the top, power, augmented now more directly by money, allows them to continue to have access to world-class medical facilities. A glaring example of health inequalities was the army of doctors who looked after Boris Yeltsin's heart condition. True, presidents and rulers the world over have whatever healthcare they need on tap, but that accorded to Yeltsin surely takes some beating. For example, he had *ten* doctors writing to his Security Services chief explaining his heart condition. Yeltsin admits to a 'whole brigade' of doctors involved in his heart bypass surgery in November 1996,

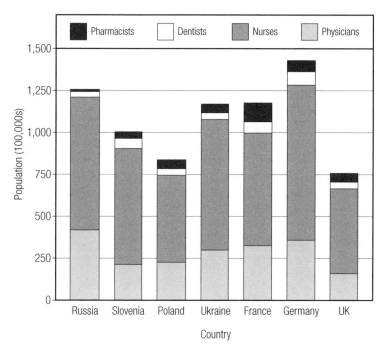

Figure 6.4   Number of Health Professionals per 100,000 Population in 2000, Selected Countries

Source: WHO 2002b, table 3.

including an American and two Germans who watched the procedure on a video monitor.[20] Any ordinary Russian person with Yeltsin's condition would most likely not be alive now.

The post-transition crisis has inevitably affected healthcare expenditure, and this may partly explain the increase in mortality. We saw in Chapter 5 that a key plank of Russia's shock therapy reforms of 1992 was the curtailing of public expenditure to rein in inflation. There has been the policy of shifting the burden of healthcare, hitherto exclusively on the state, to a health insurance system and the introduction of fees in state facilities, plus the significant expansion of the private sector.[21]

Figure 6.5 shows Russia's public expenditure on health as a percentage of GDP. After falling slightly in percentage terms in 1992, it quickly rose to over 4% between 1994 and 1997 before falling back to 3% in 2000. However, *real* expenditure fell sharply in 1992 (a massive 17% drop over 1991) but recovered during the 1993–97 period: in 1994 it actually rose 12% above the 1991 level. But there was a very sharp contraction in 1998 in the wake of the financial crisis that summer. By 2000, expenditure was just 72% of its 1991 level. The crisis and neglect of the health service is starkly indicated by the fact that only in Russia did employment fall in this sector. The switch to market prices led to an immediate collapse of Comecon trading, one consequence of which was a shortage of medical inputs, including drugs. Cost prevented these being offset by Western imports for the mass of the population. The lack of funding resulted in the reduction in immunisation rates for measles, polio and diphtheria.[22] Food poisoning has also increased owing to a loosening of hygiene and quality control standards, a reduction in the number of health inspectors, and the bribery of, and threats to, inspectors.[23] Similarly, liberalisation and deregulation in the absence of well-resourced regulatory institutions has accentuated problems of health and safety at work.

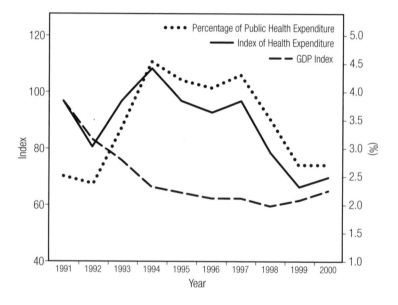

Figure 6.5   Russia's Expenditure on Public Health as a Percentage of GDP 1991–2000

Source: Derived from UNICEF 2002, tables 10.1 and 6.10.

The decline of the public health system has led to an increase in private health expenditures via 'informal payments', that is, unofficial payments to healthcare providers. Thus, in Russia in 1997, 74% of patients reported making informal payments for healthcare[24] and as such payments become the norm, it is inevitably the poorest sections of society who do not seek medical assistance. Figure 6.6 shows total expenditure on health (public and private) for a selection of countries.

Russia's expenditure is a fraction of that of developed countries, but in comparison with countries of similar GDP, it is twice that of Malaysia, but rather less than Poland's and Lithuania's. Yet we have seen that Malaysia's life expectancy at all ages is higher than Russia's. This is further evidence that health expenditure is not the decisive determinant of life expectancy. But it is certainly the case that in the context of a profound economic crisis, a weakened health service has not provided an adequate health safety net for many of those most affected.

The example of the US suggests that the manner in which health expenditure occurs is of considerable importance. Though its per capita health expenditure is twice that of France and Japan – the bulk of which (7.3% of GDP) is private – it has a lower life expectancy than both. This raises the question of the efficacy of private health care vis-à-vis a universal public health service. Beyond a certain level of development, an increase in private health expenditure does not necessarily imply an ultimate reduction in the overall mortality rate; though it almost certainly will favourably impact upon those most able to pay for private treatment. An increase in private healthcare does not compensate for the reduction in public expenditure since the latter is likely to affect the poorer sections of the population. The US provides the clearest example of this: with health expenditure of over 14% of GDP, and per capita expenditure of over $4,000, there are nevertheless some 45 million people (one-sixth of the population) without adequate health insurance. If this is true of one of the richest societies in the world, then it was even more foolish to imagine that the market model of healthcare could help mitigate the health and mortality crisis in Russia. Indeed, the market must continue to produce 'the inverse care law' where the wealthy with fewer real needs buy more health resources, whereas the poor, with more needs, buy less. The changing priorities in the organisation of Russia's healthcare therefore allows us to agree with Davis who concludes that:

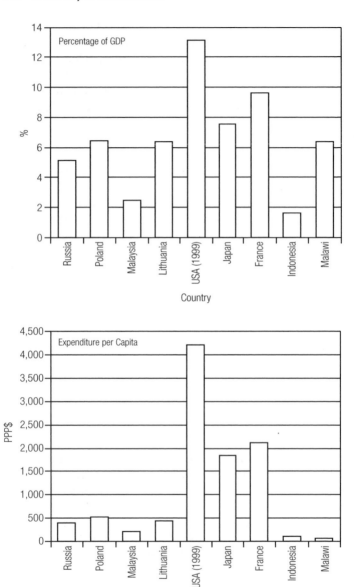

Figure 6.6   Total (Public and Private) Health Expenditure 1998, Selected Countries

Sources: UNDP 2001, pp. 158–61; Russia's figure derived from UNICEF 2001, table 6.10.

The failures of the Russian government in the health policy field were partially responsible for the rises in mortality in that country. It seems clear that reductions in health spending and deterioration in medical care in the face of rising illness in both late perestroika (1989–91) and early transition (1992–95) and the aftermath of the 1998 economic crisis facilitated the increases in mortality rates.[25]

The key role of alcoholism

In 1993, Russia overtook France as the world's heaviest drinking country, with average consumption per adult male of a bottle of vodka every two days.[26] But the societal effects of alcohol, as we shall see, are very different in these two countries. Indeed alcohol seemingly presents a puzzle: it is a source of great enjoyment for probably the majority of adults in the world in that it acts as a powerful means of relaxation, social interaction and general merriment. There is also evidence of its positive effects on health and longevity at certain levels and types of consumption (notably regular, moderate, drinking of red wine). Yet alcohol can equally be a great destroyer of lives: most commonly personal death through abuse, and deaths of others from alcohol-induced accidents. It is also an instigator of wrecked relationships including domestic violence, divorce and family breakup. As we have suggested in earlier chapters, the destructive effect of alcohol is ultimately an expression of an alienated existence where the loss of control over one's life induces a trip into 'another life' so as to abandon the strains and stresses of the present. Given the strong addictive properties of alcohol, the destructive element becomes exceedingly difficult to break. Alienation and addiction, therefore, form powerful, reinforcing factors with often truly deadly outcomes. Consequently, if hope in a genuinely rewarding life can be realised, the sense of alienation will diminish and with it nihilistic alcoholism, leaving alcohol to play a more benign social role, perhaps even leading to the sorts of beneficial consumption patterns prevalent in the Mediterranean. This might appear paradoxical but in countries such as France and Italy, which have very high levels of alcohol consumption, life expectancy is also among the highest in the world. The answer appears to lie in the fact that medical research shows that 'regular, moderate alcohol consumption [which is the norm in the Mediterranean, and indeed in much of Western Europe] and episodic, heavy consumption [so prevalent in Russia] have quite different effects on lipid metabolism, clotting, and propensity to arrhythmias [i.e. irregular heart rhythms]'.[27] In other words, beneficial effects accrue from the former type of consumption whilst harmful effects arise from the latter type.

What is clear is that the breaking free from the lethal grip of alcoholism in Russia will not be easy. A draconian curtailment of supply from official channels, as under the Gorbachev programme, will only provoke illicit production and sale that may actually worsen the situation. The real solution resides in a breakthrough in the mode of living of the mass of the population: one that engenders an expansion of real choice and material benefits and an end to the acute deprivation and poverty currently so prevalent. This combined with systematic education well into adulthood of the perils of high levels of vodka consumption, and in conjunction with health warnings and constructive advice by the health authorities, may begin to turn the tide. These policies, we argue, are a precondition for a sustained reversal of the atrocious Russian male mortality rate.[28]

Plainly, the shock therapy reforms correlate with a devastating impact on adult mortality rates as seen by the rapid rise between 1991 and 1994 and the fall in life expectancy. But Russia's life expectancy had been falling before the 1992 reforms – indeed, since 1987, after the abandonment of Gorbachev's anti-alcohol campaign.[29] The campaign had two premises. First, that drunkenness was damaging work discipline and, second, that there was a significant, direct, causal link between alcohol consumption and Russia's high male mortality rate and low life expectancy. Cutting alcohol consumption would therefore not only ratchet up productivity but also, at the same time, reduce mortality levels. Though there was little impact on productivity, the second premise was shown to be spectacularly correct when in the two years of the campaign, male life expectancy increased to an all-time high of 64.9 years. And when the campaign was abandoned because of enormous public pressure (Gorbachev's aim had been one of severely restricting the availability of alcohol in the manner of a semi-prohibition policy, rather than attempt to 'educate away' Russian men's strong predilection for alcohol), life expectancy also fell. Given such a powerful correlation, therefore, research into the link between alcohol and mortality rates post-transition, would seem to be of enormous importance. Leon et al. examined the reason for the steep rise in mortality rates from 1987 and concluded that very high alcohol consumption may be leading to a 'very large number of circulatory deaths in middle age'.[30] Also, Wasserman and Vdmik show a positive correlation between alcohol and suicide, violent causes of death and accidental poisoning, whilst Ryan points to a direct link between the latter and the diminution of the state's ability to impose control over the quality in production.[31]

Mortality rates improved between 1994 and 1998. Shkolnikov et al. argue that this was mainly due to a fall in death among middle-aged adults as a result of a decline in average alcohol consumption of 19% (estimated by the Russian Longitudinal Monitoring Survey).[32] Why this decline occurred is not precisely clear, as there was certainly no sustained anti-alcohol campaign similar to Gorbachev's. Given the importance of alcohol, the fact that the group that has been hit hardest is middle-aged males, we would expect alcohol-related diseases to be prominent in the list of 'micro' determinants of mortality.[33] As seen in Table 6.4 for both men and women, diseases of the circulatory system (which alcohol most affects – though it also affects respiratory diseases such as pneumonia) were the dominant cause accounting for between 40% and 50% of total deaths. Furthermore, alcohol plays a significant factor in 'external' causes such as motor-vehicle accidents, accidental poisoning by alcohol, accidental drowning, suicides, homicides and violent deaths. Given that middle-aged men are the heaviest drinkers – adult males consume 90% of alcohol but are only 25% of the population – the impact of all these categories of death is visited mostly upon this group.[34] The main reason for the increase in alcohol consumption according to Paniccia is 'inertia', that is, the continuance of prevailing drinking habits.[35] This might be true, but what is the reason for this? Our argument is that to better understand inertia, we need to examine societal conditions that drive certain groups to persist in self-destructive behaviour such as high levels of alcohol consumption. We discuss this further below.

'Inertia' was more crucial than the increase in the alcohol purchasing power of wages (because the price of alcohol fell faster than wages) or alcohol as a stress-reliever. Moskalewicz et al. suggest that '[i]t cannot be excluded that the stress related to current transitions led to increased consumption in some vulnerable groups like the unemployed or induced short episodes of heavy drinking that may have had negative health consequences'.[36] Note, however, that the fall in relative price was considerable. Between 1992 and 1994, at a time of hyperinflation, the price of alcohol rose by 431%, that is, by only one-third of the consumer price index increase of 1,229%.[37] This suggests that there must have been some 'price effect', notwithstanding the decline in average purchasing power.

The role of alcohol has also been highly significant in regard to mortality from 'external causes' as is evident from Table 6.5. Alcohol consumption is correlated positively with male suicide rate and, interestingly, evidence suggests that the female suicide rate may also be correlated with the *male* suicide rate.[38] The overall mortality rate from external causes remains extremely high at 5 times that of Western Europe.[39]

Death by alcohol poisoning rose by an astonishing three-fold for men and four-fold for women between 1991 and 1994 reflecting the decline in state regulation and the flourishing of homebrew (*samogon*) trading. By 1998 this had dropped sharply but was still 50% higher than in 1991 for men and 70% higher for women. Alcohol is also implicated in suicide, murder and accidental drownings where the incidence of intoxication is a common occurrence.[40]

So there seems incontrovertible evidence of the severe impact, especially on male mortality, from high alcohol consumption. Yet there is still a vested interest for the state to maintain high rates of alcohol consumption: that of tax revenue. In 1988, tax on alcohol generated an astonishing 35% of government revenue, although this had fallen to only 5% by the late 1990s as most sales were on the black market, hence avoiding tax.[41] The doubling of taxes on vodka by Yeltsin to generate additional tax revenue inevitably diverted production from registered channels to illegal trading with the associated increase in production and sale of low-quality, frequently poisonous alcohol. Clearly, the problem of alcoholism is, as we have seen, a deep-rooted one in Russian culture and custom, with roots in the peasantry of Tsarist times as we saw in Chapter 4. To a very significant extent, the individual is locked into this corrosive cultural practice that is not only completely socially accepted, but is invariably encouraged. True, the choice to 'binge drink' is made by the individual, but not to do so might risk rebuke and exclusion by friends and family. Thus social conditioning provides a very powerful impetus to an individual's decision; and this decision is potentially better carried out by those of a professional, better-educated class than by industrial and agricultural workers. Without doubt, such a pattern has been reinforced by the transition crisis.

Table 6.5 Male and Female Age-Standardised Death Rates per 100,000 at Ages 15–74 for 'External Causes' of Death in 1991, 1994 and 1998*

	Male Mortality Rates			Female Mortality Rates			Male Ratio 1998:1991	Female Ratio 1998:1991
	1991	*1994*	*1998*	*1991*	*1994*	*1998*		
Motor-vehicle accidents	51.8	45.9	37.1	0.7	11.8	11.5	0.7	0.9
Accidental poisoning by alcohol	26.7	83.2	39.4	5.9	21.9	9.9	1.5	1.7
Other accidental poisonings	16.8	26	25.2	4.1	6.4	5.5	1.6	1.3
Accidental drowning	17.3	25.1	22.0	1.9	3.1	3.3	1.3	1.7
Suicides	58.4	96.7	78.8	11.8	15.0	12.2	1.4	1.0
Homicides	31.4	66.1	45.1	8.2	17.4	12.5	1.4	1.5
Unspecified violent death[42]	28.3	75.0	58.8	6.0	16.4	12.9	2.1	2.1
Other accidents and violence	54.9	96.6	68.7	10.9	20.5	15.1	1.3	1.4
Total external causes	*294.1*	*527.7*	*382.8*	*62.3*	*114.9*	*84.0*	*1.30*	*1.35*

*There is a problem with the data. The broad headings combined do not add up to the total columns implying that there is a missing element.

Source: Shkolnikov et al. (2001).

165

Suicide and murder

The despair and criminalisation of Russian society have also given rise to very high levels of violence. In the next chapter, we examine state-related violence and death, but here we focus briefly on two types of civilian violence: suicide or self-inflicted death; and murder, the killing of others. In *A Sort of Life*, the novelist Graham Greene wrote poignantly: 'a successful suicide is often only a cry for help which hasn't been heard in time'. Such unheard cries for help in Russia have led to an increase in suicide rates across all sectors of the population, though even in the depths of hopelessness some attempt can be made to retain a semblance of dignity. In the midst of the 1998 financial crash when there were defaults on debts across the financial system, one 87-year-old woman in the St Petersburg region, not having received her pension, wrote out a note listing how much she owed and asking forgiveness for her debts before she hanged herself.[43]

Russia has the second highest suicide rate in the world after Lithuania.[44] In 2000, there were 57,000 suicides which, at a rate of 39 per 100,000, is more than double that of 1985 (and three times that of the US and five times that of Britain). However, though inordinately high, the rate remained stable in the 1990s. At approximately 20% throughout the 1990s, male suicide constitutes the highest proportion of deaths from 'external causes', and is five times the level of the female suicide rate (for which other external causes show a greater incidence). Between 1991 and 1998, the male suicide rate was between 4% and 5% of all registered causes of death (Table 6.5). The highest suicide rate, at 140 per 100,000, is for men aged 50–54.[45] This group is part of that which, as we have seen, suffers most from alcohol abuse and has the highest levels of overall mortality.

In a survey of the causes of suicide, Brainerd has linked male suicide to the state of the macroeconomy – as given by two variables: GNP per capita and the employment-to-population ratio.[46] The regressions show that a $100 increase in GNP per capita lowers the predicted male suicide rate by up to 0.2% whilst a 1% increase in the employment-to-population ratio reduces the male suicide rate by approximately 3%. In contrast, the female suicide rate appears to be relatively insensitive to economic conditions. Brainerd suggests that this is because women's non-market work is valued more than men's in transition societies. This may have some validity, but a more probable factor is that men are still considered the major breadwinners and hence a deterioration in their economic conditions is likely to have a greater impact on their social behaviour, including personal self-esteem. Feelings of hopelessness and loss of self-esteem may therefore trigger the suicide option. A further argument is that the 'care-giving' function of women (who often take care of children and elderly parents) may prevent women from committing suicide in equivalent numbers.[47] The male suicide rate for most age groups in 1998 was between six and eight times that of its female counterpart;[48] an equivalent comparison for the murder rate was three to five times higher for men. For both suicide and murder, the pattern was broadly similar to the overall mortality rate, namely that there was a steady increase between 1991 and 1994, followed by a decline, with the 1998 figure being higher than 1991. Male suicide showed an increase up to the 40–49 age group (to approximately 90 per 100,000) where it stabilised. In contrast, the female suicide rate showed a steady increase for all ages, and by 1998 it had returned to 1991 levels.

Turning now to murder, Russia's official murder rate in 1998 was 21.6 per 100,000, which equates to 33,500 murders in total. This is three times the rate of the US (6.9 per 100,000), 24 times that of Germany (0.9 per 100,000 in 1999) and an astonishing 43 times that of France (0.5 per 100,000).[49] However, Alexander Gurov, the head of the State Duma's Security Committee, argues that this is a gross *underestimate* as it takes into account only those who died on the spot. It thereby excludes 40,000 per annum who die after being injured in attacks and a further 19,000 whose cause of death is not determined, but Gurov believes that 70% of these are, in fact, murders. There are also those who simply 'disappear', many of whom may also have been murdered. This leaves the true numbers of murders at close to 100,000 per annum. Gurov argues that business-related deaths account for 40% of these, which suggests that those who want to get rich often resort to eliminating their rivals.[50] We have no way of knowing how true this figure is and 40,000 such murders seems incredible, but there is no doubt that mafia and business-related killings are rife and more than a match for anything seen in the US during the 'Roaring Twenties'.

The murder rate for men is higher at younger ages (25–50) in comparison with the male suicide rate, and falls sharply for men in their 60s and 70s. For women, however, the murder rate is fairly constant from the ages of 20 to 74. By 1998, for women, murder became almost as common a cause of death as suicide – thus the factors restricting the female suicide rate do not appear to operate for murder. The higher proportion of non-alcohol-related deaths at younger ages is a powerful reflection of the increasing crime rate in Russia.[51]

Regional variations and impoverishment

In Soviet times, life expectancy of Russians in rural areas (with lower living standards) was less than that of urban centres. In 1992, urban residents lived, on average, 2.4 years longer than their rural counterparts. Thereafter, the gap quickly narrowed so that by 1994, it was just 0.8 years as urban life expectancy fell faster than the rural. The reason for this turnaround is that in the urban areas there has been a sharp increase in labour turnover, higher levels of unemployment, an increase in stress, the mushrooming of crime, higher levels of migration and greater levels of instability in comparison with rural areas. Consequently, male life expectancy has deteriorated more in urban areas. This tends to confirm the fact that a *rise* in unemployment is a more important determinant of mortality than its *level*.[52]

Walberg et al. argue that if mortality increase is a result of impoverishment, one would expect the largest fall in life expectancy to occur in regions where decline in income has been greatest.[53] Yet in line with the above, their findings show that the largest falls in life expectancy are, in fact, in the richest regions – mainly in urban areas (including Moscow and St Petersburg) with the lowest falls in rural, poorer regions. The former were marked by high rates of labour turnover, increase in crime, and higher average but unequal distribution of household income. From this they conclude that it is the impact of the social and economic transition (especially unemployment), which they term 'lack of social cohesion', and not simply impoverishment, that provides the best explanation of a rise in mortality. They argue that mortality increase from 1991 to 1994 accords well with Durkheim's concept of 'anomic suicide'. Anomic suicide is the form of suicide associated with *anomie* or 'lack of norms' and rising uncertainty. It occurs particularly when there is a sudden disruption of normal social circumstances. Though Durkheim focused on the rate and type of suicide and its relationship with social structure, the methodology can be extended to other kinds of societal change, including disease and mortality. Wilkinson makes the point that: '[t]he evidence is overwhelming that the rates of most diseases vary from society to society in ways that reflect, and indeed are indicative of, differences in their social and economic organisation. Most of the main causes of death look no less sociological than suicide.'[54]

This therefore seems a worthwhile framework to understand the changes in Russia's mortality since 1991. Lack of social cohesion arose from the sudden change in the social order and led to widespread *anomie*. In turn, this fed ultimately into a rising mortality rate. The approach appears equally to have validity in regard to improvements in the mortality rate after 1995. This suggests that a decline in *anomie* obtained as a new social order took shape with new norms and expectations. Hence uncertainty decreased and a new social equilibrium became embedded, leading to a declining mortality rate. But Walberg et al. downplay the importance of impoverishment too much for the reason that rising unemployment and higher levels of labour turnover actually imply an *increase* in impoverishment for those afflicted.

However, the sudden deterioration of the mortality rate from 1999 onwards presents a puzzle in regard to the appropriateness of 'anomic suicide'. All other things being equal, the theory suggests that one would have expected to witness a continuing reduction in *anomie* and improvement in the mortality rate in line with the continuing adjustment of the population to the new conditions. But as we have seen, mortality indicators worsened after 1998. A possible explanation for this in 1999 is the sudden financial crisis of 1998 that could be construed as a form of a 'minor' anomic change. However, since then, the economy has picked up, albeit hesitantly, but mortality rates have continued to deteriorate. In fact, what this appears to indicate is a case of 'hysteresis', that is, after the shock of adjustment, the new political and socio-economic conditions experienced by the majority of the population remain dire. This has given rise to a new and lower equilibrium of health and life expectancy for the population in general and, as we shall see below, for working-class males in particular.

Paniccia examines the impact of impoverishment on health and mortality in transition economies and concludes that though there was a decline in calories and protein intake below recommended levels for the poorest, there have been no problems of malnutrition. Moreover, increase in impoverishment would suggest an increase in mortality of the most vulnerable groups, namely, the young and old,[55] but, as seen in Table 6.2, there is little evidence for this. However, social marginals such as vagrants and the homeless were subjected to a deterioration in health from inadequate shelter, poor hygiene, and lack of clean water that led to infectious, parasitic and water-borne diseases. The reduction of public expenditure has accentuated health problems in regard to poor water maintenance, sewage and garbage collection systems. Furthermore, the rise of the 'informal economy' has led to a fall in food hygiene from the prevalence of unregulated private food vendors that are more likely to be patronised by the poorer section of the community.[56] These factors certainly give cause to increasing the incidence of morbidity but do not necessarily lead to rising mortality. Overall, therefore, death purely as a result of severe impoverishment has been relatively rare, being confined largely to the social marginals in the richer urban centres.

Ethnic differences

Official data for the ethnic breakdown of mortality rates is not available. In a rare study of the topic it is, however, discussed by Bogoyavlensky et al.[57] The authors provide a gradient of mortality rates by regions that can be used as a proxy for ethnic differences, but with the caveat of lack of reliability. Starting with the highest, the mortality rates run from the small peoples of the North; the Tuva people; other peoples of Siberia; Kalmyks and Kazakhs; Finno-Hungarian peoples; Russians; peoples of the Volga region (except Finno-Hungarians); East Slavic peoples (except Russians); Germans; Armenians; Jews; and peoples of North Caucasus. One has to treat the situation of the North Caucasus with caution as no data is provided for Chechnya, and statistics for republics surrounding it are incomplete and unreliable due to the conflict. One statistic that is provided is that for the aboriginal peoples of the Far North. Their male life expectancy is only 44.3 years and female life expectancy 54.1 years. They also suffer an infant mortality rate of 30–35 deaths per 100,000, twice that of the Russian average. These are equivalent to the poorest peoples in the world and suggest almost complete neglect and hardship.

Stress (psychosocial factors)

The 'shock' of shock therapy was not only an economic one – it had repercussions throughout all aspects of society. The sudden changes which brought about acute uncertainty inevitably caused much stress among broad swathes of the population – above all in regard to the rapid increase in unemployment and decline in living standards – accentuated by inadequate support institutions and social safety nets, and an inability to cope in a market-dominated environment. Such stress manifests itself in physiological and psychological problems – such as cardiovascular disease, hypertension, ulcers, increased smoking and alcohol consumption, suicide and murder – that have an impact upon mortality. The importance of stress has been acknowledged in a number of studies relating to mortality and post-transition Russia.[58]

Indeed, Marmot and Bobak contend that economic hardship does not imply an increase in mortality due to increases in the diseases of poverty but rather cautiously hypothesise the importance of psychosocial (i.e. acute, stress-related) factors affecting mortality and suggest two pathways in which these can impact on disease.[59] First, a direct effect on neuroendocrine and immune systems that can ultimately lead to disease and second, an indirect, adverse effect on health behaviour (such as smoking, heavy drinking and poor diet). Stress can arise from an array of sources such as work environment, life events and difficulties, social relationships and (lack of) 'social capital' (social supports, integration and social cohesion), lack of control over one's life, unemployment and insecurity.[60] To this can be added geographical and sectoral reallocation of labour; problems in the new private sector (low stability, poor safety and social protection); and highly stressful situation of migrants and those marginalised by the reforms.[61] Notwithstanding the need for caution in the link between stress and mortality (Shkolnikov and Cornia counsel that the limitations of data prevent a definitive conclusion, but nevertheless assert that stress has played an important role in the recent health crisis),[62] this exhaustive list of potential sources does seem entirely plausible. Moreover, the impact of the early years of transition was to intensify all stress-inducing factors with stress being most frequent and pronounced among young male adults who are most likely to confront problems relating to employment, divorce (married men live longer than divorced men) and migration.[63] But we must also assume that stress-inducing factors were acute for middle-aged men given that it was this group that suffered the steepest increase in mortality. Strong corroborative evidence for the importance of stress would be provided if, in the long run, a lessening of the stress factors results in a concomitant reduction in the mortality rate; though we hasten to add that this is certainly not a realistic scenario for the foreseeable future. The close examination of stress is very useful in the post-transition period and provides many valuable insights. Nonetheless, we argue that the danger in this approach is that it takes the focus away from actual increases in poverty that have occurred and especially, on class inequalities. It is to the latter that we now turn.

Class inequalities

We have repeatedly emphasised the importance of class throughout this book and the post-transition period has proved to be no exception. In regard to the health and class nexus, the issue has long attracted considerable attention and study in the West. For example, the supreme importance of class and inequality in health, including mortality, was the focus of the powerful Black Report in Britain in 1980, that we referred to in Chapter 4; the aims and methodology of which would be highly suitable and worthwhile for any country, including Russia. Indeed, the conclusions of the report were so explosive and unpalatable to the then newly-incumbent Conservative government that they deliberately chose to snub it. The reason for this was that the report conclusively demonstrated that there were marked differences in mortality rates between occupational classes, for male and female, and at all ages:

> ... much of the evidence on social inequalities in health can be adequately understood in terms of specific features of the socioeconomic environment: features (such as work accidents, overcrowding, cigarette smoking) which are strongly class-related in Britain and also have clear causal significance ... [that can be understood] only in terms of the ... consequences of the class structure: poverty, working conditions, and deprivation in its various forms.[64]

Implicitly this was an attack on the *laissez-faire* approach and the inequalities it generates. But such an approach would soon be advocated with considerable gusto in Britain by the Thatcher government. And it was precisely this type of advice that would also be proffered to Eastern Europe and Russia a decade later. The market theorists must have been aware of the health implications of their reform programmes, and which had been so clearly set out in the Black Report and other similar works. Yet they systematically failed to convey this to the reforming governments. If the conclusions of the report were derisively ignored in Britain, they would also certainly be in Russia.

Townsend, Phillimore and Beattie, in a survey inspired by the Black Report, stress the point that social class is not simply 'just another' indicator (along with, say, employment, race or overcrowding) but is the decisive social concept, fundamental to the explanation of the distribution of health.[65] They emphasise that class is more than just 'occupational' but is defined as a total reflection of differences in rank in economic and social position – a position that approximates more to the Marxian definition than the Weberian one ordinarily used in sociological analysis. Such a wider definition proves to be a more powerful predictor of health, as Townsend et al. find in their study of health inequalities in the North-East of England. Their findings show an often extremely wide variation in health between local populations – thus in regard to mortality, the rate for wards with the worst health was almost twice that of those with the best health. Moreover, such variation corresponds closely with variation in material deprivation or affluence.[66] The conclusion is obvious and even banal but needs to be stressed: class and its corollary, material deprivation, are not just the preserve of Russia but exist even in advanced societies. That said, the poor health safety net and inadequacies of the Russian health system mean that the effects are felt more acutely there. And research shows that those at the sharp end tend to be less educated, working-class, middle-aged men who have suffered the highest level of, and greatest deterioration in, mortality during the transition period.[67] One consequence, therefore, of the changing nature of class relationships is that they are now fully out into the open. The corollary to this has been open inequalities in health and healthcare.

Siegrist combines two explanations for this: health-damaging behaviour by manual-working-class males (smoking, high alcohol consumption, fatty diet, lack of exercise and obesity) and a stressful psychosocial environment (from relative deprivation in income, work, housing, restricted social mobility and freedom, threat to personal security, social isolation and exclusion). This gives rise to anger, disappointment, helplessness and hopelessness, all of which contribute to the development of physical and mental disease. This 'social reward deficiency' may, in turn, reinforce the craving for stress-relieving, addictive, health-damaging behaviour, such as high alcohol consumption and smoking. In the context of post-transition Russia, such a framework appears persuasive and fits in well with our determinants of mortality discussed in Chapter 1.[68]

Cockerham focuses on alcohol as a 'lethal component of male lifestyle', arguing that poor health lifestyle choices are largely the outcome of 'structural conditions' or the position in a society in which an individual finds him- or herself.[69] Similarly, diet and (lack of) exercise can also be considered as being structurally conditioned – the Russian diet is notorious for its high levels of cholesterol, sugar and salt, and poor-quality (fatty) meat with low amounts of vegetables and fibre: in combination these are a sound recipe for cardiovascular disease and cancer.[70] Cockerham argues that this is consistent with Pierre Bourdieu's concept of *habitus*, that is, individuals' experiences, socialisation and class reality. In other words, to a significant degree, the choices and lifestyle of people are limited by their *habitus*, and for Russian working-class men the *habitus* provides a very narrow range of lifestyle choices. Widening such choices requires economic growth and a rise in disposable income which generates improved behaviour and a better, healthier, lifestyle. But the post-transition collapse in living standards clearly precluded this for the majority of the population. Therefore, the *habitus* became further entrenched, forcing people to cling on to lifestyles that are damaging to their health. We could think of Gorbachev's anti-alcohol campaign as an attempt to break aspects of such entrenchment, but ultimately it failed because it did not provide a real expansion of choices. The transition, especially in the early years, rather than expanding choices, further reduced them. One must therefore draw the obvious conclusion: not until there is a sustained increase in real per capita income, particularly for working-class men, will changes in lifestyle occur which lead to a consistent improvement in mortality rates and life expectancy. Till then, millions more will continue to experience an early visit to the grave.

This chapter has shown that the impact on normal mortality rate of the shock therapy reforms has been truly immense. Russia in the 1990s had witnessed the greatest peacetime increase in mortality that any modern society had ever seen. Yet this occurred in a period without autocratic rule where there was no Stalinist-type repression and mass murder. Moreover, there were no famines, no environmental disasters and no major epidemics of killer diseases. Initially, the stronger sense of optimism boosted the will to live, and hopes for a more prosperous and secure future were strong. Yet for the vast majority, these were quickly dashed. The much-vaunted new system had simply failed to deliver. For the majority, what took place had been almost unimaginable – the worsening of all the key socio-economic indicators from already low and cruel levels. This begs the obvious question that is conspicuous only by its neglect: if the old system had failed and stood condemned for its criminal disregard, then did not the same apply to the new? Mirroring their predecessors, the victims of this disregard seemed invisible to those who controlled the successor state, and to those who advised them. The hope and promise that a society might be created on the basis of fulfilling real human wants and needs was once more cast aside by Russia's post-1991 rulers who, as we have seen, proved to be just as enthusiastic about 'breaking eggs to make omelettes' as those of old.

On 17 July 1998, what were thought to be the remains of the last Tsar and his family and servants were buried in the cathedral of St Petersburg's Peter and Paul Fortress. This was a contentious ceremony. The correspondent of the *Moscow Times* correctly described it as 'modest' in comparison with Tsar Alexander III's burial in 1894 but noted that it cost 'just' 5 million roubles (or $806,000). Some were indifferent whilst others were enraged. A lone protester asked: 'Factories are closed, people are not getting their wages, so what's going on with this funeral?'[71] What was going on, in fact, was a stark example of inequalities not just in life, but also in death. Though the ceremony was boycotted by most of the political elites, Boris Yeltsin, recognising the symbolism of the event, decided to attend, declaring solemnly that Russia had finally repented for one of its 'most shameful episodes in history'. Though one can dispute the veracity of this remark, what is not in dispute is that no such repentance has been made for the tens of millions of ordinary Russians who have suffered under their rulers.

7 Yeltsin, Putin and 'Abnormal' Deaths 1992–2002

COLLECTIVE VIOLENCE AND 'INTENTIONAL' DEATHS

Post-transition Russia has been fortunate in not suffering significant numbers of abnormal deaths that have emanated from serious disasters such as famines or Chernobyl-type explosions. But as this chapter will show, Russia has incurred very large numbers of other types of abnormal deaths – the vast majority resulting from actions of the state. The fall of the Soviet state gave a huge impetus to realising important rights and freedoms. People in Russia, like its former satellites in Central Europe, wished to become a 'normal market economy' or, as they would see it, just a 'normal society'. A normal society would suggest that in regard to mortality, there would be very few abnormal deaths at the hands of the state. Certainly, as we saw in Chapter 4, abnormal mortality fell sharply after Stalin's death but remained significant. We now examine to what extent the weakening of state power since 1991 has led to the reduction in abnormal deaths.

In its analysis of violence, including violent death, the World Health Organisation (WHO), uses a two-fold typology: 'intentional' and 'unintentional'. The former closely approximates to Wheatcroft's 'deliberate and purposeful action' and the latter to his 'irresponsible acts and neglect' that we discussed in Chapter 1. Unintentional violence incorporates most normal deaths that we examined in the last chapter. Intentional violence has three main types: 'self-directed' (by suicide and self-abuse), 'inter-personal' (within families, communities, and among strangers, including murder) and 'collective violence' (by larger groups and states). It is under this third type that our category of 'abnormal' deaths largely comes, that is, intentional deaths caused by the state. These can be further categorised in terms of war-related injuries and state violence and repression, in particular from execution and imprisonment. In post-transition Russia, the most important type of violent deaths has been war-related deaths. A caveat, however, needs to be stressed: because these are still considered highly politically sensitive categories, official data is not readily available and Goskomstat's *Demographic Yearbook of Russia* does not list them under these types. Consequently, in the main, we resort to gleaning data from an array of sources of varying reliability, but which we believe to have credibility and integrity. Nonetheless, these remain estimates and approximations and, as such, are open to contention.

Table 7.1 provides a breakdown of death from war for various regions of the world. It needs emphasising that estimates for war fatalities vary enormously – as we shall shortly see with respect to Chechnya – so we need to treat these with caution.[1] The most noticeable aspect is the difference between high-income and low- and middle-income regions. Globally, deaths from war-related injuries are 0% for the former but 0.6% for the latter.[2] In terms of rankings, war is the eleventh highest cause of deaths for Africa (the region with the highest war-related mortalities) accounting for 1.6% of total deaths, the 34th highest in South East Asia (0.4% of total), and 21st in low- and middle-income Europe (0.6% of total), the region within which Russia resides.

Table 7.1   Estimated Mortality Caused by War-Related Injuries, Selected Regions

Region	Ranking	War-Related Mortality as % of Total Deaths
Africa	11	1.6
Americas (high income)	66	0.0
Americas (low/middle income)	60	0.1
South East Asia	34	0.4
Europe (high income)	68	0.0
Europe (low/middle income)	21	0.6

Source: WHO 2002a, statistical annex table A.6.

Figure 7.1 gives a breakdown of rates of mortality by 'intentional' injury. We can use this as a proxy for a comparison of global abnormal deaths, including state deaths. It is immediately striking that, of the major countries, Russia has by far the highest rate, at 54 per 100,000. This is over three times that of the US and France, and seven times that of the UK. It is also much higher than for large developing countries such as South Korea and Argentina (3.6 and five times respectively). Only other former Soviet republics such as Belarus and Ukraine come near Russia's rate: Belarus's is 76% and Ukraine's is 69% that of Russia. Undoubtedly, therefore, despite improvements in rights and freedoms, Russian society remains an extremely violent one – in 2002 it was ranked third in the world for violent deaths.[3] A good deal of this violence stems from the state, and the rest of this chapter elaborates upon the most important types of state-induced violent deaths.

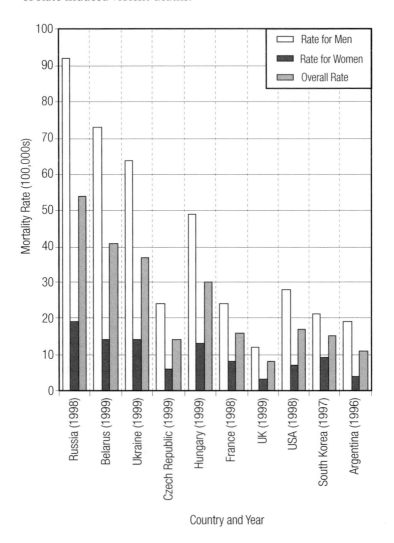

Figure 7.1   Mortality Rates by 'Intentional' Injury, Selected Countries

Source: WHO 2002a, statistical annex table A.7.

POLITICAL CRISIS AND CIVIL UNREST

Market Stalinism, like the original 'plan Stalinism', was a strictly top-down affair. No effort was made to explain to the public what the transition entailed. Optimism and support did not last long as precipitous falls in living standards soon took place. By October 1992, ten months into the reforms, opinion polls were showing that only 5% of the population was satisfied with the economic situation, 16% with their standard of living, and 10% with the political situation.[4] These figures provide evidence of the small section of the population who really gained, or who managed to shore up their living standards, in the tempestuous months of 1992. Disillusionment rapidly set in with the new political system. This was certainly no political or social revolution. Research by Olga Kryshtanovskaia showed that in early 1994, 75% of Yeltsin's presidential administration, 74% in the government (executive branch), and 83% of regional political elites had come from the Soviet-era *nomenklatura*.[5]

The economic crisis accelerated by the shock therapy reforms induced social resistance and a political crisis. Throughout 1992, there were political attacks on Boris Yeltsin by his opponents. In March 1993, a parliamentary (Federal Assembly) motion to impeach Yeltsin narrowly failed, but in the following month, Yeltsin did receive a vote of confidence in a national referendum. Buoyed by this, in September, he decided to silence his critics by dissolving the Congress of Peoples Deputies and the Supreme Soviet, and calling for new elections. Independent-minded newspapers were closed, and TV presenters dismissed. Such actions did not unduly worry his major Western supporters, who readily backed these moves.[6] But fierce opposition erupted as some deputies barricaded themselves in the White House in Moscow. The crisis deepened in October 1993 as supporters of the Supreme Soviet occupied the Moscow Mayor's office and stormed the Ostankino TV tower. Yeltsin's retaliation was swift: he declared a state of emergency that led to the arrest of 89,250 people[7] and ordered the bombardment of the parliamentary building that resulted in the deaths of, according to official figures, 147 people. In reality this action, in combination with deaths outside the TV tower, led to over 1,000 being killed, including many who were just sightseers.[8] The deputies finally surrendered, Yeltsin had his victory and became a virtual autocrat, notwithstanding the fact that he would contest (and win) presidential elections in 1996.[9] Power shifted towards the executive.

The new constitution granted Yeltsin powers that were more comprehensive than those of Communist Party General Secretaries of the 1977 USSR constitution.[10] Appointment of the Prime Minister was in his gift. He or she, in turn, selected members of the government – meaning that the entire executive was under the grip of Yeltsin. To further add insult to injury to the legislature, the constitution now granted the President powers to dissolve the new State Duma – a scenario familiar in many Third World countries where the military top brass frequently exercise such a fiat. Yet all this was meekly accepted by Yeltsin's new international allies who, only a few years earlier, had railed against precisely this sort of concentration of political power by the leaders of the one-party states of the former Eastern bloc. Opinion polls showed that 72% of Muscovites supported the assault on Parliament, still believing more in Yeltsin's credentials than those of his opponents.[11] But these events had a deeply disillusioning impact on the population. Only 53% of those eligible voted in the first multi-party elections in December 1993. The shock of these elections was that Zhirinovsky's fascist Liberal Democratic Party of Russia received 25% of the vote – twice that of the Yeltsin-supporting Democrats. But the opposition, a combination of the extreme right and nationalists (including the Communist Party) failed to successfully unite against Yeltsin.

In the absence of a strong, credible opposing candidate in the 1996 presidential elections, and with huge backing from the oligarchs, Yeltsin was re-elected. Following his sudden resignation on New Year's Eve 1999, Yeltsin then handed power onto a hand-picked successor who would take care of his and his cohorts' interests, the former KGB officer Vladimir Putin. The manner in which this was done would have, and continues to have, a devastating effect on a recalcitrant Russian republic – Chechnya, where a war of independence had been fought between 1994 and 1996. In 1999, Yeltsin contrived a resumption of war on Chechnya. This saw his popularity rise, enabling him to hand over the presidency in a baton-like manner to his protégé, Prime Minister Putin, who took over as Acting President on 1 January 2000. Boosted by the popularity of the war in Chechnya, Putin easily won the March 2000 Presidential election. To all intents and purposes he had indeed been 'Put in' to the top post in Russia by his former master. One consequence of his victory would be the continuation of the horrific abnormal death count in Chechnya.

DEATH AND DISEASE IN PRISONS

Something seemingly strange has been happening to crime and punishment in post-transition Russia. Recorded crime, after sharply increasing in 1992, declined until 1997. It rose sharply again in 1998 and 1999 before stabilising in 2000 and 2001 at just under 3 million, a 37% increase over 1991 (see Table 7.2 for an array of indicators concerning crime and imprisonment). One would think from this that the conviction rate would also rise by a similar rate. On the contrary this, in fact, more than doubled in the 1991–2001 period, from 594,000 to 1.2 million. Most of these serve prison sentences and, during their incarceration, many go on to contract disease and die.

In line with the increase in total recorded crime, recorded theft and burglary increased by 35% (to 1.8 million) in 1992 before falling to 1.2 million in 1997. The figure for 2001 (1.42 million) was only marginally more than that for 1991. Theft and burglary remain by far the largest type of criminal offence, accounting for 48% of all crime in 2001, but down from 62% in 1991. However, the numbers *convicted* for these offences have also more than doubled – from 239,000 in 1991 to 609,000 in 2001. Drug abuse saw the greatest increase in recorded crime, from 19,000 in 1991 to 242,000 in 2001, a twelve-fold increase. Most of those convicted are men. Women account for just 14% of the total, although this is significantly higher that the 9% in 1992.

For men, the highest conviction rate is for those in the age range 30–49 (36%) followed by 18–24 (31%) and 25–29 (17%). Just over half those convicted are unemployed, that is, able-bodied and not working or studying. Such a rapid increase in the conviction rate has inevitably led to a sharp increase in the numbers imprisoned: in 1991, there were 680,000 prisoners (including pre-trial detainees); by 1996, this had rapidly climbed to over 1 million, peaking at 1.05 million in 1997. Since then, there has been a gradual reduction, down to 968,000 in 2002, but this is still 42% higher than in 1991. One is tempted to think that, as in the US, locking people up has become an important method of removing them from the unemployment statistics.

What this clearly indicates is that a harsher criminal justice regime was set in place from the early years of the transition; at a time when, according to Western apologists, the supposedly more liberal Yeltsin government was fending off reactionary, conservative, elements in the parliament. In truth, as Valery Abramkin, Director and founder of Moscow Centre for Prison Reform (MCPR) (and a former dissident

Table 7.2 Various Indicators of Crime and Imprisonment in Russia 1991–2002

	1991	1992	1993	1994	1995	1996	1997	1998	1999	2000	2001
Recorded crimes (000s)	2,173	2,761	2,800	2,633	2,756	2,625	2,397	2,582	3,002	2,952	2,968
For theft	1,243	1,651	1,580	1,315	1,368	1,207	1,054	1,143	1,414	1,310	1,273
For burglary	102	165	184	149	141	121	112	122	139	132	149
For drug abuse	19	30	53	75	80	97	186	190	216	244	242
Total convictions (000s)	594	661	792	925	1,036	1,111	1,013	1,071	1,223	1,184	1,244
For theft	207	275	357	405	457	481	465	471	592	599	541
For burglary	32	41	55	59	56	56	57	58	64	65	68
For drug abuse	9	10	19	29	39	46	65	101	108	99	127
By age group (%)											
14–17	14	14	13	12	11	11	12	12	12	13	12
18–24	23	24	25	25	24	24	28	29	30	31	31
25–29	19	18	16	16	16	16	15	15	16	16	17
30–49	38	40	40	42	43	44	40	39	38	35	36
Over 50	6	5	6	6	6	6	5	5	5	5	5
Convictions of women	9	7	9	9	12	13	12	12	12	13	14
Of previously prosecuted	38	39	37	35	34	33	33	34	34	35	36
Not working or studying	21	26	35	41	44	47	46	49	51	50	51
Total prisoners (000s)	680	745	750	842	929	1,018	1,048	1,010	n/a	n/a	968*

* March 2002.

Sources: for recorded crime and convictions, Goskomstat 2000, ch. 11; for prisoners 1991–98, MCPR website; for 2002, ICPS 2002, 'Prison Brief for Russia'.

who was locked up in Moscow's notorious Butyrka prison in the early 1980s for writing 'slanderous' articles against the Soviet state) argues, there was a liberalisation in the penal system during the Gorbachev era, as the prison population was halved. 'After 1991 the economy plunged, and the authoritarian forces partially reasserted themselves.' Abramkin suggests that things have improved since 1998, when the civilian Ministry of Justice took over the GUIN (Main Directorate for the Execution of Punishments) from the 'semi-military' Ministry of Interior.[12] This might be so, but total numbers of prisoners still remain some 40% higher than in 1991. What is clear is that crime and punishment remains a central key plank of Russian society and a huge number are scarred by the penal system. Elsewhere, Abramkin provides the staggering statistic that, by the mid-1990s, ex-prisoners made up 15% or one in seven of Russia's adult population.[13]

Increasing levels of incarceration have propelled Russia into the unenviable position of having the second highest prison rate in the world at 670 per 100,000, just under the US's 690 per 100,000 (see Figure 7.2). The US is unique in that it has a rate far in excess of other developed countries: indeed its rate is over six times that of the next highest, New Zealand, which is ranked 71 at 157 per 100,000. In between are all the major developing and transition countries. The highest West European country is the UK, ranked 90, at a rate of 133 per 100,000.

Russia's 'prison-industrial complex' is very large, but unlike its US counterpart, it has not seen an expansion in capacity. The result has been intense overcrowding, especially in pre-trial detention centres. There are 1,010 prison establishments comprising 749 penal colonies, 184 pre-trial detention centres, 13 prisons, and 64 juvenile colonies (in mid-2001, there were 17,000 children serving prison sentences).[14] However, the official capacity of the prison system is given as 960,000, implying that it is operating at just over 2% above capacity. But, given numerous reports of acute overcrowding in prison cells, this suggests that the 'normal capacity' must be an extremely miserly one. The stark reality is that many are imprisoned for minor offences such as theft which, in the West at least (excepting the 'three strikes and you're out' policy of some US states) would rarely result in imprisonment. In contrast, Russia's philosophy of justice has been based on the principle of 'one strike and you're out'. Examples include a 14-year-old boy being sentenced to five years when he and his brother stole a leather jacket and ten roubles from a passer-by; a man jailed for five years for stealing three chickens and two turkeys; and a

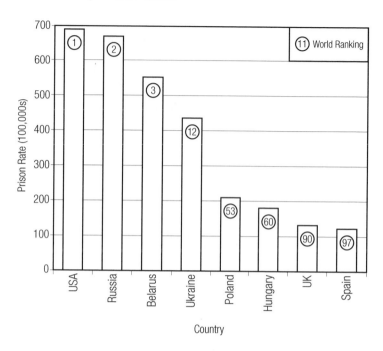

Figure 7.2   Sample Prison Rates (per 100,000) July 2002, Selected Countries

Source: ICPS 2002, *World Prison Brief*, 'Highest Prison Population rates'.

mother of three children jailed for five years for stealing a goat.[15] Such an approach to punishment stems from the profoundly illiberal doctrine at the heart of the Russian state, with precursors in its Stalinist past. A possible mitigating factor for the high incidence of crime is poverty, but given that this is largely determined by the state's socio-economic policy, it is not deemed mitigating or mitigating enough. To do so would imply casting unpleasant scrutiny over the state's responsibility and complicity in civilian crime. Consequently, up until very recently, alternatives to imprisonment were not seriously entertained nor much concern given to the more humane concept of 'restorative justice'. However, under pressure to tackle the mushrooming prison population, 75,000 prisoners were freed in the first nine months of 2002. Furthermore, a new criminal code drawn up in July 2002 does recommend the use of other forms of punishment, with the aim of reducing prison numbers by 200–250,000.[16] Whether this approach is fully accepted and implemented remains to be seen, but assuming it was, it would certainly be a progressive move even though it would still not reduce the prison population down to 1991 levels.

The callousness of the system is graphically revealed in the situation in pre-trial centres (called SIZOs) which house one-quarter of all prisoners. MCPR shows that these have less than one square metre of space per inmate, which is insufficient space for all prisoners to sit. There are insufficient beds. Sleeping is done in shifts. Rooms are damp, lacking in oxygen with no running water and insufficient washing and toilet facilities – conditions ripe for contracting illness and disease. The shocking aspect of this is that a large proportion of these prisoners – many of whom will be innocent – will not only contract some ailment(s) but also end up dying, as 2,000 SIZO prisoners did in 1994.[17] In 1998, during the financial crisis, there was hunger in detention centres. The state simply was not providing sufficient food for this category of prisoner[18] and in 1999, in St Petersburg's detentions centres, inmates were dying from the summer heat on a daily basis.[19]

Prisoners operate strict power structures that have a bearing on all aspects of prison life, including gaining access to treatment for disease. Reyes and Conix describe this hierarchy for former Soviet republics, a hierarchy that has some equivalence with social class:

> … a caste system exists in establishments for sentenced prisoners. Inmates are stratified into four groups. The 'bosses' (*blatniye*) are the upper caste – professional criminals. Then comes the silent majority of 'blokes' (*muzhiki*), non-professional criminals just in to serve their time, with no power. The third caste is the 'collaborators' (*kozly*), who are shunned because they work for the prison administration. At the bottom are the 'untouchables' (*petukhi*), the despised members of the prison society: homosexuals, sex offenders, outcasts from the other groups, and anyone who has contravened the unofficial laws of the prison hierarchy.[20]

The higher up this hierarchy, the more the likelihood of better conditions and treatment for disease. The extraordinarily high levels of captivity in filthy, unhygienic places have spawned an epidemic of disease and death, and not only within prisons. Alexander Goldfarb, a Russian microbiologist at the New York-based Public Health Research Initiative, has described the situation in Russian prisons as becoming a 'sort of a medical Chernobyl',[21] meaning that they are spreading disease, particularly multi-drug-resistant strains of TB. He estimates that the incidence of TB had tripled to 1 per 1,000 (15 times the rate in the US) by 2001 with 86,000 having active cases of TB in 2002.[22] *Almost half* the prisoners have some kind of illness and over 20,000 suffer from incurable forms of disease.[23] The GUIN operates an astonishing 83 TB hospitals and colonies, popularly referred to as 'burial zones' because so many die there. As more than 100,000 prisoners are released each year, drug-resistant strains of TB are spreading in the wider community, hence the Chernobyl analogy. Another potential timebomb is waiting to explode, that of the HIV virus: almost 22,000 prisoners were infected by it in 2002, and numbers are rising.

It is therefore no surprise that Amnesty International has described conditions in Russian prisons as being 'cruel, inhuman, or degrading'. They cite the Russian human rights commissioner's view that conditions in the penal system were 'horrible', and pre-trial detention centres as 'hotbeds of epidemics'.[24] They were also hotbeds of criminality as the Justice Ministry revealed that 33,000 of the 350,000 officers in the prison system were punished for criminal offences in 2001.[25] The conditions for prison staff are also appalling and exacerbated by the delays (of three to five months) in getting paid and not receiving payment for food and uniforms. Unsurprisingly, many resort to crime including bribery and theft to support their families. Many also pay the price for working in prisons by contracting diseases which they pass on to family members.[26] Little wonder that so many end up joining the ranks of those whom they have been monitoring and controlling.

A cynic might suspect that given such rates of disease in prisons, the government might feel that it is better to keep those infected inside in the hope that they will soon die and not communicate their diseases to hapless civilians in the outside world. And a truly obscene number do die: Amnesty estimates that approximately 10,000 people die in prison every year.[27] Unquestionably, therefore, Russia's prisons are truly dangerous places and fertile ground for state-sponsored deaths.

After the 1917 revolution, one of the central principles of the criminal justice system had been to cast aside the concept of 'punishment'. Rather than revenge and retribution, the penal codes strove for 'rehabilitation' of the offender.[28] This view of justice was decades ahead of anything seen in the advanced West, and it is only now that in some Western countries there is a serious examination of the role of rehabilitation-based restorative justice. But punishment-based justice continues to dominate the world over. Back in the 1930s, Alexander Paterson had set out the simple doctrine that 'men are sent to prison *as* punishment, not *for* punishment'. In other words, once in prison, inmates should be treated humanely and not subjected to any more suffering. But it is important to note that this 'liberal' conception of justice still represented a retreat from that of post-revolutionary Russia. The regression of the justice system in Russia accelerated rapidly in the late 1920s, as punishment of the most brutal kind soon became the norm. When applied to Russia's penal system of the 1930s and the proliferation of the Gulags, not only was this an affront to the notion of rehabilitative justice, it also massively collided with Paterson's doctrine. Though the situation in post-transition Russia has comparatively improved over the 1930s, punishment in the form of blatantly inhuman treatment of many prisoners is rife. The idea of rehabilitation does not even register on the penal radar screen. So, though there is no legal or generalised policy of prisons as institutions for further punishment, the pitiless nature of the system does precisely this for a large number of prisoners. Not surprisingly, because the prison experience tends to be a deeply cruel one, it prevents many ex-prisoners from adjusting well to the outside world. Failing to cope, many return to a life of crime and quickly end up back in prison.

TORTURE AND STATE EXECUTIONS

The late and great Polish film director Krzysztoff Kieslowski describes why he made *A Short Story about Killing* (in which the state executes a young man who brutally murdered a taxi driver) as one of the ten films in his masterful 'Decalogue':

> I think I wanted to make this film precisely because all this takes place in my name, because I'm a member of this society, I'm a citizen of this country, Poland, and if someone in this country puts a noose around someone else's neck and kicks the stool from under his feet, he's doing it my name. And I don't wish it. I don't want them to do it. I think this film isn't really about capital punishment but about killing in general. It's wrong no matter why you kill, no matter whom you kill and no matter who does the killing.[29]

The impassioned plea is moving, but one might criticise Kieslowski's naivety for thinking that state executions really do take place 'in the name of its citizens' and also because, at the time the film was made (in 1988, just before the collapse of the Communist regime) there may well have been a majority in favour of the death sentence in Poland. Nonetheless, the new Solidarity Polish government of 1989 repudiated capital punishment, and perhaps Kieslowski's powerful film had assisted in this. But no such immediate renunciation took place in Russia after 1991; the firing squads would be kept busy, albeit at a much reduced rate, as the state would go on legally killing for a few more years before a moratorium on the death penalty was introduced in 1996.

We noted above that during the Gorbachev years, the numbers in prison were sharply reduced, and the same occurred in regard to executions which, in Russia, declined from 407 in 1985 to just 15 in 1991. Death sentences passed following the collapse of the Soviet Union remained fairly constant at over 200 each year (excepting 1994 and 1998) as can be seen from Figure 7.3.

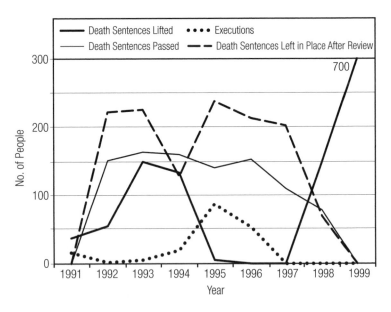

Figure 7.3   Death Sentences and Executions in Russia 1991–99

Source: Unpublished data provided by MCPR, October, 2002.

The numbers executed fell to dramatically lower levels during 1992–94 arising from legislative changes that allowed the replacement of the death penalty for life imprisonment or a minimum of 25 years. Even though there were no less than 30 types of crime punishable by death sentence, this appeared to be the first step towards its abolition. And even those awaiting their fate on death row had the chance of a presidential pardon if they chose to plea for clemency. In his *Midnight Diaries*, written after he had resigned as President, Boris Yeltsin reflected upon this particularly unpleasant aspect of his presidency:

> The green files also contained requests for pardons for those convicted of capital crimes. I dreaded those files the most. How to decide a question of life or death? How, with one stroke of a pen, to determine the fate that only God knows? These were terrible documents, chilling to the soul. A person could wind up in front of the firing squad for a crime he didn't commit. Maybe he was an awful person; maybe he was horrible. But what if he hadn't committed murder? For me, this was yet another indication of how foolproof the judicial system must be. The death sentence is utterly irreversible. If a mistake is made, it can't be fixed, and a life is on our consciences.[30]

What Yeltsin is highlighting here is one argument against the death penalty. If an error is made, there is no going back. Yet, despite this supremely compelling caveat, he supported it, and instead focused his concerns on establishing an infallible judicial system. This would be considered quite an impossible task in even the most modern, liberal, humane society, but in Russia, with its long history of use of police torture to extract confessions, and contempt for judicial niceties, this was nothing short of a joke. Andrei Babushkin, Head of the non-governmental Committee for Civil Rights, explains the *raison d'être* for the use of police torture: '[i]f the government begins fighting against torture, it will outrage law enforcement agencies, [who] do not know any other method to investigate crime'.[31] As Anatoly Pristavkin, the Chairman of the Russian Presidential Clemency Commission, put it: 'the worst thing in Russia is the high number of judicial errors. Law enforcement bodies act extremely rudely and extract confessions even from the innocent … Unjust sentences, when innocent people were executed for crimes committed by others, were everywhere ….'[32] Amnesty International has pointed out that in Russia, judges often dismiss allegations of torture out of hand, in effect rewarding the police for their abuses by accepting forced confessions as valid evidence. Methods of forcing confessions include 'beatings, electric shocks, rape, the use of gas masks to induce near-suffocation, and tying detainees in painful positions'. Most at risk from such police brutality are members of the ethnic minorities, the poor, and women.[33] The irony (if one could call it that) is that Russia is a signatory to an array of international human rights treaties including the International Covenant on Civil and Political Rights, the Convention against Torture and Other Cruel, Inhuman or Degrading Treatment or Punishment, and the International Convention on the Elimination of All Forms of Racial Discrimination.[34] Russia's very membership of these treaties and conventions severely strains their integrity and one can only wonder at the criteria required for acceptance as a signatory to them.

In reality, however, Yeltsin's angst-ridden feelings were largely set aside. Ever the populist, he recognised that violent crime was causing grave concern throughout society and a tough stance would be a certain vote-winner in the run-up to the 1996 presidential elections. He therefore ratcheted up the execution rate – as Figure 7.3 shows, 86 prisoners received bullets to the back of their heads in 1995 and a further 53 in the first few months of 1996. In the same vein, in 1995, he granted only five pardons out of 91 death-row prisoners who petitioned for clemency.[35] This was Yeltsin as the 'hard cop'. But soon a 'soft cop' side to his political character would appear. Knowing that the presidential election was in the bag, as part of moving towards Europe and the West, in February 1996, Yeltsin acceded to Russia joining Europe's major human rights organisation, the 40-nation-strong Council of Europe. A crucial condition for membership was the imposition of a moratorium on the death penalty by Russia and, within three years, its removal from the statute books. This was done despite opposition from the Communists and nationalists in the Duma, and indeed from the population at large, the majority of whom support capital punishment. Such opposition meant that by 1999, Russia still did not comply, which allowed the courts to continue to mete out death sentences. Despite this, the moratorium was upheld. Yeltsin made a surprising intervention in June 1999 with the aim of pressurising the Duma to ratify the Council of Europe's Protocol. Perhaps thinking of his legacy and with thoughts on resigning as President, he commuted every death sentence in Russia, a total of 716 death-row inmates. The Council of

Europe was impressed; other human rights NGOs were impressed, but ordinary Russians remained cynical as ever: mechanic Sergei Shutov's view of Yeltsin's motives probably had a ring of truth, 'he probably just wants to save his criminal friends'.[36]

In 1999, the Constitutional Court required that death sentences should only be given when jury trials for serious offences become generalised throughout the Federation (scheduled for 2003); for the short term at least, this banned new death sentences as most regions lack jury trials. But, in 2003 or soon after, there is every likelihood of the return of state executions. The moratorium, nonetheless, has proved manna from heaven for those on death row since 1996 (excluding Chechnya), for there have not been any state executions during this period. Putin has hitherto complied with Yeltsin's line but come under increasing pressure from right-wing deputies to rescind the moratorium. A resolution passed by the Duma in February 2002 invoked nationalist arguments for the retention of the death penalty: '[I]t is inadmissible, for the benefit of foreign policy interests, to ignore the will of the people, who will not accept the abolition of the death penalty.'[37] However, deviating from his 'strong man' image he has so far resisted – remarkably, for progressive and ethical reasons, rejecting 'populist appeals' and stating that 'only the almighty has the right to take life'.[38] But when it came to the vexed issue of Chechnya, Putin's words rang hollow and grotesque.

THE WAR IN CHECHNYA

In October 2002 Moscow experienced, to use the strikingly apposite term of Chalmers Johnson, 'blowback'.[39] On 23 October, it was claimed that up to 50 armed Chechen fighters, including women, stormed a theatre complex in the south-east of Moscow, taking hundreds of hostages. Their demand was clear: unless Russian troops were removed from Chechnya, hostages would be killed, and the hostage-takers had no qualms about dying. After a stand-off of three days, Putin's response was decisive but one that showed callous disregard for both hostages and the hostage-takers. A poisonous gas was sprayed into the building that was then stormed by special troops. This ended the crisis but at a cost of the deaths of practically all of the fighters, and also of at least 128 hostages. After at first showering the world with disinformation about the nature of deaths, refusing to provide details of the type of gas used and why, and preventing relatives from visiting hospitals and mortuaries, the

Russian government admitted that all but two of the deaths were as a result of gas poisoning. The crisis cruelly exposed how little the Russian state had travelled towards a more open government and away from the secret state. It seemed that Putin's reputation as a strong man, unflinching in his rejection of Chechen demands, had been firmly confirmed, but perhaps when Russians come to terms with the full truth, the episode may further shake his popularity (that has already taken a dive after the sinking of the submarine *Kursk* some two years earlier (which led to the loss of 118 crew), where he appeared to show lack of concern by failing to end his summer holidays to take control of the rescue bid). But there is no denying the fact that loss of innocent lives was of limited importance to the Russian state, be it those it subjugates in the peripheral regions, or those living in the metropolitan centre. What were the events that led to this desperate act of hostage-taking?

By far the major cause of abnormal deaths in Russia during the transition period has been the war in Chechnya, a small republic in the Caucasus mountains[40] with a population of just over 1 million. This has been an act of the utmost brutality by the Russian state and, *prima facie*, in terms of the drain on a dwindling budget, against its own interests. Given the collapse of the economy and the enormous squeeze on public expenditure, huge outlays on a seemingly endless war in this small republic seem paradoxical and inexplicable. But, as bloodthirsty as it has been, there is nonetheless a powerful logic to this – one that enmeshes domestic, economic, and geopolitical factors. The prime motives for this war reside in, on the one hand, the push by the military-industrial complex and the so-called 'power ministries' (military, interior and intelligence) to halt the decline in their influence following the collapse of the Soviet Union and, on the other, the importance of oil and oil pipelines in the region; indeed to ensure that a new pipeline from the Caspian Sea would be built through Russia, the most cost-effective pipeline option of which ran through Chechnya. An influential 'small triumphant war' type theory has been put forward by Pain and Popov from Yeltsin's Presidential Council who believe that the most likely explanation for the Chechen war was to improve their master's electoral chances.[41] The credibility of this theory appears to have even greater force with respect to the second war that began in 1999, for the electoral success of Yeltsin's successor and guardian Vladimir Putin.

In the early 1990s, pressure to split from the Soviet Union intensified following the breaking free of the Central European satellites. Demands arose for more sovereignty on the part of the republics of the Russian Federation – but this did not imply secession. The exception to this was Chechnya where the nationalist movement of the Pan-National Congress Executive Committee (IK OKChN) led by Jokhar Dudaev, in June 1991, pushed for 'unconditional recognition of the right of the Chechen nation to independence'.[42] On 1 November, 1991, Dudaev, after winning presidential elections with an 85% vote, declared independence (which was not recognised by the Russian parliament) and, by so doing, incurred the wrath of Boris Yeltsin who promptly imposed martial law on the Checheno-Ingushetia republic. Russia had just lost Central Europe and was about to lose the former Soviet Republics but, invoking the 'domino effect theory', allowing independence to a republic that (rightly or wrongly) was part of the Russian Federation proper was deemed a step too far. The line was, therefore, drawn at preserving the current territorial integrity of Russia. The downward spiral to all-out war soon began. Chechnya also provided a useful distraction from the economic mess and political repression that followed the storming of the White House in the autumn of 1993 as 3,500 residents, mostly from the Caucasus, were deported from Moscow ostensibly to counter the rising crime rate in the city. This was to boost the arguments of racists and fascists in the coming elections and the politics of the 'Red–Brown' alliance of former Stalinists and fascists.[43]

During 1994, there was a veering away from the relatively 'softly-softly' approach that had hitherto been adopted by the Russian government and instead a tough signal was sent out by Deputy Premier Sergey Shakrai that Russia was prepared to use force to defend its interests in the Caucasus. This at first seemed to be directly contradicted by Boris Yeltsin who, in the summer, whilst troops were being sent to the Chechen border, announced that forcible intervention in Chechnya was impermissible. His words meant little. It was Chechen independence that was impermissible. This implied that Dudaev's separatist government had to be forcibly removed. The military assault duly began on 18 December 1994 as more than 30,000 Russian soldiers marched into Chechnya. Bombers followed suit by attacking the capital city Grozny's TV tower, gas lines and power stations, and tanks rolled into the city. The assault on Grozny (condemned as 'terror bombing' by Western news agencies at the time) was the heaviest artillery bombardment since the Second World War. Around 4,000 shells per hour rained down, destroying the foundations and ravaging the water supplies and sewage systems.[44]

Casualties quickly mounted – the Russian human rights campaigner Sergei Kovalyo estimated that 24,000 civilians had been killed by February 1995.[45] Less than a month before the attack, Minister of Defence General Pavel Grachev had proclaimed that the Chechen problem could be solved in one hour by one parachute regiment. However, after less than a month's fighting his assessment had changed to a war lasting for several years, with the implication that Russia was about to experience a 'new Afghanistan' with all the brutalities, death and destruction of the decade-long war that had helped to weaken the Soviet Empire in the 1980s. And, to a significant extent, this proved correct. But support for the war was shallow: most democratic opposition parties *opposed* the war, as did the Communist Party, and even some Russian nationalist groups such as Don Cossacks. Opinion polls suggested that once the war started, support quickly plummeted (e.g. in Moscow 70% opposed the war whilst only 13% approved of it).[46]

If Chechens were being expelled from Moscow, captured Chechen fighters were being sentenced to death in Chechnya following a change in the Russian penal code. Such a breach of the Geneva Convention and Vienna Agreement on Standard Minimum Rules for Treatment of Prisoners was undoubtedly due to the effective resistance mounted by the Chechens. This was a familiar scenario of smaller numbers of highly committed fighters proving a strong match for a larger, better equipped army, but one comprising very young, uncommitted, conscripted soldiers; many of whom were soon to die. The 'return of bodybags' syndrome further sapped support for the war with opposition to it being led by mothers of soldiers – though there seemed to be little opposition to the *manner* in which the war was being conducted; a fact linked to the blanket ban in the media of the reality of this war (truth has always been a major casualty of the Chechen war). However, stories of atrocities – men thrown into mud-pits, electric shock treatment, widespread rape and summary executions – were coming out.

But the ferocity of Chechen fighters, mounting casualties, the assassination of Dudaev (in April 1996), and Yeltsin's victory in the Presidential elections in July 1996 were factors that quickly drove the process to a peace settlement. A cease-fire agreement was signed in August and all Russian combat troops would be withdrawn by December 1996. In effect, this was tantamount to a humiliating defeat for the Russian state (albeit a temporary one). The agreement was that Chechnya's future would be reached via mutual consent by

31 December 2001. Echoing memories of Afghanistan, the world's second largest military power was unable to subdue this tiny, obstinate republic to its will.

In regard to the total casualties of the war, there have been a number of estimates from various individuals and organisations involved in the conflict. John Dunlop has succinctly surveyed all the best available sources and come to reasonable conjectures of the fatalities broken down in terms of Russian soldiers, Chechen fighters and civilians.[47] The military newspaper *Krasnaya zvezda* in October 1996 estimated that 2,941 soldiers of the Russian Ministry of Defence were killed, but this did not include internal troops or border guards. The MVD (Ministry of Internal Affairs) estimated that 1,087 internal troops died, giving a total of 4,028 from official sources. A slightly higher figure of 4,379 was arrived at by the 'Memorial' Society, the Russian human rights organisation, but they stressed that this was an incomplete list as it excluded soldiers 'missing without trace', held in captivity, and deserters. Moreover, wounded soldiers dying in hospitals were not counted, nor were those whose bodies were not recovered. The callous disregard the Russian military has had for its own soldiers is indicated by the minimal effort made in identifying dead soldiers as this was thought too costly, and funds to do this properly were inadequate.[48] Unidentified dead soldiers were not included in the official death toll. A self-respecting army should know precisely whom it sends out to battle, and the exact numbers who die in the process. The fact that such lacunae exist is one more disgrace to a thoroughly disgraceful episode of Russia's post-transition history.

Krivosheev, using official sources, provides a total of 5,552 Russian troop casualties broken down into the following categories: killed at the front (4,513); died of wounds in hospitals (338); died of illness and accidents (191); missing (486); in captivity (24). But given the incentive for the Russian army not to reveal the true extent of their losses, these are probably underestimates. Adding estimates for those dying from wounds, illnesses and accidents, Dunlop arrives at a much higher total of 7,500 dead.

Estimating the number of Chechen fighters killed is much more difficult as these include regular and irregular (temporary volunteers) soldiers. The official estimate by the Russian Ministry of Defence was that 15,000 were killed, which seems highly exaggerated and not based on any evidence. On the other hand, the estimate by the former acting President of Chechnya was that 3,000 died, which is probably on the low side. A more accurate figure of 4,000 is that provided by Aslan Maskhadov when he was Chechen military Chief of Staff, during the normalisation of relations after the war.[49]

Finally, in regard to civilian losses, estimates vary widely. Official sources are just not interested in civilian casualties, and no effort is made to count up the toll. The estimate by Russian General Anatolii Kulikov of 18,000 killed in total, that is, both civilian and military losses, appears to have been plucked from thin air, and he himself confesses that this may well be an understatement – and so should be treated with extreme scepticism. Maskhadov's estimate is more than six times this at 120,000 civilians including children, whilst acting President Yanderbiev is a little under this at 100–120,000. Madina Magomadova, head of the Mothers of Chechnya Committee, in September 1996, when the war had ended, estimated that 'some 75,000 had been killed by January [1996] and that the toll has risen since'. But perhaps the figure which seems to have credibility is that of 70–90,000 by General Lebed, and a similar figure (80,000) is provided by Vladimir Maksimenko of the Russian Academy of Sciences.[50] Yurii Deryugin, a colonel in the military reserves, summed up the first Chechen war thus: 'The military actions in Chechnya are unprecedented in their barbarism … If in the Vietnam War for each soldier who died, 9–10 civilians also died, then in Chechnya, there have died 15–17 adults plus 1–2 children.'[51] If we assume 80,000 civilians died, the total deaths in the first war were 91,500.

The toll of deaths in the capital Grozny was particularly high, perhaps accounting for half of all deaths. In 1990, Russians, Ukrainians and Belorussians comprised 56% of Grozny's population, whereas ethnic Chechens totalled only 31%, with ethnic Ingush comprising 5%.[52] This suggests that very many Russians must have voted for Dudaev in the Presidential elections and supported Chechen independence. However, with the onset of war, many ethnic Chechens fled to rural villages of relatives, an escape route not available to ethnic Russians who remained trapped in the city. Consequently, the large majority of those killed in Grozny were bound to be ethnic Russians and other Slavs. If we assume that half of all civilian deaths were in Grozny, then perhaps more than half of all deaths were of ethnic Russians, a fact not publicised much by the Russia government or media.[53] There is an irony in this in that throughout Russia there was racist scapegoating of Chechens under the banner of Russian nationalism, but no such discrimination existed in the killing fields within Chechnya itself.

In retrospect, the 'Chechen problem' had been put on ice. However, three years after the peace agreement Yeltsin decided to warm it up again. In August 1999, Chechen guerrilla forces of Bayev and the Arab Islamist Khattab moved into neighbouring Dagestan in an attempt to spread revolt beyond Chechnya. However, Dagestani forces rebuffed these. But the consequences for Chechnya were dire, as this became the pretext for the resumption of the assault on it and a renewed invasion. Soon after the war began there were bomb explosions in Moscow, first in the Manezh shopping centre near to the Kremlin which injured 40 people and, in September 1999, in blocks of flats that killed 212 people. No definitive conclusion exists as to who was responsible though many are now convinced that it was the work of elements within the Russian state. Boris Kagarlitsky has argued that the bombs had been planted with the connivance of the military intelligence (GRU) using Chechen activists.[54] Chechen president Maskhadov went further by arguing that this was done on Putin's order.[55] There have even been suggestions that elements within the Russian state had financed Basayev and Khattab's incursions, which, moreover, had been warned about in advance by Maskhadov.[56] Given the explosive nature of these allegations, it is indicative and a damning indictment that they have not been thoroughly investigated. Russia now has a cowed and pusillanimous media and will not allow NGOs to carry out any investigations. But there has been great reluctance on the part of Western media organisations to show any real interest in the Chechen disaster. This stems partly from obstacles put in their way by the authorities, but also from the way in which the Chechen war has been accepted as an internal Russian matter and so regarded as off-limits for searching examination. The line drawn by the Russian state regarding its territorial boundaries, no matter the torn history of republics such as Chechnya, is one fully accepted by the leading Western powers and their leaders, which the media meekly accepts. Sammut has levelled the charge that whilst the Russian government has discouraged foreign assistance, equally, the international community did not respond to pleas for assistance made by Maskhadov during the 'peace years', highlighting again the unwritten 'off-limits' accord. The Western neglect of Chechnya then intensified after the attacks in the US on 11 September 2001. In the frenzy of denunciations against the attacks on the World Trade Center, Putin cynically argued that Chechen fighters had links with Osama bin Laden and his Al Qaeda network. In the new supercharged atmosphere of unity in the 'War against Terror', criticisms from mainstream politicians and commentators became completely muted, leaving the abuses to continue.

The Russian government quickly utilised the widespread revulsion at Chechens and Caucasians by blaming Chechen separatists for the Moscow bombs. The population was whipped up into supporting the new war against those the government denounced as 'bandits' and 'terrorists'. The ground assault began on 30 September. In sharp contrast to the first war, there was little opposition to the second invasion. Once more, the slaughter has been immense, though estimates vary widely of the fatalities. In May 2002, the Interfax Military News Agency cited an official of the Ministry of Defence saying that 2,498 servicemen had been killed and 6,325 had been injured. These figures did not include Interior Ministry troops that make up a large part of the federal forces serving in Chechnya.[57] However, a more reliable figure is probably that of the Mothers of Soldiers Committee who put the figure at 7,000 soldiers dead.[58] The Command of the Joint Group of Federal Forces in Chechnya announced that almost 13,000 Chechen fighters had been killed, but this is probably an exaggerated figure. As with the first war, no official figures on losses among the local population are available. A confidential dossier compiled by the News Services and Military Expert Advisory group to the German Chancellor's Office estimates the deaths of 10,000 Russian soldiers and 80,000 Chechens.[59] It is difficult to assess how reliable these figures are but they seem to be on the higher end of estimates for casualties.

Dunlop estimates that by early 2002, the death list was as follows: 20–25,000 civilians, 8,000 Russian military and police, and 8,000 Chechen fighters. Thus 36–41,000 had been killed in the second war after two and half years' fighting, a toll that will inevitably keep on rising as long as the war continues. By the end of 2002, we estimate deaths from the two wars as follows: 17,000 Russian forces, 13,000 Chechen fighters, and 160,000 civilians, a grand total of 190,000 dead. This is over 15% of the total population. In fact, the number of Russian personnel killed in Chechnya is probably higher than the numbers killed in Afghanistan – a war that spanned ten years.

The problems in 2001 of the Russian military were succinctly described in an editorial in the *Wall Street Journal* following the shooting down of a Russian MI-26 helicopter which killed 116 people. Former Prime Minister Primakov is quoted as saying that the military is no longer under civilian rule. Given the full support from Putin, this is highly contentious, for it implies that the ex-KGB man is completely in the pocket of the military. But equally, given the power of the military-industrial complex and Primakov's inside-knowledge, his assertion is certainly plausible. Moreover, it might also help explain the threats made against Georgia by Putin in September 2002 when he accused Georgia of harbouring fleeing Chechen fighters.

Of the recruits sent to Chechnya, 20% had drug- and alcohol-related problems, and one-third had not completed primary education. Roads and airfields were too damaged to use, and there was a widespread shortage of fuel and spare parts. With soldiers reduced to eating grass, it is hardly surprising that morale has been abysmally low.[60] Despite the shortages, the cost of the war has been enormous, imposing a great strain on public finances. Vishnevsky has estimated that during 1999–2000 this mounted to $8.8 billion, a sum greater than the annual budget for both Moscow and St Petersburg. The corruption and criminalisation of the political and business segments of society has also seen the same developing in the armed forces in Chechnya. Indeed, crime and corruption of an astonishing variety has become rife, including money embezzled by high-ranking officials, the massive theft of oil, bribes to bypass military checkpoints, the selling of bodies to relatives, and the kidnapping of civilians. A report in *Die Welt* claims that 4 billion roubles in the 2002 budget for reconstruction in Chechnya have 'trickled away without any noticeable improvements on the ground'.[61] Ordinary soldiers have also been affected as they find senior officers pocketing a proportion of their wages.[62] It naturally follows that a corrupt, brutalised and demoralised army will resort to the utmost barbarism with scant regard for the conventional rules of military engagement.

Although there have been restrictions on observers in Chechnya, numerous reports detailing the atrocities have been made available, particularly by NGOs. An example is the following from Human Rights Watch. This provides harrowing details gleaned from interviews conducted with Chechens from the village of Alkhan-Yurt, which the Russians occupied in December 1999:

> On December 1, after weeks of heavy fighting, Russian forces took control of Alkhan-Yurt, a village with a peacetime population of about 9,000 that is located just south of Grozny.
>   During the two weeks that followed, Russian forces went on a rampage in the village, summarily executing at least fourteen

civilians. They first expelled, temporarily, hundreds of civilians from Alkhan-Yurt, and then began systematically looting and burning the village, killing anyone in their way. Among the dead were: centenarian Nabitst Kornukayeva, and her elderly son Arbi, who were found shot to death in the yard of their looted home; fifty-seven-year-old Khamid Khazuyev, who was shot in the yard of his home when he tried to stop looting soldiers; Akhanpash Dudayev, sixty-five, who was killed in his basement, and his body burned in his looted home; and Taus Sultanov, forty-nine, who was shot in a cellar and left to bleed to death while soldiers robbed other civilians with him of their belongings. The killings went on for more than two weeks, without any apparent attempt by Russian authorities to stop it. Aindi Altimirov, the last to die, was killed and beheaded by Russian soldiers on December 18.

Nearly every villager ... said he or she had personally seen Russian soldiers looting homes. Villagers described how they watched, powerless, as soldiers loaded household goods – furniture, clothing, refrigerators, televisions, and the like – onto military trucks and stolen vehicles and hauled away their loot ... According to many witnesses, soldiers also committed rape in Alkhan-Yurt. One woman gave Human Rights Watch the names of two women she personally knew who she said were raped, while a second witness told Human Rights Watch that five or six women had been raped, and that she was forced to hide her own daughters in a hidden earthen pit to prevent a similar fate. A third witness gave detailed information about a gang rape of a forty-two-year-old woman by a group of seven 'kontraktniki,' or contract soldiers. Distinct from recruits and officers, kontraktniki are men who sign short-term contracts for military service.[63]

Amnesty International's 2002 report on Russia confirmed the findings of Human Rights Watch. Human rights abuses were rife in Chechnya: 'arbitrary detention; torture including rape; ill-treatment; "disappearances"; extra-judicial executions; and the use of official secret detention centres that often amounted to little more than pits in the ground'. It noted that Novaia gazeta journalist Anna Politkovskaya was detained and threatened whilst investigating claims of torture in Chechnya.[64] Politkovskaya has bravely reported on war crimes in Chechnya, for which she was awarded the Index on Censorship's Most Courageous Defence of Expression award in March 2002 and the International Women's Media Foundation's

Courage in Journalism Award in October 2002. One of her reports describes a rampaging operation by Russian soldiers in Staiye Atagi, a village south of Grozny, in search of 'illegal bandit formations' during late January to early February 2002. This involved extortion, looting and rape.[65]

Not surprisingly, therefore, survival itself has become a struggle for Chechens as their republic has been reduced to a vast, deadly rubble. For those who manage to avoid being killed, life is extremely perilous: practically everyone has been displaced from their home; refugee camps in neighbouring Ingushetia and Georgia lack basic utilities, and the land is cluttered with landmines.[66] The impact on the environment has been devastating, with 30% of the territory an ecological disaster zone and a further 40% suffering unfavourable ecological conditions. A shocking 80% of the population suffer from TB, heart disease and various blood disorders, and all forms of cancer.[67] Though official statistics do not give mortality rates for Chechnya,[68] all this inevitably means that normal mortality for all ages and both genders must also be very high and life expectancy very low – indeed the lowest in Russia. Ultimately, it is the Russian state and its policy on Chechnya that is responsible for this catastrophe – a policy alarmingly similar to the policies of the ostensibly more brutal regimes of the Stalinist past.

So has Russia, over a decade after the fall of the Soviet Union, come full circle? Has it cast aside its new, liberal, democratic ways for a return to the old brutal Stalinist past, at the heart of which was a merciless police-military apparatus? As we have already indicated, the answer must be no. In the brutality of the repressive aspects of the state apparatus, there is, in fact, little departure from the original point of the circle. Steeped in their old traditions and practices, the policies of those in power remain cruel and intolerant, and continue to kill in large numbers. The bulk of those subjected to these outrages have been the weak and dispossessed. The strong and wealthy have, almost in their entirety, escaped unscathed, even when their *raison d'être* has been looting and crime. As with normal mortality, the key determinant of incurring an abnormal type of death is class, although the deaths in Chechnya have also stemmed from the targeting of a certain ethnic type. In conclusion, therefore, the abnormal death count in the transition years has certainly been high, but its distribution is also a highly unequal one.

8   Conclusion

CLASS, INEQUALITY, AND A 'QUIET VIOLENCE'

People with handwritten signs are commonplace in Moscow. Sometimes they are asking for work, sometimes they are begging. You can easily pass them by. But sometimes an image remains. In September 2002, a girl in her teens was standing in a Moscow Metro station with a sign which read '*Pomagaete, umiraet Mama*' – 'Help me, my mother is dying'. An hour later she had gone, replaced by a cripple. Good pitches on the Moscow Metro have to be shared.

There has been enough said in the first part of this book to show why the system before 1991 never deserved the name of socialism. So, far from having illusions about that society, our focus on the inequalities of life and death under the old regime make our judgements much harsher than those of most of its critics. But the change was not supposed to lead to what Russia has become. The 'fly-in, fly-out' consultants and the governments they worked with said that the transition would create a new and better Russia. It has merely juggled around those at the top while subjecting the mass of the population to immiseration and turmoil.

This could only happen because of the confusion over the nature of the USSR. If this was 'socialism' then the only alternative seemed to be 'capitalism'. It is easy to understand why people in Russia and the former USSR felt like this. They had been brought up on the lie – and by the 1980s, many looked with envy on the achievements of the advanced West. It is less easy to forgive the way in which they were encouraged in this illusion by people in the West who should have known better. But the collapse of Russian control in Eastern Europe and then within the USSR itself occurred at a peculiar time. During the 1980s, in the West, there had been a resurgence of the right and free market ideologies. Sections of the left had lost much of their confidence and themselves came to believe that 'there was no alternative' to the free market. By generally accepting that Russia was in some sense socialist, they too were pushed to a belief in the market as a salvation.

Even if we accept the premise that Russia was 'socialist' – which we do not – there were serious problems with the view that the market was a cure-all. First, while advanced Western capitalism was more successful than the system in the East, and while there were pockets of growth elsewhere, it was by no means clear that the global capitalist system had, or has, the capacity to generalise these gains.[1] Second, to the extent that advanced capitalism had developed a more 'civilised face' that people in the former Soviet bloc admired, this was not a gift of the gods or the economists. It had emerged from generations of struggle to tame and impose a degree of order. Governments acted, either directly or indirectly, because they were pushed to do so by groups (and most notably the labour movement in all its forms) who were prepared to fight for something better, sometimes at considerable personal cost. This idea and sense of history was missing in the transition. In the first 'period' the belief was that 'institutions' would automatically build themselves. But the destructive impact of the transition demobilised society, weakened the capacity to protest, and prevented a strong and independent labour movement from being built that could not only counteract the power of the employer in the workplace, but also hound and harry governments. In the second period (roughly from the mid to late 1990s) institutions were suddenly remembered, but now it was imagined that they could simply be dropped into place from above. The talk was all of 'regulatory structures' and careful intervention, as if a technocratic mantra would succeed in reining in the abuse of power.[2]

But a third problem went deeper still. Posing the issue in terms of two alternatives inevitably legitimises one at the expense of the other. But what if both sides are compromised? The history of Western capitalism is also built on exploitation, oppression and injustice. All of these have led to mass death and not least in the twentieth century. That century saw the 'high noon' of colonialism and imperialism. It brought two world wars and a mass of smaller wars. Political rights have been unevenly and belatedly extended. Civil disorder is sometimes brutally put down even in the most 'democratic' of societies. Legalised racism survived in 'the leader of the free world', the US, into the 1960s. The West largely turned a blind eye to the same in South Africa until 1990. Racism today survives informally everywhere in institutions and everyday practices. Above all, for all the talk of its disappearance, Western societies remain moulded by powerful class mechanisms. These continue to produce serious inequalities in life and death. Indeed in the last decades these inequalities have if anything increased.

The charge against capitalism is not that it has not allowed improvement. Capitalism has been progressive in the way that it has developed and integrated the productive structure, the likes of which had never been seen before. But because capitalism is a class society, its achievements are always contradictory and uneven – the true potential that exists remains unrealised. Nowhere is this more true than for life expectancy. In one of his more recent surveys of inequality and health, Wilkinson points to eight major studies which show the high correlation which exists between income inequality and mortality. Behind the analysis of patterns of disease and death, he suggests that 'instead of exposure to toxic materials and mechanical dangers, we are discovering the toxicity of social circumstances and patterns of social organisation'.[3]

If we are faced with a choice between two societies, one more unequal than the other, then, other things being equal, we should prefer the more equal one, not only for the better life it provides but also because of the way in which such a society extends life. But the same logic that leads us to prefer the more equal should also lead us to struggle for the even more equal. But here problems occur over how far we can push this struggle, yet still remain within the limits of capitalism. Wilkinson argues that 'health and quality of life in modern societies [are] primarily dependent on distributional justice and levels of what might be called "social capital"'.[4] But this is an evasion. While distributive justice is not narrowly determined by production, it is rooted in it. It might be possible to pay those in charge of production less, but so long as power ultimately resides in control of the means of production by the few, then the many will be at a disadvantage. This spills over into a second difficulty. While the state can to some extent mitigate market-determined inequalities, it can and does reproduce within itself and society at large more fundamental competitive divisions. Or, to ask the perennial question: whose interest does the state serve? Therefore, capitalism is not simply a market phenomenon; it is also a state one. The history of Russia as we have tried to show is evidence of this. Wilkinson's powerful defence of equality is therefore weakened by his neglect of production and his analysis of the state.[5]

Life expectancy has dramatically improved in many societies in the twentieth century. Much of this has been a product of an epidemiological shift that has involved the elimination or reduction of infectious diseases. This part of the demographic transition has clearly reflected social improvements – and we have traced some of these in Russia in the previous chapters. Today material factors remain important. When societies experience crisis, infectious disease can return, as is evident with the return of tuberculosis, and new ones can strike, as with AIDS. We reject the view that beyond a certain point standards of living and per capita output cease to be relevant issues. But we share the view that at higher levels of development, other factors come more into play in explaining premature death. In particular, as we have seen in Russia, degenerative diseases, accidents of all types, suicide, murder and state death become more important. But these are socially conditioned and structured causes of premature death. They do not strike equally. Wilkinson is right to say that this type of disease and death is a product not of affluence but of the poor and relative poverty in affluent societies. To understand why, we have to also see how behaviour and lifestyle is socially moulded and conditioned. This is what Wilkinson and others have tried to do and there is much in the analysis on which we happily draw and endorse. But, as with the evasion over capitalism and the state, so there is also a reluctance to make class this central issue. What we are seeing are not failures of 'community' and 'social cohesion' but the varying consequences of class society and the injuries and deaths it produces.

In an account that has been too much neglected, Richard Sennett and Jonathan Cobb refer to 'the hidden injuries of class', a term the observant reader will recall us using before. What Sennett and Cobb mean by this is that class relations come to mark the inner emotional lives that we lead. We get caught between a rhetoric of equality and opportunity and the very different reality. The conflict of classes becomes internalised, a 'struggle between men leads to a struggle within each man'.[6]

In saying this, it is far from our intention to endorse every argument made by Sennett and Cobb. Some we would strongly contest. But their central point, that class has both a material and an emotional effect, is one we would strongly support. Two societies more than any other in the past century have used the rhetoric of classlessness – the US and Russia. Yet Russia, no less than the US, can, as we have argued, be understood as a class society. The rhetoric of classlessness suggests that we are all equal, all invested with the same power to realise dignity, honour and respect. Yet the reality of class is power and powerlessness. We become pawns of a world over which we have little control. This poses the question, 'What am I worth?' As Sennett and Cobb put it: 'what happens to the dignity men see in themselves and in each other, when their freedom is checked by class?' All of us have a sense of this dilemma, but it is socially structured in two crucial ways. The less real power we have, the greater the dilemma. The less understanding we have of the dilemma, the greater the individual emotional impact. Seeing your situation as a product of class, organising and struggling against it cannot heal all the wounds but it can help to mitigate them. Accepting the legitimacy of the system, not having the capacity to struggle collectively, will tend to throw even more weight on the inner emotional life and encourage people to turn in on themselves. Instead of honour, respect and dignity that comes with some sense of power, powerlessness gives rise to feelings of anxiety, inadequacy, humiliation, guilt and even, as Sennett and Cobb show, to a sense of shame. These tend to feed into personal behaviour and its counter-cultures. Collectively, this is tantamount to a 'quiet violence'. The issue, therefore, is not the way that some disembodied behaviour or lifestyle affects people and leads to ill health and premature death, but the way that class, materially and 'spiritually', moulds our inner and outer life. But there is also a dialectic at work here because class can also be turned from a point of weakness to a point of strength. There is no reason why we should live in a world that denies us material equality and with it an equality of dignity, honour and respect in life and death. But challenge to injustices and for improvements has historically come from struggle on class lines.

A CENTURY OF STATE MURDER?

In this book we have tried to show how the history of Russia fits into this perspective. In 2000, a monograph of some 80 pages edited by three Russian authors came out that also examined death in Russia. These authors made the point that 'from the 1930s to 1980s when the concept of the "social homogeneity of Soviet society" dominated ideology, the few research findings dealing with social differences in death rates in Russia were not published'.[7] Our aim in this book has been to bring to light precisely such differences for the whole of the twentieth century and to make an explicit link of these with the policies of the state. The problems of reliable data and widespread gaps still exist, but using whatever is available it is clearly discernible that the class hierarchy in life engenders a class hierarchy in death, and the state has been centrally implicated in this. Pre-1917, class divisions in Russia were out in the open and viewed by most as natural and timeless, and the core duty of the Russian state was to take care of the Tsar's empire and keep in check his increasingly restive subjects. The 1917 revolution represented a massive assault on this and called time on Tsarism. Unlike any revolution before, its avowed aim was to do away not only with the obscene class privileges of the monarchy but to attempt to move to a world without classes. In the most difficult of circumstances, the years 1917–28, albeit with weakening vigour, were about moving towards this goal. But in the face of civil war and foreign intervention, the obstacles proved too great. The revolution, isolated and without assistance from the advanced countries, quickly degenerated. Yet in this brief period, notwithstanding the disruption and hardship, heroic attempts were made to transform the lot of the common people and to honestly establish an accurate demographic picture of the country.

From 1928 and the launch of Stalin's First Five Year Plan, the whole dynamic of Russian society changed. Gone were the ideals of the revolution, the attempt to liberate humanity, *all* of humanity from want and suffering. Ruthless oppression and exploitation returned with a vengeance. Sharp class relations, albeit in a different form, reasserted themselves as a new bureaucratic class, *de facto*, the ruling class, beholden to a tyrannical dictator, with distinct interests, ruled over the mass of workers and peasants. The objectives of the regime became very different to that of the 1917 revolutionaries. The aim now was to militarily compete with the Western powers, no matter the cost, the waste and death this entailed. Marx had famously described in *Capital* the dynamic of the capitalist system: '[a]ccumulate, accumulate! That is Moses and the Prophets.'[8] From 1928 onwards, Russia accumulated, industrialised, collectivised and, in the process, brutalised and destroyed millions of lives. The country was called the 'Soviet Union'. The word 'soviet' means 'council' (especially workers' council), that is, a democratic forum for discussion, debate, voting and decision making. But all this was completely stamped out and it seemed as though even the word 'democracy' had been erased from the Russian dictionary. Yet this was done by a state that still baldly proclaimed itself to be a 'workers' state' or a 'people's democracy', founded on the principle of egalitarianism. But all the facts belied it. Only when focusing on the mass of society was some semblance of equality discernible, but this was an equality of poverty, of denial of the most basic material goods, of the abrogation of an array of rights and of ruthless exploitation. What confused so many was that unlike Western capitalism with its transfer of private property rights via kinship and nepotism, class rule in Russia depended on control of state property. This indeed was true but the bureaucratic ruling class meticulously ensured that those joining its ranks were absolutely trustworthy, and so were carefully handpicked via the *nomenklatura* mechanism. The prize was not only power and influence, but also an array of privileges that expanded the further up the hierarchy one reached. These became of such magnitude that they would surely have kept directors of large Western corporations more than content.

This was not the only anomaly. Stalinist Russia had, and post-Stalinist Russia to this day still has, the iconography of Lenin liberally scattered throughout the country. Yet, there has always been a sharp contradiction between the 'visible' statues, portraits, images, and the mausoleum of Lenin and the 'invisible', submerged *ideas* of Lenin. This stark reality is perhaps best demonstrated by a simple but powerful quote from one of Lenin's most famous works, on a topic that has been a core part of this book, and one of enormous importance not just to Russians but to the people the world over. The topic is that of the state. On the eve of the October Revolution, Lenin wrote in *State and Revolution* that: 'so long as the state exists there is no freedom. When there is freedom, there will be no state.'[9] This strikingly explicit statement (significantly, from a trenchant critic of anarchism) appears decidedly utopian at the turn of the twenty-first century. But we wonder how many Soviet citizens knew this or how many Russians know this now? Perhaps most do not care for such theorising. Yet there can be no denying that the state built up on the wreckage of the revolution must, *by definition*, have been in sharp contrast to what Lenin had envisaged – a vision, we should add, Lenin had built on Marx and Engels's view of the 'withering away of the state' under Communism. In reality, the new state's *raison d'être* became the rejection of all forms of freedom, and whose baleful legacy still lingers. Certainly, Lenin's body needs to be buried, as he had wished, but his life and ideas equally need to be unburied and critically understood in the proper context. As we saw in Chapter 4, there was a thaw in the repressive nature of the Soviet state after Stalin's death in 1953 but, to a significant extent, it remained a police state. And though the post-1991 Russian state certainly grants more rights and freedoms, so that there has been a 'withering away of the police state', nonetheless it has scant regard for Lenin's notion of freedom or even of the basic norms of liberal democracy and human rights. And it has been this abject neglect of the freedoms of people that has led to the appalling levels for the indicator of the ultimate unfreedom that has been discussed at length in this book – death.

The right had long criticised the authoritarianism, repression and denial of human rights of the former Soviet Union. The Stalinist left, eager to defend what they thought was socialism, had no satisfactory answers to this except to denounce the critics as capitalist, imperialist apologists. But such *ad hominem* defences were always inadequate given that the truth had long been available from reports by dissidents, émigrés, and refugees fleeing the brutal regimes of the Eastern bloc. However, there was a mirror attitude on the part of apologists for the West – a stony silence on their part in regard to the ills of these purportedly advanced, 'civilised' countries. The double standards involved, as noted in Chapter 1, were enormous and, moreover, they continue. Suddenly, from 1989 for Central Europe and from 1992 onwards for Russia, criticisms of the new regimes from the right became muted and little effort was made to closely examine the 'vale of tears' that had quickly arisen. Stephen Cohen, in fact, goes further to argue that Western complicity in this was immense;[10] an argument we have also stressed in this book. Whereas in the past, the second superpower had received an unrelenting and intense attention by Western political leaders and, consequently, was given enormous amounts of coverage by the media and academia, now the region has been shunted to the sidelines only to surface when events such as the sinking of the *Kursk* submarine or the hostage-taking in Moscow occur. Crumbling economies and societies that pose no external threat do not command much attention. Indeed, Russian and East European studies has now largely become a Cinderella subject in political discourse and academic teaching and research.

This book has shown the historically high levels of normal and abnormal mortality that have afflicted Russia throughout the twentieth century. The leitmotif has been the class-based inequality that has resulted. In the 'classless workers' state' of Soviet times, collation of data and their analysis in terms of class was a taboo subject. But anyone who cared to dig a little would soon have discovered a great collision between the rhetoric and reality. For the stark reality was that workers, as if human detritus, headed for the grave at a far quicker speed than the bureaucratic class that ruled over them; and with far less pomp and circumstance. The anonymous author of the English summary of Shkolnikov et al.'s rediscovery of the role of social inequality in death writes of their work that:

> The key finding in the analysis of the death rate variation by education and occupation is a clear similarity between the situation in Russia and that of other industrialized countries. In Russia the difference in mortality rates, as profiled in these two indicators are at least as high as in the West.[11]

This comment derives from Shkolnikov et al.'s discussion of the pre-1991 situation. We have argued that the explanation of these gaps is to be found in class, despite the pretensions of so many commentators that inequalities did not take a class form. The challenge to those who reject our argument is to explain how the similarities in the social variation in life expectancy can exist if there is not a shared similarity in socio-economic processes. Not only do class inequalities help throw light on health inequalities and variations in deaths, but health inequalities throw light on the issue of class. As Wilkinson puts it, 'health is telling a story about the major influences on the quality of life in modern societies and it is a story which we cannot afford to ignore'.[12]

With the collapse in 1991, however, class and inequality could be more openly discussed. But what the more accurate data revealed was not flattering: in this freer, purportedly more liberal society, male workers' tryst with the cemetery began to occur at an even quicker and alarming rate. What explains this? Surely the two systems are entirely different? Certainly it is easier to comprehend the naked brutality of the Stalinist system. Its real ideology and practice was crystal clear. Resort to whatever repression was needed, eliminate any opposition and denounce them as 'counter-revolutionaries'; and orient the whole of society to heavy industrial and military production. The corollary was that everything else was relegated to the 'residual principle' – the most damning indictment of the priorities of the ruling class, state and society. This necessitated systematically starving the people of so much that is body- and mind-enhancing, in sum, life-improving. All the key determinants of mortality were held down. Even when they significantly improved, as they did after the war, mortality rates remained high in comparative terms and class gradients remained steep.

But much more surprising is the outcome of the new system. The hideous priorities of the *ancien régime* have been removed, and with it the abhorrent residual principle. And repression and violence have, outside Chechnya, subsided. Yet the results have been devastating for the majority of the population. Social inequality in the post-1991 Russia has led to sharper gradients in health and mortality. And the indignity of inequality is carried to the grave. Today in Moscow, demand for graves is very high. Status, money and connections are the best guarantors of obtaining a good site at the cemetery for one's own or a relative's coffin. Moreover, the average cost of a funeral at 5,000 roubles (almost two months' average wages), is prohibitively expensive for many.[13] This might explain why the cremation rate has reached 60%. In St Petersburg, the mafia has taken over the lucrative funeral business, meaning that bribes are often paid for the burial of loved ones. Nominally, the city authorities charge the same price on a cemetery plot regardless of the location, but bribery can get you a better plot. The solution, according to an officer of the Bureau of Funeral Services, is simple: 'change the law and allow a system where those with money can pay more for a better location, and those with less will have to find another plot'.[14] There is actually no guarantee that this will pull the rug from the mafia's feet, but the remark does express with stark honesty the justification of intense inequity even in death.

The hopelessness and despair so rampant in modern Russia has spawned an array of purported remedies, religions, cults, etc., as coping mechanisms. Most common, as we have stressed at some length, is alcohol which remains without doubt the major 'opium of the people'. It is as deeply ingrained in the male Russian working class and rural culture as the alcohol is in their veins, corroding life and body at one and the same time. But it is by no means the only opiate, real or proverbial. Other drugs are also consumed in abundance, including the real opium from which heroin is made. Heroin addiction is spreading and, though not immediately life-threatening, through the use of contaminated needles it is generating an HIV epidemic that is remorselessly laying in store a death explosion. More conventional and not physiologically damaging release-mechanisms have also proliferated. Religions have made a comeback. Though the Soviet state had accorded sole privileges to the Russian Orthodox Church, religion had been systematically repressed. This forced other religions, especially evangelical faiths, underground, and, within a deeply oppressive society, these became important means of obtaining solace and comfort, thereby ensuring their survival. After 1991, freedom of religious expression was restored and most people in Russia admitted to having a faith: this in a country that had for decades been officially deemed as 'atheistic'. In 2002, an opinion poll showed that atheists comprised only 31% of the population. The majority (58%) considered themselves Orthodox; 5%, Muslim; 1%, non-orthodox Christian; 2%, other religions; and 4%, undecided. At the same time, however, adherence to the faith is not strong and may actually have waned since 1991. Thus, in 2002, only 6% attended a house of worship more than once a month.[15]

But there has been a proliferation of myriad non-traditional religions, belief systems and therapies, many emanating from the West but with Eastern origins, and others with roots in the occult and paranormal, so that the competition in obscurantist 'mumbo-jumbo' has intensified. These include astrology, extra-sensory perception (ESP), faith-healing, fortune-telling, the Moonies, New Age paganism, psychics, Scientology, White Brotherhood (a racist appeal to Slav nationalism), etc. This is surely not an exhaustive list and no doubt others will also sprout on what is now very fertile terrain.

Another avenue of salvation is rather more disturbing, that of the flight to reactionary politics. The political terrain has a centre of gravity that is firmly right-wing, authoritarian and deeply national-istic. The scapegoating of outsiders, 'the other', has become sanctioned from the top. Life for non-ethnic Russian minorities – most of whom suffer from the double burden of class and ethnicity – is barely tolerable. Though data on ethnic differences is sparse, the reality must be indubitably worse for non-Slavic peoples in all socio-economic indicators. The race card has reached such proportions that, in the virtual absence of progressive parties and politics, there is a real threat of death, destruction and ethnic cleansing in the event of serious civil unrest breaking out. All this means that divide-and-rule politics by the government and deflection from culpability and responsibility for the corruption and mayhem is made easier.

So at the beginning of the new millennium, an honest examination tells us that Russia is not in a good state. The high hopes and expectations of 1991 seem a distant memory and disillusion-ment is truly profound. In fundamental respects, the reason for this is a familiar one: a minority has a tight grip over the state and society, and rules over the population with contempt and callousness. Stunted, shortened lives and cynicism are a natural product of this. It is not surprising then that so many decide not to bother to vote, a precious right gained after the collapse of the Soviet Union. Selfdisenfranchisement is rife and seems set to continue but this is in essence an expression of lack of real power. There is an argument which suggests that people who are socially, politically and intellectually engaged with the world around them tend to live longer (whether the same is true for those who systematically engage in 'other-worldly solutions' is not clear). Apart from the various factors we have looked at to account for the catastrophic decline in life expectancy during the 1990s, perhaps we need to add this one. Far too many Russians are disengaged from society and this perhaps also suggests that their will to survive and live longer has diminished. But we do not want to end on such a pessimistic note. We acknowledge that the subject of this book has been a bleak one, even though death comes to us all. But by writing of death in a country that arguably over the course of the twentieth century witnessed more premature and unnecessary deaths than any other in history, we want to make the case for life. A future that encompasses life filled with good health, longevity and meaning in Russia and elsewhere, and one that attempts to ceaselessly banish the sorts of outrages we have discussed at length in this book. A Russian artist was once asked why he seemed to paint death so often. The question surprised him. He painted death, he said, in order to create life. It is in this spirit that we have written this book.

Appendix:
Basic Data on the Prison Camp System under Stalin

Table A1   Basic Data on the Prison Camp System under Stalin

	Sentences for Counter-Rev. Crimes	Judicial Executions	Prisons*	Camps 31 Dec.*	Colonies*	Special Settlements*	Colony Deaths	Prison Deaths	Camp Deaths
1929	56,220	2,109							
1930	208,069	20,201							
1931	180,696	10,651		212,000					7,238
1932	141,919	2,728		268,700		1,317,022			13,267
1933	239,664	2,154		334,300		1,142,084			67,297
1934	78,999	2,046		510,307		1,072,546			26,295
1935	267,076	1,229		725,483		973,693	4,331		28,328
1936	274,670	1,118		839,406		1,017,133	5,884		20,595
1937	790,665	353,074		820,881			8,123		25,376
1938	554,258	328,618		996,367		997,329	14,799		90,546
1939	63,889	2,552		1,317,195			7,723	7,076	50,502
1940	71,806	1,649	186,278	1,344,408	315,584	997,513	6,761	3,277	46,665
1941	75,411	8,011	470,693	1,500,524	429,205		15,000	19,867	100,997
1942	124,406	23,278	268,532	1,415,596	361,447		103,673	29,788	248,887
1943	78,441	3,579	237,534	983,974	500,208		100,840	20,792	166,967

Year							
1944	75,109	3,029	151,296	663,594	516,225	55,525	8,252	60,948
1945	123,248	4,252	275,510	715,506	745,171	37,221	6,834	43,848
1946	123,294	2,896	245,146	600,987	509,696	12,641	2,271	18,154
1947	78,810	1,105	293,135	808,839	894,667	22,193	4,146	35,668
1948	73,269	-	280,374	1,108,057	1,061,195	24,055	1,442	27,605
1949	75,125		231,047	1,216,361	1,140,324	13,967	982	15,739
1950	60,641	475	198,744	1,416,300	1,145,051	9,983	668	14,703
1951	54,775	1,609	164,679	1,543,382	997,378	8,079	424	15,587
1952	28,800	1,612	152,614	1,713,614	796,174	7,045	370	13,806
1953			152,290	1,731,693	740,554	4,304	240	5,825

* Readers are reminded that these are figures at one point of the year, not during the course of the year, but the whole system was in continual movement and therefore numbers passing through it are much higher.

Sources: Compiled from the data reported in *Naselenie Rossii* 2001, and Getty et al. 1993. There are minor differences in these sources. Where these occur we have taken the data from the more recently published source.

Notes

CHAPTER 1

1. S. Courtois, N. Werth et al., *The Black Book of Communism* (Cambridge, MA: Harvard University Press, 1998).
2. United Nations Development Programme, *Human Development Report for Central and Eastern Europe and the CIS* (Geneva: UN, 1999), pp. iv, 5–10.
3. D. Huff, *How to Lie with Statistics* (London: Penguin, 1991).
4. A. Blum, *Naître, Vivre et Mourir en URSS 1917–1991* (Paris: Plon, 1994), p. 40.
5. See R.S. Clem (ed.), *Research Guide to the Russian and Soviet Censuses* (Ithaca, NY: Cornell University Press 1986).
6. F. Lorimer, *The Population of the Soviet Union* (Geneva: League of Nations, 1946), p. xiii.
7. Quoted in Blum, *Naître*, p. 40.
8. Ibid., p. 16.
9. A. Solzhenitsyn, 'How people read *One Day*. A survey of letters' in L. Labedz (ed.), *Solzhenitsyn. A Documentary Record* (London: Penguin, 1972), p. 55.
10. J. Glover, *Humanity: A Moral History of the Twentieth Century* (London: Jonathan Cape, 1999).
11. S. Wheatcroft, 'The scale and nature of German and Soviet repression and mass killings 1930–1945', *Europe-Asia Studies*, vol. 48, no. 8, 1996, pp. 1319–53.
12. A.J.P. Taylor, *English History 1914–1945* (Oxford: Oxford University Press, 1965), p. 683. For a classic analysis of the mechanisms of the Bengal famine see A. Sen, *Poverty and Famines: An Essay on Entitlement and Deprivation* (Oxford: Oxford University Press, 1981).
13. Readers with no Russian should note that Gos. Kom. Rossiiskoi federatsii po statistike, *Naselenie Rossii za 100 let 1897–1997* (Moscow, 1998), has a Russian and English text.
14. D.M. Heer, 'The demographic transition in the Russian Empire and the Soviet Union', *Journal of Social History*, vol. 1, no. 3, 1966, pp. 193–240.
15. B. Kerblay, *Contemporary Soviet Society* (London: Methuen, 1983), p. 26.
16. R.G. Wilkinson, *Unhealthy Societies. The Afflictions of Inequality* (London: Routledge, 1996).
17. M. Prowse, 'Is inequality good for you?', *Financial Times*, 7/8 December 2002, pp. 12–13.
18. R. Lewontin, *The Doctrine of DNA* (London: Penguin, 1991), p. 42.
19. See B.N. Mironov, 'New approaches to old problems: the well-being of the population of Russia from 1871 to 1910 as measured by physical stature', *Slavic Review*, vol. 58, no. 1, spring 1999, pp. 1–26; S.G. Wheatcroft, 'The great leap upwards: anthropometric data and indictors of crises and

secular change in soviet welfare levels, 1880–1960, *Slavic Review*, pp. 27–60, plus subsequent discussion.
20. A. Sen, 'The economics of life and death', *Scientific American*, May 1993, p. 21.
21. Ibid., p. 25.

CHAPTER 2

1. For one version of the Orthodox funeral service, see <web.ukonline.co.uk/ephrem/funeral.htm>
2. R.S. Wortman, *Scenarios of Power: Myth and Ceremony in Russian Monarchy: Volume Two: From Alexander II to the Abdication of Nicholas II* (Princeton, NJ: Princeton University Press, 2000).
3. See A. Maylunas and S. Mironenko, *A Life Long Passion. Nicholas and Alexandra. Their Own Story* (London: Weidenfeld and Nicolson, 1996), pp. 91–100.
4. T. Trice, 'Rites of protest: populist funerals in Imperial St Petersburg, 1876–1878', *Slavic Review*, vol. 60, no. 1, spring 2001, p. 84.
5. Maylunas and Mironenko, *A Life Long Passion*, pp. 154, 137.
6. Ibid., p. 245.
7. See C. Merridale, *Night of Stone. Death and Memory in Russia* (London: Granta, 2000), passim.
8. Tsentralnyi statisticheskii komitet, *Ezhegodnik Rossii, 1904 g.* (St Petersburg, 1905) p. 82.
9. S.A. Novoselskii, *Voprosy demograficheskoi i sanitarnoi statistiki* (Moscow: Medgiz, 1958) contains a summary of Novoselskii's analysis, 'Smertnost i prodozhitelnost zhizni v Rossii', pp. 54–64.
10. Quoted in N.A. Semashko, 'Friedrich Erismann. The dawn of Russian hygiene and public health', *Bulletin of the History of Medicine*, vol. XX, no. 1, June 1946, p. 6.
11. E.J. Dillon, 'The first Russian census', *The Contemporary Review*, vol. lxxii, no. 6, December 1897, p. 839. For an historical discussion see L. Schwartz, 'A history of Russian and Soviet censuses', in R.M. Clem (ed.), *Research Guide to the Russian and Soviet Censuses* (London: Cornell University Press, 1986).
12. Novoselskii, *Voprosy demograficheskoi*, p. 127.
13. Entsiklopedeskii Slovar, 'Rossiia', vol. 27 (St Petersburg: Brokhaus & Efron, 1899), pp. 94–5.
14. E.J. Dillon, 'The first Russian census', p. 845.
15. A. Kahn, 'Natural calamities and their effect on the food supply in Russia', *Jahrbucher fur Geschicte Osteuropas*, vol. 16, 1968, pp. 353–77.
16. For annual statistics of recorded cholera deaths see L. Tarassevich, 'Epidemics in Russia since 1914', League of Nations Health Section, *Epidemiological Intelligence*, no. 2, 1922, p. 39. For infectious diseases 1900–20 see p. 34.
17. K.D. Patterson, 'Typhus and its control in Russia, 1870–1940', *Medical History*, vol. 37, 1993, pp. 361–81.

18. K.G. Vasil'ev and A.E. Segal, *Istoriia epidemii v Rossii* (Moscow: Medgiz, 1960).

19. S. Hoch, 'Famine, disease and mortality patterns in the parish of Borshevka, Russia, 1830–1912', *Population Studies*, vol. 52, 1998, pp. 357–68.

20. A.I. Lapina, *Orgnaizatsiia borby s tuberkulezom v SSSR* (Moscow: Meditsina, 1969), pp. 6–11.

21. S. Hoch, 'Famine, disease', p. 361.

22. More babies were conceived in September–April when food stocks were higher and there was less work. The Church frowned on sex in the major fasts before Christmas and in Lent. The late spring and early summer saw food supplies at their lowest and agricultural labour rising to a peak. See R.E.F. Smith and D. Christian, *Bread and Salt: A Social and Economic History of Food and Drink in Russia* (Cambridge: Cambridge University Press, 1984), pp. 335–8.

23. N. Frieden, *Russian Physicians in an Era of Reform and Revolution, 1856–1905* (Princeton, NJ: Princeton University Press, 1981), p. 364.

24. G.A. Friedman, 'Recollections of cholera epidemics in Russia', *Medical Record* (New York), 19 August 1911, p. 370.

25. S. Hoch, 'Famine, disease'; S.G. Wheatcroft, 'Crises and the condition of the peasantry in late imperial Russia', in E. Kingston-Mann and T. Mixter (eds), *Peasant Economy, Culture and Politics of European Russia, 1800–1921* (Princeton, NJ: Princeton University Press, 1991), pp. 128–72.

26. F.D. Markuzon, 'Sanitarnaia statistika v gorodakh prerevolutsionnoi Rossii', in A.B. Burtakov (ed.), *Ocherki po istorii statistiki SSSR* (Moscow Gosurdarstvennoe statisticheskoe izdatelstvo, 1955), pp. 121–62.

27. Novoselskii, *Voprosy demograficheskoi*, 'Vliianie ekonomicheskikh uslovii na chastotu otdelnikh prichin smerti', pp. 76–86.

28. A. Kahn, 'Government policies and the industrialisation of Russia', *Journal of Economic History*, vol. 27, no. 4, December 1967, p. 463.

29. Quoted in G. Freeze, *From Supplication to Revolution. Documentary Social History of Imperial Russia* (New York: Oxford University Press, 1988), pp. 265–6.

30. Novoselskii used registered cause of death data and summed the numbers for smallpox, measles, scarlatina, diphtheria, whooping cough and all forms of typhus. Novoselskii, *Voprosy demograficheskoi*, p. 72.

31. See M. Haynes and R. Husan, 'Whether by visible or invisible hand: the intractable problem of Russian and East European catch-up', *Competition and Change*, vol. 6, no. 3, 2002c, pp. 269–87.

32. See, for example, M.R. Haines, 'Socio-economic differentials in infant and child mortality during mortality decline: England and Wales 1890–1911', *Population Studies*, vol. 49, no. 2, July 1995, pp. 297–315.

33. Calculated from P. Gregory, *Russian National Income, 1885–1913* (Cambridge: Cambridge University Press, 1982), pp. 56–9, 256, 263. Local government expenditure on health and education was two-thirds higher than national government spending.

34. Summaries of some of the annual army sanitary reports can be found in *The Lancet*, 29 August 1896, pp. 613–14; 27 November 1897, pp. 1412–13; 17 January 1903, pp. 198–9.

35. G.F. Krivosheev, *Rossiia i SSSR v voinakh XX veka. Poteri vooruzhennuikh sil. Statisticheskoe issledovanie* (Moscow: Olma-Press, 2001), pp. 43, 594.

36. Quoted in P. Vinogradov, 'Russia', *Encyclopedia Britannica*, vol. 32 (new vol. 3) (London: Encyclopedia Britannica Company Ltd, 1922), pp. 308–40.

37. See P. Waldron, 'States of emergency: autocracy and extraordinary legislation, 1881–1917', *Revolutionary Russia*, vol. 8, no. 1, June 1995, pp. 1–25.

38. Quoted in Semashko, 'Friedrich Erismann', p. 6.

39. Serious pogroms occurred in 1871 in Odessa, in 1881–82 in various towns in the south and east. In 1891–92, Jews were expelled from Moscow. The Kishniev pogrom in 1903 killed up to 45. But this was small compared to pogroms in 1905–06 which may have killed up to 10,000. In 1905 in Baku there was considerable Azeri-Armenian violence which left 1,500 dead.

40. W.B. Lincoln, *In War's Dark Shadow. The Russians before the Great War* (New York and Oxford: Oxford University Press, 1994), p. 331.

41. R.F. Leslie, *The History of Poland Since 1863* (Cambridge: Cambridge University Press, 1980), p. 78 et seq.

42. Lincoln, *In War's Dark Shadow*, p. 310.

43. A. Ascher, *The Revolution of 1905: Russia in Disarray* (Stanford, CA: Stanford University Press, 1988), p. 172.

44. R. Service, *The Russian Revolution 1900–1927*, second edition, (Basingstoke: Macmillan, 1991), p. 16.

45. These included in 1901 N.P. Bogolepov, Minister of Education; 1902 D.S. Sipyagin, Minister of Interior; 1903 Prince Golitsyn, Viceroy of the Caucasus (wounded); 1904 V.K. Plehve, Minster of Interior, N. Bobrikov, Governor General of Finland.

46. F. Lorimer, *The Population of the Soviet Union: History and Prospects* (Geneva: League of Nations, 1946), pp. 41–2.

47. Andreev et al. (1993) started their reconstruction of population history in 1922 because the years 1914–21 were so confused.

48. P. Von Hindenburg, *Out of My Life* (London: Cassell & Co., 1920), p. 273.

49. In their enthusiasm to tie down the range of losses the authors give overly misleadingly exact figures. We have rounded them to the nearest 1,000 so as to better reflect the likely errors involved. They also refer to 238,000 not returning from captivity, but the basis of this figure is also unclear.

50. S. Kohn, *The Cost of the War to Russia. The Vital Statistics of European Russia during the World War, 1914–1917* (New Haven, CT: Yale University Press, 1932), p. 136.

51. See P. Gatrell, 'Refugees in the Russian Empire, 1914–1917. Population displacement and social identity', in E. Acton (ed.), *Critical Companion to the Russian Revolution, 1914–1921* (London: Edward Arnold, 2001).

52. Kohn, *Cost of the War*, pp. 32, 124–5.

53. Ibid., pp. 37–41.

54. Lorimer, *Population*, p. 30; M. Buttino, 'Study of the economic crisis and depopulation of Turkestan, 1917–1920', *Central Asian Survey*, vol. 9, no. 4, 1990; M. Buttino, 'Economic relations between Russia and Turkestan,

1914–1918, or How to start a famine', in J. Pallot (ed.), *Transforming Peasants* (Basingstoke: Macmillan, 1998).

55. L.E. Heenan, *Russian Democracy's Fatal Blunder. The Summer Offensive of 1917* (London: Praeger, 1987), p. 121.

56. Z.P. Solovev, *Voprosii zdravookhrareniia* (Moscow, 1940), p. 147.

57. See M. Haynes, 'The Debate on popular violence and the Popular Movement in the Russian Revolution', *Historical Materialism*, no. 2, summer 1998, pp. 185–214.

58. V.I. Lenin, *Collected Works* (Moscow: Foreign Languages Publishing House, 1965), vol. 26, pp. 19–21.

59. A. Ransome, 'Russia', *Encyclopedia Britannica*, 12th edition, new vol. 3 (London: Encyclopedia Britannica Company Ltd, 1928), p. 413.

60. Quoted in B.M. Khromov and A.V. Sveshnikov, *Zdravookranenie Leningrada* (Leningrad: Lenizdat, 1969), p. 59.

61. J. Glover, *Humanity: A Moral History of the Twentieth Century* (London: Jonathan Cape, 1999).

62. Quoted in I.S. Ratkovskii and M.V. Khodiakov, *Istoriia Sovietskoi Rossii* (St Petersburg: Lan, 2001), p. 67.

63. On Clausewitz see M. Howard, *Clausewitz* (Oxford: Oxford University Press, 1983), pp. 43, 26.

64. A. Mayer, *The Furies. Violence and Terror in the French and Russian Revolutions* (Princeton, NJ: Princeton University Press, 2000), p. 23.

65. Lenin, *Collected Works*, vol. 30, pp. 180–2, 222–3, 234–5, 326–8.

66. Ratkovskii and Khodiakov, *Istoriia Sovietskoi*, p. 67.

67. Ransome, 'Russia', p. 417.

68. Quoted in D. Koenker 'Urbanisation and deurbanisation in the Russian revolution and civil war', *Journal of Modern History*, vol. 57, no. 3, September 1985, p. 441.

69. 'Amenorrhea', *Bolshaya sovetskaia entsiklopediia*, 1926, vol. 2, p. 398.

70. The total number of deaths from any disease obviously depends on morbidity multiplied by the case fatality rate. The case fatality rate of malaria was low, for typhus in these years it was 10–15%, for smallpox it was over 30%, but the smallpox epidemic recorded less than 500,000 in these years compared to the much larger typhus epidemic.

71. Patterson, 'Typhus and its control'.

72. Lenin, *Collected Works*, vol. 30, p. 278.

73. I.A. Dobreitsera, 'Bor'ba s epidemiiami', in *Piat' let sovetskoi meditsini 1918–1923* (Moscow: RSFSR Narodnuii Komissariat Zdravookhraneiya, 1923), pp. 121–30. O.V. Baroian in his *Itogy poloveknoi borby s infektsiiami SSSR* (Moscow: Meditsina, 1968) offers various long-run disease series but it is not clear how these are calculated and, while their rough order of magnitude seems correct, they are usually lower than the contemporary ones reported here, subsequent data reported to the League of Nations and more recently quoted figures from the archives. While Baroian's book retains some value in an otherwise neglected field we have preferred not to use his series.

74. C. Davis, 'Economic problems of the Soviet health service', *Soviet Studies*, vol. xxxv, no. 3, 1983, pp. 343–61.

75. Tarassevich, 'Epidemics in Russia'.

76. H.H. Fisher, *The Famine in Soviet Russia, 1919–1923: The Operations of the American Relief Administration* (New York: Macmillan Co., 1927).

77. Poland had effectively achieved independence as a result of the war and German occupation. Romania took Bessarabia and Turkey the Pashalik of Kars. The October Revolution led directly to the independence of Finland and by a more convoluted route to the independence of the Baltic states.

78. Lorimer, *Population*, p. 41.

79. Ibid., p. 114.

80. S.G. Wheatcroft and R.W. Davies, 'Population', in R.W. Davies, M. Harrison and S. Wheatcroft (eds), *The Economic Transformation of the Soviet Union, 1913–1945* (Cambridge: Cambridge University Press, 1994), p. 65.

81. Quoted in V. Serge, *Russia Twenty Years After* (New York: Humanities Press, 1996), p. 155.

82. Ibid., p. 152.

83. For a discussion of this process see M. Haynes, *Russia: Class and Power 1917–2000* (London: Bookmarks, 2002), chapter 3.

84. Davis, 'Economic problems', pp. 346–7.

85. Quoted in S. Cohen, *Bukharin and the Bolshevik Revolution. A Political Biography* (London: Wildwood House, 1974), pp. 290–2.

CHAPTER 3

1. V. Serge, *Russia Twenty Years After* (New York: Humanities Press, 1996), p. 163.

2. G. Ofer, 'Soviet economic growth 1928–1985', *Journal of Economic Literature*, vol. xxv, no. 2, December 1987, p. 1784.

3. M. Harrison, 'Providing for defence', in P. Gregory (ed.), *Behind the Facade of Stalin's Command Economy* (Stanford, CA: Hoover Institution, 2001), pp. 81–100; N.S. Simonov, 'Mobpodgotovka: mobilisation planning in inter-war industry', in J. Barber and M. Harrison (eds), *The Soviet Defence-Industry Complex from Stalin to Khrushchev* (London and Basingstoke, Macmillan, 2000), pp. 205–22.

4. 'The share of consumption to GNP is lower in the Soviet Union than in most countries, typically by at least ten GNP points, which are taken up … by investment and defence.' Ofer, 'Soviet economic growth', p. 1790.

5. See 'Demograficheskoe protsessi v 30e gody' in *Naselenie Rossii v XX veke. Istoricheskie ocherki, tom 1. 1900–1939* (hereafter *Naselenie Rossii tomi*) (Moscow: Rosspen, 2000), pp. 336–44.

6. The 1939 census showed 159.1 million civilians, 2.1 million in distant regions, 2.1 million in the military and 3.7 million in the 'special contingent' under NKVD control (i.e. the Gulag). The addition of another 2.8 million was not entirely arbitrary. 1.14 million were added to account for those not counted because they were not at home and then a further 1% correction made for other undercounting. However, these adjustments are not now accepted.

7. For a discussion of the different possibilities see B.A. Anderson and B.D. Silver, 'Demographic analysis and population catastrophes in the USSR', *Slavic Review*, vol. 44, no. 3, 1985, pp. 517–36.

8. E.M. Andreev, L.E. Darskii and T.L. Kharkova, *Naselenie Sovetskogo Soyuza 1922–1991* (Moscow: Nauka, 1993), p. 4; C. Merridale, *Night of Stone. Death and Memory in Russia* (London: Granta, 2000), p. 198.

9. For the use of the Andreev et al.'s figure see N. Gavrilova, *Naselenie Moskvy: istoricheskii rakurs* (Moscow: Mosgoarkhiv, 2001), p. 51. For some of the problems see M. Ellman, 'A note on the number of 1933 famine victims', *Soviet Studies*, vol. 43, no. 2, 1991, pp. 375–9 and his further comments in 'On sources: a note', *Soviet Studies*, vol. 44, no. 5, 1992, pp. 913–15.

10. These are the figures offered by S.G. Wheatcroft and R.W. Davies in their 1994 summary, 'Population', in R.W. Davies (ed.), *The Economic Transformation of the Soviet Union, 1913–1945* (Cambridge: Cambridge University Press, 1994). Stephen Rosefielde who had earlier argued for much higher figures essentially accepts them. See his 'Stalinism in post-communist perspective: new evidence on killings, forced labour and economic growth in the 1930s', *Europe-Asia Studies*, vol. 48, no. 6, 1996, pp. 959–87.

11. See S. Maksudov, *Poteri naseleniia SSSR* (Benson, VT: Chalidze Publishers, 1989).

12. Rosefielde mistakenly says that 9 million of the excess deaths were adult and 0.7 million children. He achieves this by subtracting a now erroneous *old* estimate of Lorimer by excess child mortality from the total *new* estimate of excess mortality. See Rosefielde, 'Stalinism', p. 972.

13. See M. Haynes, *Russia Class and Power 1917–2000* (London: Bookmarks, 2002).

14. See J.L. Scherer and M. Jakobson, 'The collectivisation of agriculture and the Soviet prison camp system', *Europe-Asia Studies*, vol. 45, no. 3, 1993; G. Bordygov, 'The policy and regime of extraordinary measures in Russia under Lenin and Stalin', *Europe-Asia Studies*, vol. 47, no. 4, June 1995, pp. 615–32.

15. Serge quotes *Pravda* on the supposed positive effect of the death sentences in the first of the great purge trials, 'Our muscles acquire new vigour, our machines turn faster, our hands are nimbler ... We shall break new industrial records.' Serge, *Twenty Years*, p. 236.

16. These included Stalin's wife Nadezhda in 1932; 1933, Skrypnik; 1935, Lomindaze Tomsky; February 1937, Sergo Ordzhonokidze (but possible murder); 1937, Jan Gamarnik, A.G. Cherviakov.

17. The figure of 3.6 million is usually given for 1921–45 but this is misleading as the number of arrests before 1928 was less than 100,000. By giving figures for the years 1921–45 as if it were a unified period the decisive shift of 1928–29 is minimised. S. Wheatcroft, 'The scale and nature of German and Soviet repression and mass killings 1930–1945', *Europe-Asia Studies*, vol. 48, no. 8, 1996, p. 1334. See also 'Massovye repressii: zakluchennye', in *Naselenie Rossii tom 1*, pp. 311–30. On arrests and death penalties in the 1920s see p. 316.

18. See *Naselenie Rossii tom 1*, p. 321, for the limited data which we have.

19. Serge, *Twenty Years*, p. 219.
20. Because arrests were dominated by 'criminal' offences most sentences were non-custodial. This was especially so of the criminalisation of labour discipline which led to 10.9 million arrests for lateness alone between 1940 and 1952. The whole purpose was to force workers to work. But the increasingly repressive character of the regime increased the share of custodial sentences to 24.3% in 1933 and 47% in 1939. J.A. Getty, G.T. Rittersporn, and V.N. Zemskov, 'Victims of the Soviet penal system in the pre-war years: a first approach on the basis of archival evidence', *American Historical Review*, vol. 98, no. 4, 1993, p. 1019. Most NKVD arrests resulted in sentences. 0.21 million were found not guilty or fined. 0.4 million were exiled. 2.2 million were imprisoned and 0.8 million were executed. Wheatcroft, 'Scale and nature', p. 1336.
21. After 1945 some longer sentences were also served in labour colonies.
22. See *Naselenie Rossii tom 1*, pp. 312–13 for the size of the major camp complexes.
23. Even in years of fewer executions most were 'political' at the hands of the NKVD. Murder was not a capital offence at this time.
24. Getty et al., 'Victims', passim. For deaths in the 1930s by camp complex see *Naselenie Rossii tom 1*, p. 319.
25. M. Ellman, 'Soviet repression statistics: some comments', *Europe-Asia Studies*, vol. 54, no. 7, 2002, pp. 1151–72.
26. Getty et al., 'Victims', p. 1022.
27. Ibid., p. 1028.
28. Wheatcroft, 'Scale and nature', p. 1334
29. This was how it was described in the Riutin platform, a shorter English version of which is in E. Mawdsley, *The Stalin Years. The Soviet Union 1929–1953* (Manchester: Manchester University Press, 1998), p. 127.
30. '"Kulatskaia ssuilka" v 1930e gody: chislennost, rasselenie, sostav', in *Naselenie Rossii tom 1*, pp. 277–310.
31. Serge, *Twenty Years*, p. 168.
32. Wheatcroft, 'Scale and nature', p. 1337.
33. F. Lorimer, *The Population of the Soviet Union: History and Prospects* (Geneva: League of Nations, 1946), p. 140.
34. For a discussion of the issues see M.B. Tauger, 'Natural disaster and human actions in the Soviet famine of 1931–1933', *The Carl Beck Papers*, no. 1506 (Pittsburgh, PA: Center for International Studies, University of Pittsburgh, 2001).
35. 'Demograficheskie posledsteviia sploshnoi kollektivizatsii i golod 1932–1933 gg', in *Naselenie Rossii tom 1*, pp. 265–76.
36. We can also add that it does a service to those Ukrainian Stalinists who ate well and prospered while ordinary people in the Ukraine suffered.
37. See, for example, the comments in Tauger, 'Natural disaster' passim; Ellman, 'Soviet repression statistics', passim.
38. Serge, *Twenty Years*, p. 26.
39. 'Industrializatsiia i urbanizatsiia: demograficheskie posledsteviia', in *Naselenie Rossii tom 1*, pp. 219–42.
40. N. Mandelstam, *Hope Against Hope: A Memoir* (London: Collins & Harvill, 1971), p. 301.

41. T. Sosnovy, 'The Soviet urban housing problem', *American Slavic and East European Review*, vol. xii, no. 2, December 1952, p. 295; *Naselenie Rossii tom 1*, pp. 239–40.

42. Quoted in J. Barber and R.W. Davies, 'Employment', in R.W. Davies (ed.), *The Economic Transformation of the Soviet Union, 1913–1945* (Cambridge: Cambridge University Press, 1994), pp. 103–4.

43. L. Trotsky, *The Revolution Betrayed* (New York: Pathfinder, 1972b), passim.

44. Serge, *Twenty Years*, p. 44.

45. Ibid., p. 26.

46. Ibid., p. 11.

47. Zhiromskaia quotes rates of workplace deaths at 75 and 90 per 1,000 workers for 1935–36. This rate is so astronomical it may be a misprint. V.B. Zhiromskaia, *Demograficeshkaia istoriia Rossii v 1930-e gody* (Moscow: Rosspen, 2001).

48. Quoted in G. Rimlinger, 'The trade union in Soviet social insurance: historical development and present functions', *International and Labor Relations Review*, vol. 14, no. 3, 1961, p. 406.

49. Quoted in G. Rimlinger, *Welfare Policy and Industrialisation in Europe, America and Russia* (Chichester: John Wiley, 1971), p. 279.

50. Quoted in M.G. Field, 'Post Communism medicine: morbidity, mortality and the deteriorating health situation' in J.R. Miller and S.L. Wolchik (eds), *The Social Legacy of Communism* Cambridge: Cambridge University Press, 1994), p. 187.

51. Quoted in I. Deutscher, *Stalin* (Harmondsworth: Penguin, 1966), p. 549.

52. G.F. Krivosheev, *Rossiia i SSSR v voinakh XX veka. Poteri vooruzhennuikh sil. Statisticheskoe issledovanie* (Moscow: Olma-Press, 2001), p. 594 gives 189 Soviet army personnel lost in Spain. There were also non-army Soviet deaths.

53. Ibid., pp. 166–83, 594–5.

54. Ibid., pp. 184–88, 595.

55. Ibid., p. 188.

56. *Keesings Contemporary Archives*, 8–15 June 1940, p. 4089.

57. Krivosheev, *Rossiia i SSSR*, pp. 188–212, 595.

58. In April 1990 Gorbachev publicly apologised to Poland for the massacre, ending the decades of denial that the massacre was the work of the Russian secret police. For an account by the leading Russian investigator, see N.S. Lebedeva, 'Chetvertuii razdel Polshi i Katuinskaia tragediia', in Y. Afanasiev (ed.), *Drugaia voina 1939–1945* (Moscow: Rossiskii Gosudarstvennuii Gumantitarnuii Universitet, 1996).

59. Andreev et al., *Naselenie Sovetskogo*.

60. For an explanation of the different ways in which war deaths can be analysed see M. Haynes, 'Counting Soviet deaths in the Great Patriotic War: a note', *Europe-Asia Studies*, vol. 55, no. 2, 2003, pp. 303–9.

61. O. Bartov, *Hitler's Army: Soldiers, Nazis, and War in the Third Reich* (New York and Oxford: Oxford University Press, 1991), p. 87.

62. W. Benz, *The Holocaust. A Short History* (London: Profile Books, 2000), pp. 74–87.

63. Estimates from Lorimer, *Population*, p. 194, adjusted to take account of lower 1939 population figure.
64. Krivosheev, *Rossiia i SSSR*, p. 595.
65. Quoted in D.A. Volkogonov, *Stalin: Triumph and Tragedy* (London: Weidenfeld and Nicolson, 1995), p. 460.
66. Hitler's allies included Finland. There the war became known as the 'Continuation War' from 1941–45. Finland, as an ally or co-belligerant, recovered land lost and more, but did not directly assist the Nazis in the Siege of Leningrad.
67. See 'Tragicheskie posledstviia blokady Leningrada', in *Naselenie Rossii v XX veke. Istoricheskie ocherki, tom 2. 1940–1959* (hereafter *Naselenie Rossii tom 2*) (Moscow: Rosspen, 2001), pp. 40–6.
68. Ibid., pp. 82–127. W. Moskoff, *The Bread of Affliction: The Food Supply in the USSR during World War II* (Cambridge: Cambridge University Press, 1990), passim.
69. See 'Spetspolselensty i ssylnye. Zakluchennye', in *Naselenie Rossii tom 2*, pp. 166–96 and especially table 47 at p. 195.
70. M. Djilas, *Conversations with Stalin* (Hardmondsworth: Penguin, 1969), pp. 87–8.
71. Kalingrad (the former Königsberg) and the Carpatho-Ukraine from Czechoslovakia. In the Far East the brief campaign against Japan yielded Manchuria, the Kuriles Islands, Southern Sakhalin and four small islands.
72. A. Bergson, *The Real National Income of Soviet Russia Since 1928* (Cambridge, MA: Harvard University Press, 1961), p. 46.
73. See Krivosheev, *Rossiia i SSSR*, passim.
74. Quoted in M. Charlton, *The Eagle and the Small Birds. Crisis in the Soviet Empire From Yalta to Solidarity* (London: British Broadcasting Corporation, 1984), p. 55.
75. See *Naselenie Rossii tom 2*, p. 15, for the numbers.
76. P. Polian, *He po cvoei vole ... Istoriia i geografiia preinuditelnostuikh migratsii v SSSR* (Moscow: OGI-Memorial, 2001), p. 240; *Naselenie Rossii tom 2*, p. 155.
77. There was thus now a more marked national pattern in the postwar camps than before 1941. See *Naselenie Rossii tom 2*, p. 188.
78. Ellman, 'Soviet repression statistics'.
79. Polian, *He po cvoei vole*, p. 239.
80. F. Chuev, *Molotov Remembers* (Chicago, IL: Ivan R. Dee, 1993), p. 325.
81. Stalin's daughter Svetlana fell in love with a Jew whom Stalin then sent to the camps.
82. The uncertainty again reflects registration difficulties. See M. Ellman, 'The 1947 Soviet famine and the entitlement approach to famines', *Cambridge Journal of Economics*, vol. 24, no. 5, 2000a, pp. 603–30.
83. Calculated from Goskomstat, *Naselenie Rossii za 100 let (1897–1997)* (Moscow: Goskomstat, 1998), p. 176.
84. Sosnovy, 'Soviet urban housing problem', p. 295.
85. E. Radzinsky, *Stalin* (London: Sceptre, 1996), p. 522.
86. S. Allilueva, *Twenty Letters to a Friend* (Harmondsworth: Penguin, 1968), p. 18.

CHAPTER 4

1. See R. Medvedev, *Khrushchev* (Oxford: Blackwell, 1982), pp. 207–11.
2. See Y. Yevtushenko, *The Poetry of Yevgeny Yevtushenko*, ed. G. Reavey (London: Marion Boyars, 1981), pp. 161–5. 'Turksib' refers to the building of the railway to link Turkestan cotton and Siberian grain; 'Magnita' refers to the industrial centre of Magnitogorsk.
3. For a brief analysis of the film and its role see N. Galichenko, *Glasnost Soviet Cinema Responds* (Austin: University of Texas Press, 1991), pp. 1–2, 59–62. The film was only shown after getting the high level backing of the reformist foreign minister Eduard Shevardnadze and the mobilisation of powerful artistic support. Once released it packed cinemas everywhere and became the best-known cultural expression of the attempt to come to terms with the past and its living dead.
4. On Beria's arrest and execution see 'Beria's arrest: from the unpublished memoirs of Marshall Moskalenko', *Moscow News*, no. 23, 1990, pp. 8–9.
5. N.S. Khrushchov (sic), *Report on the Programme of the Communist Party of the Soviet Union and reply to discussion* (London: Soviet Booklets, 1961), p. 115. Khrushchev also named Voroshilov, Bulganin, Pervukhin, Saborov and Shepilov as members of the 'group', but they had even milder punishments.
6. V.N. Zemskov, 'Massovoe osvobozdenie spetsposelentsev i ssylnykh 1954–1960 gg', *Sotsiologicheskie issledovaniia*, no. 1, 1991, pp. 5–26. There is a convenient list of the release pattern in *Naselenie Rossii v XX veke. Istoricheskie ocherki, tom 2. 1940–1959* (Moscow: Rosspen, 2001), pp. 180–1.
7. For one account see M. Haynes, *Russia: Class and Power 1917–2000* (London: Bookmarks, 2002), pp. 124–8.
8. W. Adams, 'The death penalty in Imperial and Soviet criminal law', *American Journal of Comparative Law*, vol. 18, 1970, pp. 575–94; G.P. van Den Berg, 'The Soviet Union and the death penalty', *Soviet Studies*, vol. 35, no. 2, April 1983, p. 163; G.P. van den Berg, *The Soviet System of Justice: Figures and Policy* (Dordecht: Martinus Nijhoff, 1985).
9. See V. Vitaliev, *Special Correspondent. Investigating the Soviet Union* (London: Hutchinson, 1990), p. 66.
10. For some of the first public discussions of the criminal subculture and its relationship to those in power, see Vitaliev, *Special Correspondent*, pp. 65–145. For an earlier 'exotic' account of crime see Y. Brokhin, *Hustling on Gorky Street. Sex and Crime in Russia Today* (London: W.H. Allen, 1976).
11. Vitaliev gives the example of the search for a serial killer in Belorussia where one of the accused committed suicide in jail, a second was found guilty and executed and then the real killer was found. Vitaliev, *Special Correspondent*, p. 135.
12. A. Pristavkin, 'Death penalty in Russia' (1998) at Moscow Centre for Prison Reform website.
13. Medvedev, *Khrushchev*, pp. 219–20; Khrushchov, *Report on the Programme*, p. 115.

14. A. Marchenko, *My Testimony*. Trans. M. Scammell. (Harmondsworth: Penguin, 1971). Marchenko was jailed six times for dissent. He died in prison in 1986 on the eve of the Gorbachev reforms. He was finally recognised in the USSR in 1989. See *Current Digest of the Soviet Press*, vol. xli, no. 43, 1989, p. 25.

15. L.I. Shelley, *Policing Soviet Society. The Evolution of State Control* (London: Routledge, 1996), pp. 181–4.

16. S.H. Baron, *Bloody Saturday in the Soviet Union. Novocherkassk, 1962* (Stanford, CA: Stanford University Press, 2000), pp. 67–9. There were also many seriously wounded.

17. R. Leger Sivard, *World Military and Social Expenditures 1987–1988* (Washington, DC: World Priorities, 1987), pp. 12–13.

18. Quoted in J. Granville, 'In the line of fire: the Soviet crackdown on Hungary, 1956–57', *Journal of Communist Studies and Transition Politics*, vol. 13, no. 2, June 1997, pp. 67–107.

19. J. Pilger, *Distant Voices* (London: Vintage, 1992), p. 155.

20. Sivard, *World Military*, pp. 12–13.

21. Quoted in Pilger, *Distant Voices*, p. 14.

22. G.F. Krivosheev, *Rossiia i SSSR v voinakh XX veka. Poteri vooruzhennykh sil. Statisticheskoe issledovanie* (Moscow: Olma-Press, 2001), pp. 534–40; V. Konovalov, 'Legacy of the Afghan war: some statistics', *Radio Liberty Report on the USSR*, vol. 1, no. 14, 7 April 1989, pp. 1–3.

23. S. Alexiyevich, *Zinky Boys: Soviet Voices from a Forgotten War* (London: Chatto & Windus, 1992); A. Heinamaa, *The Soldiers Story: Soviet Veterans Remember the Afghan War* (Berkeley: University of California Press, 1994).

24. N.A. Khalidi, 'Afghanistan: demographic consequences of war 1978–1987', *Central Asian Survey*, vol. 10, no. 3, 1991, pp. 101–25; M. Sliwinski, 'The decimation of Afghanistan', *Orbis*, vol. 33, no. 1, winter 1988–89, pp. 39–56. There is a good bibliography of the USSR's Afghan war in L.W. Adamec, *Dictionary of Afghan Wars, Revolutions and Insurgencies* (London: Scarecrow Press, 1996), pp. 344–64.

25. C. Merridale, *Night of Stone. Death and Memory in Russia* (London: Granta, 2000), pp. 351–2.

26. Khrushchov, *Report on the Programme*, pp. 69, 11.

27. Y. Lisitsin, *Health Protection in the USSR* (Moscow: Progress, 1972), p. 64; O.V. Baroian, *Itogi poluvekovoi borbi s infektsiiami v SSSR* (Moscow: Meditsina, 1968), p. 77.

28. See N. Krementsov, 'The war on cancer and the Cold War: a Soviet case', in I. Löwy and J. Krige (eds), *Images of Disease. Science, Public Policy and Health in Post-War Europe* (Luxembourg: European Communities, 2001), pp. 213–26.

29. See L.C. Chen, A. Kleinman and N.C. Ware (eds), *Health and Social Change in International Perspective* (Boston, MA: Harvard School of Public Health, 1994), esp. pp. 3–50.

30. N. Eberstadt, 'Health and morbidity in Eastern Europe, 1965–85', *Communist Economies*, vol. 2, no. 3, 1990, pp. 203–5.

31. J. Cairns, 'The cancer problem', *Scientific American*, vol. 233, no. 5, 1975, pp. 64, 70.

32. R.G. Wilkinson, 'Income distribution and life expectancy', *British Medical Journal*, vol. 304, 18 January 1992, pp. 165–8; R.G. Wilkinson, *Unhealthy Societies. The Afflictions of Inequality* (London: Routledge, 1996), pp. 72–112.

33. D.P. Forster, 'Income distribution and life expectancy', *British Medical Journal*, vol. 304, 14 March 1992, p. 715.

34. M. Bobak and M. Marmot, 'East–West mortality divide and its potential explanations: proposed research agenda', *British Medical Journal*, vol. 312, 17 February 1996, p. 425.

35. Haynes, *Russia: Class and Power*, pp. 146–7.

36. V.M. Moiseenko (ed.), *Naselenie Moskvy* (Moscow: Moscow University Press, 1992), pp. 87–91.

37. W.W. Kingkade, 'Soviet mortality by cause of death: an analysis of years of potential life lost', in W. Lutz, S. Scherbov and A. Volkov (eds), *Demographic Trends and Patterns in the Soviet Union Before 1991* (London: Routledge, 1991); J. Cairns, 'The cancer problem'.

38. Khrushchov, *Report on the Programme*, p. 78.

39. M. Field, 'The health crisis in the former Soviet Union: a report from the "post-war" zone', *Social Science and Medicine*, vol. 41, no. 11, 1995, p. 1470.

40. Quoted in D. Lane, *Soviet Society under Perestroika* (London: Unwin Hyman, 1991), p. 321.

41. Quoted in E. Mezentseva and N. Rimachevskaya, 'The Soviet country profile: health of the USSR population in the 70s and 80s – an approach to comprehensive analysis', *Social Science and Medicine*, vol. 31, no. 8, 1990, p. 869.

42. J. Eyer and P. Sterling, 'Stress related mortality and social organisation', *Review of Radical Political Economy*, vol. 9, no.1, spring, 1977.

43. P. Townsend, P. Phillimore and A. Beattie, *Health and Deprivation: Inequality and the North* (London and New York: Routledge, 1988).

44. Bobak and Marmot, 'East–West mortality divide', p. 424.

45. L. Trotsky, *Problems of Everyday Life* (New York: Pathfinder, 1972a), passim.

46. *Moscow News*, 22 November 1987.

47. See P. Rutland, 'Labour movements and unrest', *Soviet Economy*, winter 1990.

48. *Ekonomicheskiia gazeta*, no. 40, October 1988, p. 18.

49. See F. du Plessix Grey, *Soviet Women. Walking the Tightrope* (London: Virago, 1991), pp. 158–66.

50. Vitaliev, *Special Correspondent*, p. 24.

51. In April 1971, 35% of urban housing had no baths, 27% had no toilet and 23% of all urban housing lacked running water. G.B. Smith, *Soviet Politics: Continuity and Contradiction* (Basingstoke: Macmillan, 1988), p. 254.

52. *Ocherki istorii Tumenskoi oblasti* (Tumen: Komitet po pechati i massovoi informatsii administratsii Tumenskoi oblasti, 1994), p. 225.

53. S. Orlov, 'The medicalised sobering stations: a history of a unique Soviet practice', in Löwy and Krige (eds), *Images of Disease*, pp. 353–62.

54. See Vitaliev, *Special Correspondent*, pp. 30–2.

55. V. Shkolnikov, F. Meslé and Jacques Vallin, 'Health crisis in Russia. I. recent trends in life expectancy and causes of death from 1970 to 1993';

'II. Changes in causes of death: a comparison with France and England and Wales (1970 to 1993)', *Population: An English Selection*, vol. 8, 1996, p. 133.

56. Z. Medvedev, *Nuclear Disaster in the Urals*, trans. G. Saunders (New York: Viking Press, 1989).

57. R. MacKay (ed.), *Letters to Gorbachev. Life in Russia Through the Postbag of Argumenty i fakty* (London: Michael Joseph, 1991), pp. 80–1.

58. Quoted in J. Chinn, 'The aging Soviet society', in H. Desfosses (ed.), *Soviet Population Policy. Conflicts and Constraints* (Oxford: Pergamon, 1981), pp. 56–7.

59. *Ekonomicheskiia gazeta* no. 18, April 1990.

60. The figures understate spending as some was undertaken by trade unions.

61. M. Field, 'Post Communism medicine: morbidity, mortality and the deteriorating health situation', in J.R. Miller and S.L. Wolchik (eds), *The Social Legacy of Communism* (Cambridge: Cambridge University Press, 1994), p. 179.

62. C. Davies quoted in Lane, *Soviet Society*, pp. 317–18.

63. Field, 'The health crisis'.

64. D. Hearst, 'Propping up the President', *Guardian*, 18 July 1996.

65. V.A. Velkoff and J.E. Miller, 'Trends and differentials in infant mortality in the Soviet Union, 1970–1990: how much is due to misreporting?', *Population Studies*, vol. 49, 1995, pp. 241–58.

66. E. Wnuk-Lipinski and R. Illsley, 'International comparative analysis', *Social Science and Medicine*, vol. 31, no. 8, 1990, p. 882.

CHAPTER 5

1. Quoted in V. Vitaliev, *Special Correspondent. Investigating the Soviet Union* (London: Hutchinson, 1990), p. 240. The Memorial Society must be distinguished from another organisation, Pamyat ('Memory') which was a right-wing, anti-semitic group committed to a defence of past greatness.

2. Ibid., pp. 179–83.

3. See *Literaturnaiia gazeta*, no. 4, 27 January 1988, on comparative health.

4. *Moscow Times*, 15 December 2000; 29 April 2002.

5. D. Leon, L. Chenet, V. Shkolnikov, S. Zakharov, J. Shapiro, G. Rakhmanova, S. Vassin and M. McKee, 'Huge variation in Russian mortality rates 1984–94', *The Lancet*, vol. 50, 9 August 1997, p. 384.

6. *Moscow News*, no. 17, 1988.

7. N. Eberstadt, 'Health and mortality in Central and Eastern Europe: retrospect and prospect', in J.R. Miller and S.L. Wolchik (eds), *The Social Legacy of Communism* (Cambridge: Cambridge University Press, 1994), p. 223.

8. A. Aganbegyan, *The Challenge: Economics of Perestroika* (London: Hutchinson, 1987), p. 6.

9. M. Goldman, *Lost Opportunity: What has Made Economic Reform in Russia so Difficult?* (London and New York: W.W. Norton, 1996), table 4.1, p. 76.

10. Ibid., pp. 21–3.

11. J. Winiecki, *Resistance to Change in the Soviet Economic System: A Property Rights Approach* (London and New York: Routledge, 1991), p. xiii.

12. Aganbegyan, *The Challenge*, fig. 1, p. 2.

13. A. Maddison, *The World Economy: A Millennial Perspective* (Paris: OECD, 2001), table C1-b, p. 374.

14. Cited in M. Pomer, 'Introduction', in L. Klein and M. Pomer (eds), *The New Russia: Transition Gone Awry* (Stanford, CA: Stanford University Press, 2001), p. 3. The collection of papers edited by Klein and Pomer is the first really serious attempt by mainstream economists to acknowledge and attempt to understand Russia's disastrous transition. Including the preface, it has papers by four Nobel Prize winners for economics. The book can be viewed as an important challenge to the 'Washington Consensus', many of whose leading acolytes advised on the transition.

15. Cited in S. Hedlund, *Russia's 'Market' Economy: A Bad Case of Predatory Capitalism* (London: UCL Press, 1999), pp. 90–1.

16. J. Leitzel, *Russian Economic Reform* (London and New York: Routledge, 1995), p. 27.

17. B. Yeltsin, 'Speech to Congress of People's Deputies', *Izvestia*, 29 October 1991, translated in *Current Digest of the Soviet Press*, vol. 43, no. 43, pp. 1–6.

18. L. Nelson and I. Kuzes, *Radical Reform in Yeltsin's Russia: Political, Economic and Social Dimensions* (Armonk, NY and London: M.E. Sharpe, 1995), p. 16.

19. A. Aslund, *How Russia Became a Market Economy* (Washington, DC: Brookings Institution, 1995), p. 139.

20. UN ECE, *Economic Survey of Europe in 1992–1993* (New York: UN, 1993), fn 371, p. 161.

21. Though energy prices were still regulated, they were massively increased between December 1991 and December 1992: the price of oil increased 84-fold; gas, 15-fold, and coal, 55-fold (ibid., fn 185, p. 106).

22. The Gini coefficient of income (index of concentration of incomes) characterises the level of deviation of the actual volume of distribution of incomes of population from the line of their even distribution. The value of coefficient may vary from 0 to 1, and the higher the value of the indicator, the less even the distribution of income in the society. Note that the Gini coefficient of *earnings* may show even greater inequality for Russia in the 1990s.

23. UN ECE, *Economic Survey of Europe*, no. 1 and nos 2–3 (New York: UN, 2000), p. 100.

24. UN ECE, *Economic Survey of Europe in 1992–1993*, p. 165.

25. Aslund, *How Russia Became a Market Economy*, p. 144.

26. J. Blasi, M. Kroumova and D. Kruse, *Kremlin Capitalism: The Privatization of the Russian Economy* (Ithaca, NY and London: Cornell University Press, 1997), p. 33.

27. Olga Kryshtanovskaia estimated that two-thirds of new businessmen came from the *nomenklatura*. Cited in T. Gustaffson, *Capitalism Russian-Style* (Cambridge: Cambridge University Press, 1999), p. 111.

28. Blasi et al., *Kremlin Capitalism*, p. 48.

29. S. Glinkina, A. Grigoriev and V. Yakobidze, 'Crime and corruption', in Klein and Pomer (eds), *The New Russia*, p. 239.
30. Blasi et al, *Kremlin Capitalism*, p. 46.
31. The total value of Russian industry was estimated at under $12 billion, less than that of US cereal firm Kellogg or the beer company, Anheuser-Busch (D. Hoffman, *The Oligarchs: Wealth and Power in the New Russia* Oxford: Public Affairs, 2002, p. 207).
32. Glinkina et al., 'Crime and corruption', pp. 237–42.
33. Brief descriptions of the main oligarchs are given in ibid., pp. 244–5; for a fascinating account of six of these, see Hoffman, *The Oligarchs*.
34. EBRD, *Transition Report 2000* (London: EBRD, 2000), p. 204.
35. UNICEF, *Social Monitor 2002* (Florence: UNICEF Innocenti Research Centre, 2002), table 10.9, p. 87.
36. Gustaffson, *Capitalism Russian-Style*, p. 25.
37. G. Arbatov, 'Origins and consequences of "shock therapy"', in Klein and Pomer (eds), *The New Russia*, fn 3, p. 178.
38. V. Mikhalev, 'Poverty and social assistance', in Klein and Pomer (eds), *The New Russia*, table 16.1, p. 255 – data refer to 1994–95.
39. Ibid., p. 253.
40. Perhaps a comparison of the real earnings of the *nomenklatura* in 1989 with the poorest (or indeed those on average earnings) might not show quite the same differential.
41. UNICEF, *A Decade of Transition* Regional Monitoring Report No. 8, (Florence: UNICEF Innocenti Research Centre, 2001), fig. 2.1, p. 26 and table 2.7, p. 27. Note that collation of reliable data on income inequality is extremely difficult; consequently, the figures provided are estimates (ibid., box 2.1, p. 27). Nonetheless, the trend is unmistakeable and the general conclusion of rising inequality holds.
42. S. Clarke, *The Formation of a Labour Market in Russia* (Cheltenham: Edward Elgar, 1999), pp. 97–8.
43. J. Klugman, J. Micklewright and G. Redmond, *Poverty in the Transition: Social Expenditures and the Working-Age Poor*, Innocenti Working Paper No. 91 (Florence: UNICEF, 2002), p. 29.
44. UN ECE, *Economic Survey of Europe*, 2000, no. 1 and nos 2–3, p. 131.
45. Ibid., chart 4.2.5, p. 134.
46. Inflows of foreign direct investment in 2000 were $2.7 billion; this contrasts with $4.6 billion into the Czech Republic and $10 billion into Poland (UNCTAD, *World Investment Report 2001: Promoting Linkages* (New York and Geneva: UN, 2001), fig. 1.22, p. 34).
47. UN ECE, *Economic Survey of Europe*, no. 1 and nos 2–3, table 4.5.3, p. 151.
48. See R. Husan, 'Reflections on the significance of market failures in Eastern Europe', *Review of Policy Issues*, vol. 2, no. 1, 1996, pp. 81–8.
49. O. Williamson, 'Vertical integration and related variations on a transaction-cost economies theme', in J. Stiglitz and G. Mathewson (eds), *New Developments in the Analysis of Market Structure* (London and Basingstoke: Macmillan, 1986), pp. 149–74.
50. O. Bogomolov, 'Neoliberalism', in Klein and Pomer (eds), *The New Russia*, p. 55.

51. Cited in Klugman et al., *Poverty in the Transition*, p. 23.
52. K. Polanyi, *The Great Transformation* [1944] (Boston, MA: Beacon Hill, 1957), p. 130.
53. D. Crouch, 'The crisis in Russia and the rise of the right', *International Socialism*, vol. 66, 1995, p. 44.
54. S. Clarke, P. Fairbrother and C. Borisov, *The Workers' Movement in Russia* (Cheltenham: Edward Elgar, 1995), passim.
55. UN ECE, *Economic Survey of Europe in 1992–1993*, p. 161.
56. Mikhalev, 'Poverty and social assistance', p. 251.
57. UN ECE, *Economic Survey of Europe in 1992–1993*, pp. 166–8.
58. One of the key Western economic advisers, Jeffrey Sachs, in December 1991, believed that $15–$20 billion per annum in international support was possible but did not explicitly argue that the reforms would fail in its absence (Aslund, *How Russia Became a Market Economy*, fn 38, p. 333). In reality, such level of support proved a pipe-dream.

CHAPTER 6

1. WHO, *European Health Report 2002* (Geneva: WHO, 2002b), p. 70.
2. Ibid., fig. 7, p. 14.
3. See M. Ellman, 'The social costs and consequences of the transformation process', in UN ECE, *Economic Survey of Europe*, nos 2–3 (New York: UN, 2000), p. 133.
4. Note that Rosefielde estimates 'probable premature deaths and birth deficits' in Russia for 1990–98 at between 2.9 million (without migration) and 6.1 million (with actual migration). Given the unreliability of migration data, we need to treat the latter figure with caution. See S. Rosefielde, 'Premature deaths: Russia's radical economic transition in Soviet perspective', *Europe-Asia Studies*, vol. 53, no. 8, 2001, p. 1161.
5. UNICEF, *Crisis in Mortality, Health, and Nutrition*, Regional Monitoring Report No. 2 (Florence: UNICEF International Child Development Centre, 1994), pp. 43–6.
6. WHO, *European Health Report 2002*, p. 11.
7. M. Marmot and M. Bobak, 'Psychosocial and biological mechanisms behind the recent mortality crisis in Central and Eastern Europe', in G. Cornia and R. Paniccia (eds), *The Mortality Crisis in Transitional Economies* (Oxford: Oxford University Press, 2000b), p. 131.
8. See UNICEF, *Crisis in Mortality*, p. 37.
9. V. Shkolnikov and G. Cornia, 'Population crisis and rising mortality in transitional Russia', in Cornia and Paniccia (eds), *The Mortality Crisis*, p. 263.
10. T. Tulchinsky and E. Varavikova, 'Addressing the epidemiologic transition in the former Soviet Union: strategies for health system and public health reform in Russia', *American Journal of Public Health*, vol. 86, no. 3, 1996, p. 316.
11. C. Williams, 'Abortion and women's health in Russia and the Soviet successor states', in R. Marsh (ed.), *Women in Russia and Ukraine* (Cambridge: Cambridge University Press, 1996), p. 138.

12. G. Cornia, 'Short-term, long-term, and hysterisis mortality models: a review', in Cornia and Paniccia (eds), *The Mortality Crisis*, fig. 3.1.
13. R. Paniccia, 'Transition, impoverishment, and mortality: how large an impact?' in Cornia and Paniccia (eds), *The Mortality Crisis*, p. 116.
14. Ibid.
15. It is the unchanging rate of neoplasms (in comparison, all other categories show dramatic changes) that leads Leon et al. to deduce that Russian statistics are reasonably reliable. This is also suggested by the fact that 94% of all deaths are medically certified. See D. Leon, L. Chenet, V. Shkolnikov, S. Zakharov, J. Shapiro, G. Rakhmanova, S. Vassin and M. McKee, 'Huge variation in Russian mortality rates 1984–94: artefact, alcohol, or what?', *The Lancet*, vol. 350, 9 August 1997, pp. 383–8.
16. L. Tichonova, H. Borisenko, H. Ward, A. Meheus, A. Gromyko and A. Renton, 'Epidemics of syphilis in the Russian Federation: trends, origins, and priorities for control', *The Lancet*, vol. 350, 19 July 1997, p. 210.
17. See *Moscow Times*, 16 May 2002; 13 September 2002.
18. Shkolnikov and Cornia, 'Population crisis', p. 262.
19. D. Barr and M. Field, 'The current state of health care in the former Soviet Union: implications for health care policy and reform', *American Journal of Public Health*, vol. 86, no. 3, 1996, p. 308.
20. B. Yeltsin, *Midnight Diaries* (London: Weidenfeld and Nicolson, 2000), p. 46.
21. C. Davis, 'The health sector: illness, medical care, and mortality', in B. Granville and P. Oppenheimer (eds), *Russia's Post-Communist Economy* (Oxford: Oxford University Press, 2001), table 17.4, pp. 499–503.
22. UNICEF, *Crisis in Mortality*, p. 70.
23. Ibid., p. 60.
24. UNICEF, *A Decade of Transition*, Regional Monitoring Report No. 8 (Florence: UNICEF Innocenti Research Centre, 2001), fig 3.10, p. 58.
25. Davis, 'The health sector', pp. 517–18.
26. S. White, *Russia Goes Dry: Alcohol, State, and Society* (Cambridge: Cambridge University Press, 1996), p. 165.
27. V. Shkolnikov, M. McKee and D. Leon, 'Changes in life expectancy in Russia in the mid-1990s', *The Lancet*, vol. 357, 24 March 2001, p. 919.
28. We do not dwell on another health-damaging activity that Russian men in particular conduct in abundance, that of smoking (the reasons for this are similar to those for heavy drinking). There is little evidence to suggest that smoking can explain excess deaths in the 1990s, though in conjunction with high levels of alcohol intake it can accentuate the proclivity to heart disease. Indeed, evidence suggests mortality from lung cancer has actually been falling for reasons to do with the decline in the uptake of smoking during the severe economic hardship of the late 1940s and early 1950s (V. Shkolnikov and M. McKee, 'Understanding the toll of premature death among men in Eastern Europe', *British Medical Journal*, vol. 323, 3 November, 2001, pp. 1051–5; also see Table 6.4 for decline in neoplasms). However, it is estimated that 20% of Russians will eventually die from tobacco-related causes (W.C. Cockerham, *Health and Social Change in Russia and Eastern Europe* (London and New York: Routledge, 1999), p. 114) so that it is obviously the case the types of

measures needed to tackle alcoholism will also be needed to tackle smoking.

29. Leon et al., 'Huge variation in Russian mortality rates'; White, *Russia Goes Dry*.
30. Ibid.
31. D. Wasserman and A. Vdmik, 'Changes in life expectancy in Russia', *The Lancet*, vol. 357, 23 June 2001; M. Ryan, 'Russian report: alcoholism and rising mortality in the Russian Federation', *British Medical Journal*, vol. 310, 11 March 1995, pp. 648–50.
32. Shkolnikov et al., 'Changes in life expectancy'.
33. Shkolnikov and Nemtsov estimate that excessive alcohol consumption is the single most important determinant of mortality (cited in Cockerham, *Health and Social Change*, p. 111).
34. This is based on the assumption that under-15s do not drink and women, half the population, consume only 10% of the total (ibid.).
35. Cited in G. Cornia and R. Paniccia, 'The transition mortality crisis: evidence, interpretation and policy responses', in Cornia and Paniccia (eds), *The Mortality Crisis*, p. 30.
36. J. Moskalewicz, B. Wojtyniak and D. Rabczenko, 'Alcohol as a cause of mortality in societies undergoing rapid transition to market economy', in Cornia and Paniccia (eds), *The Mortality Crisis*, p. 90. Though Simpura et al. dispute the notion that alcohol relieves stress and hardship (cited in ibid., p. 90).
37. Moszkalewicz et al., 'Alcohol as a cause of mortality', p. 90.
38. See E. Brainerd, 'Economic reform and mortality in the former Soviet Union: a study of the suicide epidemic in the 1990s', *European Economic Review*, vol. 45, 2001, pp. 1007–19.
39. Shkolnikov and McKee, 'Understanding the toll of premature death'.
40. Shkolnikov and McKee, 'Understanding the toll of premature death', p. 1052.
41. Cockerham, *Health and Social Change*, p. 113.
42. The high increase in 'unspecified violent deaths' leads Shkolnikov et al. 'Changes in life expectancy' to conclude that there may have been systematic changes in certification or coding of cause of death due to, for example, lack of resources or a demoralised forensic and police service in the early years of transition. Similarly, Gavrilova et al. (p. 404) suggest that murder and suicide deaths have been under-reported in order to avoid criminal investigation and thereby save costs (N. Gavrilova, V. Semyonova, G. Evdokushkina and L. Gavrilov, 'The response of violent mortality to economic crisis in Russia', *Population Research and Policy Review*, vol. 19, no. 5, pp. 397–419).
43. *Izvestia*, 9 September 1998.
44. WHO, *European Health Report 2002*.
45. Brainerd, 'Economic reform and mortality', p. 1011.
46. These are for the years 1988–98. Though they unfortunately include pre-transition years, the validity of the findings is not damaged. Brainerd's results also show a positive correlation of suicide to divorce rates – though it can be argued that the divorce rate itself can be considered a function of the state of the macroeconomy (ibid.).

47. Gavrilova et al., 'The response of violent mortality', p. 411.
48. Ibid., table 4, p. 408.
49. WHO, *World Report on Violence and Health* (Geneva: WHO, 2002a), statistical annex, table A.8.
50. *Moscow Times*, 9 October 2002.
51. Gavrilova et al., 'The response of violent mortality', p. 413.
52. Cornia and Paniccia, 'The transition mortality crisis', pp. 17, 31–3.
53. P. Walberg, M. McKee, V. Shkolnikov, L. Chenet and D. Leon, 'Economic change, crime, and mortality crisis in Russia: regional analysis', *British Medical Journal*, vol. 317, 1 August 1998, pp. 312–18.
54. R. Wilkinson, *Unhealthy Societies. The Afflictions of Inequality* (London: Routledge, 1996), p. 15.
55. Shkolnikov and Cornia, 'Population crisis'.
56. Paniccia, 'Transition', passim.
57. D. Bogoyavlensky, V. Shkolnikov and E. Andreev, 'Ethnic differences', in V. Shkolnikov, E. Andreev and T. Maleva (eds), *Neraventsvo i smertnost v Rossii* (Moscow: Carnegie, 2000).
58. For example: UNICEF, *Crisis in Mortality*; Marmot and Bobak, 'Psychosocial and biological mechanisms'; Shkolnikov and Cornia, 'Population crisis'.
59. Marmot and Bobak, 'Psychosocial and biological mechanisms', fig. 6.2, p. 132.
60. Ibid.
61. Shkolnikov and Cornia, 'Population crisis'.
62. Ibid.
63. UNICEF, *Crisis in Mortality*, p. 68.
64. Black Report, 1980, pp. 198–9, reprinted in P. Townsend, N. Davidson and M. Whitehead, *Inequalities in Health* (Harmondsworth: Penguin).
65. P. Townsend, P. Phillimore and A. Beattie, *Health and Deprivation: Inequality and the North* (London and New York: Routledge, 1988), p. 10.
66. To derive material deprivation, Townsend et al. used an 'Overall Deprivation Index' with four components: unemployment, non-ownership of car, non-ownership of house, and overcrowding (ibid.). It should, of course, be immediately pointed out that were a similar index to be calculated for Russia (as well as for other transition economies) the first and fourth components would certainly be legitimate, but the second and third clearly would not given the wide disparities in living standards of the two countries.
67. See W. Cockerham, 'Health lifestyles in Russia', *Social Science and Medicine*, vol. 51, no. 9, 2000, pp. 1313–23; J. Siegrist, 'Place, social exchange and health: proposed sociological framework', *Social Science and Medicine*, vol. 51, no. 9, 2000, pp. 1283–93.
68. Eberstadt has suggested that it is increased individual liberty that has led to higher mortality rates, similar to increased black mortality immediately after emancipation in the 1860s (cited in L. Chen, F. Wittgenstein and E. McKeon, 'The upsurge of mortality in Russia: causes and policy implications', *Population and Development Review*, vol. 22, no. 3, 1996, fn 16). Apart from the mistaken analogy (Russians pre-1992 were not slaves), this seems bizarre. There might be some truth in the suggestion if there

had been, for example, strict prohibition of alcohol prior to the breakup of the Soviet Union followed by its complete liberalisation in 1992, and a sudden upsurge in drinking. But even during Gorbachev's anti-alcohol campaign, alcohol was widely available, increasingly from illicit *samogon* distilling (White, *Russia Goes Dry*, p. 121) with still very high (albeit reduced) levels of consumption (Moskalewicz et al., 'Alcohol as a cause of mortality', table 4.2, p. 91). But, as noted, this campaign had ended by 1988. Indeed, there are simply no significant causes of 'destructive behaviour' related to increased liberty (meaning freedoms) that have led to rising mortality. Even in regard to black mortality post-emancipation, a better explanation is provided by Meeker who argues that life expectancy declined sharply due to an increase in infectious diseases emanating from a decline in health and nutrition of free blacks for reasons of lack of medical care, no land (hence decline in their food production and intake), and poor housing (cited in Cornia, 'Short-term, long-term, and hysteresis mortality models', p. 69).

69. Cockerham, 'Health lifestyles in Russia'.
70. UNICEF, *Crisis in Mortality*, p. 29.
71. *Moscow Times*, 18 July 1998.

CHAPTER 7

1. C. Murray, G. King, A. Lopez, N. Tomijima and E. King, 'Armed conflict as a public health problem', *British Medical Journal*, vol. 324, 9 February 2002, pp. 346–9, provide a very helpful discussion in regard to data problems relating to death and injury inherent in wars.
2. Though we need to remember that developed countries, notably the US, regularly engage in wars outside their own countries, thereby inflicting war-related deaths on their 'enemies'.
3. WHO, *World Report on Violence and Health* (Geneva: WHO, 2002a).
4. UN ECE, *Economic Survey of Europe in 1992–1993* (New York: UN, 1993), p. 10.
5. Cited in L. Nelson and I. Kuzes, *Radical Reform in Yeltsin's Russia: Political, Economic and Social Dimensions* (Armonk, NY and London: M.E. Sharpe, 1995), p. 69.
6. See M. Light, 'Democracy Russian style', *World Today*, vol. 49, no. 11, 1993, pp. 228–31.
7. D. Crouch, 'The crisis in Russia and the rise of the right', *International Socialism*, vol. 66, 1995, p. 17.
8. Arun Mohanty, who was an eye-witness, estimates that as many as 1,300 were killed (personal communication).
9. J. Blasi, M. Kroumova and D. Kruse, *Kremlin Capitalism: The Privatization of the Russian Economy* (Ithaca, NY and London: Cornell University Press, 1997), pp. xvii–xviii; B. Yeltsin, *Midnight Diaries* (London: Weidenfeld and Nicolson, 2000), pp. xiii–xiv.
10. Nelson and Kuzes, *Radical Reform*, p. 40.
11. Light, 'Democracy Russian style'.
12. Cited in K. Krajik, 'Russia's prison meltdown', 2002, MCPR website.

13. V. Abramkin, *In Search of a Solution: Crime, Criminal Policy and Prison Facilities in the Former Soviet Union* (Moscow: MCPR, 1996), p. 32.
14. ICPS, 'Prison brief for Russia', 2002.
15. *Moscow Times*, 1 June 2001. A further shocking fact about these cases is that Putin refused to grant them a pardon.
16. *Russia Journal Daily*, 20 October 2002.
17. See MCPR website, 'work of MCPR', 2002.
18. There was also malnutrition of children living in prison camps with their convicted mothers (ibid.).
19. *BBC Monitoring Former Soviet Union – Political*, 29 June 1999.
20. H. Reyes and R. Conix, 'Pitfalls of tuberculosis programmes in prisons', *British Medical Journal*, vol. 315, November 1997, pp. 1447–50.
21. See Krajick, 'Russia's prison meltdown'.
22. MCPR website.
23. *BBC Monitoring International Reports*, 16 July 2002; *Agence France Presse*, 19 November 1999.
24. Amnesty International, *Annual Report 2002*, 'Russian Federation', Amnesty International website.
25. *Moscow Times*, 29 May 2002.
26. Abramkin, *In Search of a Solution*, p. 41.
27. Official figures for deaths in prisons are extremely difficult to obtain, suggesting that the government has put a D-notice on them.
28. See M. Haynes, *Russia: Class and Power 1917–2000* (London: Bookmarks, 2002), pp. 111–13.
29. Cited in D. Stok (ed.), *Kieslowski on Kieslowski* (London and Boston, MA: Faber and Faber, 1995), p. 160.
30. Yeltsin, *Midnight Diaries*, p. 119.
31. Cited in *Moscow Times*, 29 May 2002.
32. A. Pristavkin, 'Death penalty in Russia', 1998, MCPR website.
33. Amnesty International 'Human rights in the Russian Federation', 2002, Amnesty International website.
34. Russia is also a signatory to the Convention on the Elimination of all Forms of Discrimination against Women. This is farcical given that it does not have a law that recognises domestic violence as a distinct crime. The result is that the incidence of men beating or raping wives is absolutely shocking and an estimated 14,000 (*sic*) women die at the hands of their husbands or relatives each year. Amnesty International, *Annual Report 2002*.
35. Amnesty International, *Annual Report 2002*.
36. *Moscow Times*, 4 June 1999.
37. Ibid., 18 February 2002.
38. *Russia Journal Daily*, 13 March 2002.
39. Cited by T. Ali, in regard to 11 September, in *Clash of Fundamentalisms* (London and New York: Verso, 2002), p. 292.
40. In fact, other parts of the Caucasus have also seen conflict: civil war in Georgia and separatist conflicts in Abkhazia and South Ossetia; war between Armenia and Azerbaijan over the Armenian enclave of Nagorny Karabakh and between Ingushetia and North Ossetia. These have led to tens of thousands killed (see R. Ferguson, 'Chechnya: the empire strikes

back', *International Socialism*, vol. 86, 2000, p. 58) and to the creation of nearly 2 million refugees and internally displaced persons (D. Sammut, 'Population displacement in the Caucasus – an overview', *Central Asian Survey*, vol. 20, no. 1, 2001, p. 55).

41. See R. Seely, *Russo-Chechen Conflict 1800–2000: A Deadly Embrace* (London: Frank Cass, 2001), pp. 202–3. Seely provides an interesting account of the various theories of the Chechen war.

42. B. Fowkes (ed.) *Russia and Chechnya: The Permanent Crisis* (Basingstoke: Palgrave, 1998), p. 13. The chronology of the first Chechen conflict in P. Siren and B. Fowkes, 'An outline chronology of the recent conflict in Chechnya', in Fowkes (ed.) *Russia and Chechnya*, pp. 170–82 provides a very good summary of the key events.

43. See Crouch, 'The crisis in Russia', for a discussion of this.

44. Ferguson, 'Chechnya'.

45. Seely, *Russo-Chechen Conflict*, p. 261.

46. Ibid., pp. 234–5.

47. J. Dunlop, 'How many soldiers and civilians died during the Russo-Chechen war of 1994–96?' *Central Asian Survey*, vol. 19, nos 3–4, 2000, pp. 329–39.

48. Comment made by retired Lieutenant-General Lebed, in ibid., p. 331.

49. Ibid., pp. 335–6.

50. Ibid., p. 337. Dunlop's own estimate for civilian losses is much lower, 'probably exceeding 35,000', though he does not explain how this figure is derived (ibid., p. 338).

51. Cited in ibid., p. 338.

52. Ibid., p. 334.

53. However, Russian ethnographer Valerii Tishkov and Caucus specialist Sergei Arutyanov have accepted such figures (ibid., p. 335).

54. Cited by Seely, *Russo-Chechen Conflict*, p. 308.

55. A. Maskhadov, 'Open letter to the French philosopher Andre Glucksman', *Central Asian Survey*, vol. 19, nos 3–4, 2001, p. 311.

56. See J. Dunlop, 'The forgotten war', *Hoover Digest*, no. 1, 2002a.

57. Personal correspondence with OSCE, October 2002.

58. S. Lambroschini, 'War in Chechnya continues to grind on', *Johnson's Russia List*, no. 5, 16 February 2001.

59. *Die Welt am Sonntag*, 31 October 2002.

60. *Wall Street Journal*, editorial, 4 October 2002.

61. From the confidential dossier compiled by the News Services and Military Expert Advisory group to the German Chancellor's Office cited above in *Die Welt*. Our thanks to Silke Machold for translating this piece.

62. J. Dunlop, 'Chechnya in a new global context', IREX Policy Forum, 4 March 2002b.

63. Human Rights Watch, 'Russian soldiers enter Alkhan-Yurt', 2002, Human Rights Watch website.

64. Amnesty International Report on the Russian Federation, 2002, Amnesty International website.

65. A. Politkovskaya, 'Chechnya: new atrocities exposed', Chechen Republic Online, 28 March 2002. But she also describes extortion on the part of the wahhabis, or Islamist groups, as well as, incredibly enough, of the

collusion between the latter and Russian soldiers, concluding that 'bandits on both sides profit'.

66. A census conducted in Chechnya on 12–13 October 2002 has aroused deep suspicion owing to the provisional results that show the population to be 1.08 million, a figure similar to the prewar estimated one. Given that over 150,000 are likely to have been killed, 300,000 ethnic Russians have left, and that there are 150,000 refugees registered in Ingushetia alone, this far exceeds the expected figure of between 600–800,000. Ruslan Badalov ascribes political motives for this result, implicitly suggesting that the figures have been systematically falsified. See T. Aliev, 'Chechnya population inexplicably swells', *Moscow Times*, 22 October 2002.

67. Ibid.

68. The Goskomstat *Demographic Yearbook of Russia 2001* (Moscow: Goskomstat 2001a) leaves blank spaces for Chechnya. See, for example, tables 5.8 and 6.3, pp. 189, 229.

CHAPTER 8

1. See M. Haynes and R. Husan, 'National Inequality and the Catch-Up Period: Some "Growth Alone" Scenarios', *Journal of Economic Issues*, vol. xxxiv, no. 3, September 2000, pp. 693–705; and M. Haynes and R. Husan, 'Somewhere over the rainbow: the post Soviet transition and the mythical process of convergence', *Post-Communist Economies*, vol. 14, no. 3, September 2002b, pp. 381–98.

2. See M. Haynes and R. Husan, 'Market failure, state failure, institutions, and historical constraints in the East European transition', *Journal of European Area Studies*, vol. 10, no. 1, 2002a, pp. 105–29.

3. R.G. Wilkinson, *Unhealthy Societies. The Afflictions of Inequality* (London: Routledge, 1996), p. 9.

4. Ibid.

5. This also leads Wilkinson to implicitly overestimate some of the earlier mortality improvements in the former USSR.

6. R. Sennett and J. Cobb, *The Hidden Injuries of Class* (London: Faber & Faber, 1993), p. 98.

7. V. Shkolnikov, E. Andreev and T. Maleva (eds), *Neravenstvo i smertnost v Rossii* (Moscow: Carnegie Centre), English summary.

8. Marx (1867), *Capital, Volume 1* (Harmondsworth: Penguin and New Left Review, 1988), p. 742.

9. V.I. Lenin, *State and Revolution* (1917) in *Selected Works*, vol. 2 (Moscow: Progress Publishers, 1977), p. 308.

10. S. Cohen, *Failed Crusade: America and the Tragedy of Post-Communist Russia* (London and New York: W.W. Norton, 2000).

11. Shkolnikov et al. *Neravenstvo*.

12. Wilkinson, *Unhealthy Societies*, p. 6.

13. *Moscow Times*, 4 October 2002.

14. Ibid., 8 April 2000.

15. Ibid., 23 September 2002.

Bibliography

Abramkin, V. (1996) *In Search of a Solution: Crime, Criminal Policy and Prison Facilities in the Former Soviet Union* (Moscow: Moscow Centre for Prison Reform).

Adamec, L.W. (1996) *Dictionary of Afghan Wars, Revolutions and Insurgencies* (London: Scarecrow Press).

Adams, W. (1970) 'The death penalty in Imperial and Soviet criminal law', *American Journal of Comparative Law*, vol. 18, no. 3, pp. 575–94.

Aganbegyan, A. (1987) *The Challenge: Economics of Perestroika* (London: Hutchinson).

Agence France Presse (1999) 19 November.

Alexiyevich, S. (1988) *War's Unwomanly Face* (Moscow: Progress).

Alexiyevich, S. (1992) *Zinky Boys: Soviet Voices from a Forgotten War* (London: Chatto & Windus).

Ali, T. (2002) *Clash of Fundamentalisms* (London and New York: Verso).

Aliev, T. (2002) 'Chechnya population inexplicably swells', *Moscow Times*, 22 October.

Allilueva, S. (1968) *Twenty Letters to a Friend* (Harmondsworth: Penguin).

Amnesty International (2002) *Annual Report 2002*, 'Russian Federation', available at
<www.amnesty.org/web/ar2002.nsf/eur/russian+federation!Open>

Anderson, B.A. and Silver, B.D. (1985) 'Demographic analysis and population catastrophes in the USSR', *Slavic Review*, vol. 44, no. 3, pp. 517–36.

Andreev, E.M., Darskii, L.E. and Kharkova, T.L. (1993) *Naselenie Sovetskogo Soyuza 1922–1991* (Moscow: Nauka).

Andreev, E.M., Darskii, L.E. and Kharkova, T.L. (1998) *Demograficheskaia istoriia Rossii: 1927–1959* (Moscow: Informatika).

Anon. (1922) 'Statistics of the Russian famine since 1891', *Russian Information and Review*, vol. 1, no. 9, 1 February, p. 202.

Arbatov, G. (2001) 'Origins and consequences of "shock therapy"', in L. Klein and M. Pomer (eds), *The New Russia: Transition Gone Awry* (Stanford, CA: Stanford University Press), pp. 171–8.

Ascher, A. (1988) *The Revolution of 1905: Russia in Disarray* (Stanford, CA: Stanford University Press).

Aslund, A. (1995) *How Russia Became a Market Economy* (Washington DC: Brookings Institution).

Barber, J. and Davies, R.W. (1994) 'Employment', in R.W. Davies (ed.), *The Economic Transformation of the Soviet Union, 1913–1945* (Cambridge: Cambridge University Press).

Barber, J. and Harrison, M. (1991) *The Soviet Home Front, 1941–1945* (London: Longman).

Baroian, O.V. (1968) *Itogi poluvekovoi borbi s infektsiiami v SSSR* (Moscow: Meditsina).

Baron, S.H. (2000) *Bloody Saturday in the Soviet Union. Novocherkassk, 1962* (Stanford, CA: Stanford University Press).

Barr, D. and Field, M. (1996) 'The current state of health care in the former Soviet Union: implications for health care policy and reform', *American Journal of Public Health*, vol. 86, no. 3, pp. 307–11.

Bartov, O. (1991) *Hitler's Army: Soldiers, Nazis, and War in the Third Reich* (New York and Oxford: Oxford University Press).

BBC Monitoring Former Soviet Union – Political (1999) 29 June.

BBC Monitoring International Reports (2002) 16 July.

Benz, W. (2000) *The Holocaust. A Short History* (London: Profile Books).

Berg, G.P. van den (1983) 'The Soviet Union and the death penalty', *Soviet Studies*, vol. 35, no. 2, pp. 154–74.

Berg, G.P. van den (1985) *The Soviet System of Justice: Figures and Policy* (Dordrecht: Martinus Nijhoff).

Bergson, A. (1961) *The Real National Income of Soviet Russia Since 1928* (Cambridge, MA: Harvard University Press).

Black Report (1980) (*Report of the Working Group on Inequalities in Health*) Reprinted in P. Townsend, N. Davidson and M. Whitehead (1988), *Inequalities in Health* (Harmondsworth: Penguin).

Blasi, J., Kroumova, M. and Kruse, D. (1997) *Kremlin Capitalism: The Privatization of the Russian Economy* (Ithaca, NY, and London: Cornell University Press).

Blum, A. (1994) *Naître, Vivre et Mourir en URSS, 1917–1991* (Paris: Plon).

Bobak, M. and Marmot, M. (1996) 'East–West mortality divide and its potential explanations; proposed research agenda', *British Medical Journal*, vol. 312, 17 February, pp. 421–5.

Bogomolov, O. (2001) 'Neoliberalism', in L. Klein and M. Pomer (eds), *The New Russia: Transition Gone Awry* (Stanford, CA: Stanford University Press), pp. 53–9.

Bogoyavlensky, D., Shkolnikov, V. and Andreev, E. (2000) 'Ethnic differences', in V. Shkolnikov, E. Andreev and T. Maleva (eds), *Neraventsvo i smertnost v Rossii* (Moscow: Carnegie).

Bolshaia sovetskaia entsklopediia (1926) 'Amenorrhea', vol. 2 (Moscow), p. 398.

Bordygov, G. (1995) 'The policy and regime of extraordinary measures in Russia under Lenin and Stalin', *Europe-Asia Studies*, vol. 47, no. 4, June, pp. 615–32.

Borokhod, D.Z. (1990) 'Obrazovanie i prodolzhitelnost zhizni gorozhan Kazakhstan', *Sotsiologicheskie issledovaniia*, no. 9, pp. 98–101.

Brainerd, E. (2001) 'Economic reform and mortality in the former Soviet Union: a study of the suicide epidemic in the 1990s', *European Economic Review*, vol. 45, pp. 1007–19.

Brokhin, Y. (1976) *Hustling on Gorky Street. Sex and Crime in Russia Today* (London: W.H. Allen).

Bulgakov, M. (1975) *A Country Doctor's Notebook* (London: Collins).

Buttino, M. (1990) 'Study of the economic crisis and depopulation of Turkestan, 1917–1920', *Central Asian Survey*, vol. 9, no. 4.

Buttino, M. (1998) 'Economic relations between Russia and Turkestan, 1914–1918, or How to start a famine', in J. Pallot (ed.), *Transforming Peasants* (Basingstoke: Macmillan).

Cairns, J. (1975) 'The cancer problem', *Scientific American,* vol. 233, no. 5, pp. 51–9.

Charlton, M. (1984) *The Eagle and the Small Birds. Crisis in the Soviet Empire From Yalta to Solidarity* (London: British Broadcasting Corporation).

Chen, L.C, Kleinman, A. and Ware, N.C. (eds) (1994) *Health and Social Change in International Perspective* (Boston, MA: Harvard School of Public Health).

Chen, L., Wittgenstein, F. and McKeon, E. (1996) 'The upsurge of mortality in Russia: causes and policy implications', *Population and Development Review,* vol. 22, no. 3, pp. 517–30.

Chinn, J. (1981) 'The aging Soviet society', in H. Desfosses (ed.), *Soviet Population Policy. Conflicts and Constraints* (Oxford: Pergamon).

Chuev, F. (1993) *Molotov Remembers* (Chicago, IL: Ivan R. Dee).

Clarke, S. (1999) *The Formation of a Labour Market in Russia* (Cheltenham: Edward Elgar).

Clarke, S., Fairbrother, P. and Borisov, V. (1995) *The Workers' Movement in Russia* (Cheltenham: Edward Elgar).

Clem, R.S. (ed.) (1986) *Research Guide to the Russian and Soviet Censuses* (Ithaca, NY: Cornell University Press).

Cockerham, W.C. (1999) *Health and Social Change in Russia and Eastern Europe* (London and New York: Routledge).

Cockerham, W.C (2000) 'Health lifestyles in Russia', *Social Science and Medicine,* vol. 51, no. 9, pp. 1313–23.

Cohen, S. (1974) *Bukharin and the Bolshevik Revolution. A Political Biography* (London: Wildwood House).

Cohen, S. (2000) *Failed Crusade: America and the Tragedy of Post-Communist Russia* (London and New York: W.W. Norton).

Cornia, G. (2000) 'Short-term, long-term, and hysteresis mortality models: a review', in G. Cornia and R. Paniccia (eds), *The Mortality Crisis in Transitional Economies* (Oxford: Oxford University Press), pp. 59–80.

Cornia, G. and Paniccia, R. (2000a) 'The transition mortality crisis: evidence, interpretation and policy responses', in G. Cornia and R. Paniccia (eds), *The Mortality Crisis in Transitional Economies* (Oxford: Oxford University Press).

Cornia, G. and Paniccia, R. (eds) (2000b) *The Mortality Crisis in Transitional Economies* (Oxford: Oxford University Press).

Courtois, S., Werth, N. et al. (1998) *The Black Book of Communism* (Cambridge, MA: Harvard University Press).

Crouch, D. (1995) 'The crisis in Russia and the rise of the right', *International Socialism,* vol. 66, pp. 3–53.

Davies, R.W., Harrison, M. and Wheatcroft, S. (1994) *The Economic Transformation of the Soviet Union, 1913–1945* (Cambridge: Cambridge University Press).

Davies. S. (1997) *Popular Opinion in Stalin's Russia, 1934–1941* (Cambridge: Cambridge University Press).

Davis, C. (1983) 'Economic problems of the Soviet health service', *Soviet Studies,* vol. xxxv, no. 3, pp. 343–61.

Davis, C. (2001) 'The health sector: illness, medical care, and mortality', in B. Granville and P. Oppenheimer (eds), *Russia's Post-Communist Economy* (Oxford: Oxford University Press).

Dennis, M. (2000) *The Rise and Fall of the GDR 1945–1990* (London: Longman).

Deutscher, I. (1966) *Stalin* (Harmondsworth: Penguin).

Die Welt am Sonntag, 'Der verlorene Krieg', 31 October 2002.

Dillon, E.J. (1987) 'The first Russian census', *Contemporary Review*, vol. lxxii, no. 6, December.

Djilas, M. (1969) *Conversations with Stalin* (Harmondsworth: Penguin).

Dobreitsera, I.A. (1923) 'Bor'ba s epidemiiami', in *Piat' let sovetskoi meditsini 1918–1923* (Moscow: RSFSR Narodnuii Komissariat Zdravookhraneiya), pp. 121–30.

Dunlop, J. (2000) 'How many soldiers and civilians died during the Russo-Chechen war of 1994–96?' *Central Asian Survey*, vol. 19, nos 3–4, pp. 329–39.

Dunlop, J. (2002a) 'The forgotten war', *Hoover Digest*, no. 1, available at <www.hoover.stanford.edu/publications/digest/021/dunlop.html>

Dunlop, J. (2002b) 'Chechnya in a new global context', IREX Policy Forum, 4 March, available at <www.irex.org/publications-resources/policy-papers/Chechnya-forum.pdf>

Eberstadt, N. (1990) 'Health and mortality in Eastern Europe, 1965–85', *Communist Economies*, vol. 2, no. 3, pp. 347–71.

Eberstadt, N. (1994) 'Health and mortality in Central and Eastern Europe: retrospect and prospect', in J.R. Miller and S.L. Wolchik (eds), *The Social Legacy of Communism* (Cambridge: Cambridge University Press), pp. 196–225.

Ellman, M. (1991) 'A note on the number of 1933 famine victims', *Soviet Studies*, vol. 43, no. 2, pp. 375–9.

Ellman, M. (1992) 'On sources: a note', *Soviet Studies*, vol. 44, no. 5, pp. 913–15.

Ellman, M. (2000a) 'The 1947 Soviet famine and the entitlement approach to famines', *Cambridge Journal of Economics*, vol. 24, no. 5, pp. 603–30.

Ellman, M. (2000b) 'The social costs and consequences of the transformation process', in UN ECE, *Economic Survey of Europe*, nos 2–3, ch. 5.

Ellman, M. (2002) 'Soviet repression statistics: some comments', *Europe-Asia Studies*, vol. 54, no. 7, pp. 1151–72.

Ellman, M. and Maksudov, S. (1994) 'Soviet deaths in the Great Patriotic War: a note', *Europe-Asia Studies*, vol. 46, no. 4, pp. 671–80.

Entsiklopedicheskii slovar (1899) (St Petersburg: Brokhaus & Efron) vol. 27, 'Rossiia'.

European Bank for Reconstruction and Development (EBRD) (2000) *Transition Report 2000* (London: EBRD).

European Bank for Reconstruction and Development (EBRD) (2001) *Transition Report 2001* (London: EBRD).

European Bank for Reconstruction and Development (EBRD) (2002) *Transition Report 2002* (London: EBRD).

Eyer, J. and Sterling, P. (1977) 'Stress related mortality and social organisation', *Review of Radical Political Economy*, vol. 9, no. 1, spring, pp. 1–44.

Ferguson, R. (2000) 'Chechnya: the empire strikes back', *International Socialism*, vol. 86, pp. 51–69.

Fesbach, M. (1983) 'Issues in Soviet health problems'. US Congress Joint Economic Committee, *Soviet Economy in the 1980s: Problems and Prospects*, Part 2 (Washington DC: US Government Printing House).

Fesbach, M. and Friendly, A., Jr (1992) *Ecocide in the USSR* (New York: Basic Books).

Field, M. (1994) 'Post Communism medicine: morbidity, mortality and the deteriorating health situation', in J.R. Miller and S.L. Wolchik (eds), *The Social Legacy of Communism* (Cambridge: Cambridge University Press), pp. 178–95.

Field, M. (1995) 'The health crisis in the former Soviet Union: a report from the "post-war" zone', *Social Science and Medicine*, vol. 41, no. 11, pp. 1469–78.

Fisher, H.H. (1927) *The Famine in Soviet Russia, 1919–1923: The Operations of the American Relief Administration* (New York: Macmillan Co.).

Forster, D.P. (1992) 'Income distribution and life expectancy', *British Medical Journal*, vol. 304, 14 March, pp. 715–16.

Fowkes, B. (ed.) (1998) *Russia and Chechnya: the Permanent Crisis* (Basingstoke: Macmillan).

Freeze, G. (1988) *From Supplication to Revolution. Documentary Social History of Imperial Russia* (New York: Oxford University Press).

Frieden, N. (1981) *Russian Physicians in an Era of Reform and Revolution, 1856–1905* (Princeton, NJ: Princeton University Press).

Friedman, G.A. (1911) 'Recollections of cholera epidemics in Russia', *Medical Record* (New York), 19 August.

Galichenko, N. (1991) *Glasnost Soviet Cinema Responds* (Austin: University of Texas Press).

Gatrell, P. (2001) 'Refugees in the Russian Empire, 1914–1917. Population displacement and social identity', in E. Acton (ed.), *Critical Companion to the Russian Revolution, 1914–1921* (London: Edward Arnold).

Gavrilova, I.N. (2001) *Naselenie Moskvy: istoricheskii rakurs* (Moscow: Mosgoarkhiv).

Gavrilova, N., Semyonova, V., Evdokushkina, G. and Gavrilov, L. (2000) 'The response of violent mortality to economic crisis in Russia', *Population Research and Policy Review*, vol. 19, no. 5, pp. 397–419.

Geller, I.M. (1989) 'Uroven obrazovania kak faktor prodolzhitelnosti zhizni', *Demograficheskie issledovaniia*, vol. 13, pp. 101–8.

Getty, J.A. and Manning, R.T. (1994) *Stalinist Terror: New Perspectives* (Cambridge: Cambridge University Press).

Getty, J.A., Rittersporn, G.T. and Zemskov, V.N. (1993) 'Victims of the Soviet penal system in the pre-war years: a first approach on the basis of archival evidence', *American Historical Review*, vol. 98, no. 4, pp. 1017–49.

Glinkina, S., Grigoriev, A. and Yakobidze, V. (2001) 'Crime and corruption', in L. Klein and M. Pomer (eds), *The New Russia: Transition Gone Awry* (Stanford, CA: Stanford University Press), pp. 233–49.

Glover, J. (1999) *Humanity: A Moral History of the Twentieth Century* (London: Jonathan Cape).

Goldman, M. (1996) *Lost Opportunity: What has Made Economic Reform in Russia so Difficult* (London and New York: W.W. Norton).

Goskomstat (1998) *Naselenie Rossii za 100 let (1897–1997)* (Moscow: Goskomstat).

Goskomstat (2000) *Rossiiskii Statisticheskii Ezehgodnik 2000* (Moscow: Goskomstat).

Goskomstat (2001a) *Demographic Yearbook of Russia 2001* (Moscow: Goskomstat).

Goskomstat (2001b) *Handbook Russia 2001*, available at <www.gks.ru/scripts/eng/1c.exe?XXXX09F.3.1/010090R>

Goskomstat (2002) *Russia in Figures 2002* (on CD-ROM) (Moscow: Goskomstat).

Granville, J. (1997) 'In the line of fire: the Soviet crackdown on Hungary, 1956–57', *Journal of Communist Studies and Transition Politics*, vol. 13, no. 2, June, pp. 67–107.

Gregory, P.R. (1982) *Russian National Income, 1885–1913* (Cambridge: Cambridge University Press).

Grey, F. du Plessix (1991) *Soviet Women. Walking the Tightrope* (London: Virago).

Gustaffson, T. (1999) *Capitalism Russian-Style* (Cambridge: Cambridge University Press).

Haines, M.R. (1995) 'Socio-economic differentials in infant and child mortality during mortality decline: England and Wales 1890–1911', *Population Studies*, vol. 49, no. 2, July, pp. 297–315.

Harrison, M. (2001) 'Providing for defence', in P. Gregory (ed.), *Behind the Facade of Stalin's Command Economy* (Stanford, CA: Hoover Institution), pp. 81–100.

Haynes, M. (1998) 'The debate on popular violence and the Popular Movement in the Russian Revolution', *Historical Materialism*, no. 2, summer, pp. 185–214.

Haynes, M. (2002) *Russia: Class and Power 1917–2000* (London: Bookmarks).

Haynes, M. (2003) 'Counting Soviet deaths in the Great Patriotic War: a note', *Europe-Asia Studies*, vol. 55, no. 2, pp. 303–9.

Haynes, M. and Husan, R. (2000) 'National inequality and the catch-up period: some "growth alone" scenarios', *Journal of Economic Issues*, vol. xxxiv, no. 3, September, pp. 693–705.

Haynes, M. and Husan, R. (2002a) 'Market failure, state failure, institutions, and historical constraints in the East European transition', *Journal of European Area Studies*, vol. 10, no. 1, pp. 105–29.

Haynes, M. and Husan, R. (2002b) 'Somewhere over the rainbow: the post Soviet transition and the mythical process of convergence', *Post-Communist Economies,* vol. 14, no. 3, September, pp. 381–98.

Haynes, M. and Husan, R. (2002c) 'Whether by visible or invisible hand: the intractable problem of Russian and East European catch-up', *Competition and Change*, vol. 6, no. 3, pp. 269–87.

Hearst, D. (1996) 'Propping up the President', *Guardian*, 18 July.

Hedlund, S. (1999) *Russia's 'Market' Economy: A Bad Case of Predatory Capitalism* (London: UCL Press).

Heenan, L.E. (1987) *Russian Democracy's Fatal Blunder. The Summer Offensive of 1917* (London: Praeger).

Heer, D.M. (1966) 'The demographic transition in the Russian Empire and the Soviet Union', *Journal of Social History*, vol. 1, no. 3, pp. 193–240.

Heinamaa, A. (1994) *The Soldiers Story: Soviet Veterans Remember the Afghan War* (Berkley, CA: University of California Press).

Herlihy, P. (1978) 'Death in Odessa: a study of population movements in a nineteenth century city', *Journal of Urban History*, vol. 4, no. 4, pp. 417–42.

Heretz L. (1997) 'The pyschology of the White Movement', in V.N. Brovkin (ed.), *The Bolsheviks in Russian Society. The Revolution and The Civil Wars* (New Haven, CT: Yale University Press).

Hindenburg, P. Von (1920) *Out of My Life* (London: Cassell & Co.).

Hoch, S. (1998) 'Famine, disease and mortality patterns in the parish of Borshevka, Russia, 1830–1912', *Population Studies*, vol. 52, pp. 357–68.

Hoffman, D. (2002) *The Oligarchs: Wealth and Power in the New Russia* (Oxford: Public Affairs).

Howard, M. (1983) *Clausewitz* (Oxford: Oxford University Press).

Huff, D. (1991) *How to Lie with Statistics* (London: Penguin).

Human Rights Watch (2000) 'No happiness remains: civilian killings, pillage, and rape in Alkhan-Yurt, Chechnya', available at <www.hrw.org/reports/2000/russia_chechnya2/>

Husan, R. (1996) 'Reflections on the significance of market failures in Eastern Europe', *Review of Policy Issues*, vol. 2, no. 1, pp. 81–8.

Hutchinson, J.F. (1980), 'Science, politics and the alcohol problem in post-1905 Russia', *Slavonic and East European Review*, vol. 58, no. 2, April, pp. 232–54.

Hutchinson, J.F. (1990) *Politics and Public Health in Revolutionary Russia, 1890–1918* (Baltimore, MD: Johns Hopkins University Press).

International Centre for Prison Studies (ICPS) (2002) *World Prison Brief*, 'Highest prison population rates' and 'Prison brief for Russia', available at <www.kcl.ac.uk/depsta/rel/icps/worldbrief/europe_records.php?code=43>

Kahn, A. (1967) 'Government policies and the industrialisation of Russia', *Journal of Economic History*, vol. 27, no. 4, December, pp. 460–77.

Kahn, A. (1968) 'Natural calamities and their effect on the food supply in Russia', *Jahrbucher für Geschicte Osteuropas*, vol. 16, pp. 353–77.

Kerblay, B. (1983) *Contemporary Soviet Society* (London: Methuen).

Khalidi, N.A. (1991) 'Afghanistan: demographic consequences of war 1978–1987', *Central Asian Survey*, vol. 10, no. 3, pp. 101–25.

Khlopin G. and Erisman, F. (1899) 'Meditsina i narodnoe zdravie v Rossii', in *Entsiklopedicehskii slovar*, vol. 27, pp. 214–27.

Khromov, B.M. and Sveshnikov, A.V. (1969) *Zdravookranenie Leningrada* (Leningrad: Lenizdat).

Khrushchov (sic) N.S. (1961) *Report on the Programme of the Communist Party of the Soviet Union and reply to discussion* (London: Soviet Booklets).

Kingkade, W.W. (1991) 'Soviet mortality by cause of death: an analysis of years of potential life lost', in W. Lutz, S. Scherbov and A. Volkov (eds), *Demographic Trends and Patterns in the Soviet Union Before 1991* (London: Routledge).

Klein, L. and Pomer, M. (eds) (2001) *The New Russia: Transition Gone Awry* (Stanford, CA: Stanford University Press).

Klugman, J., Micklewright, J. and Redmond, G. (2002) *Poverty in the Transition: Social Expenditures and the Working-Age Poor*, Innocenti Working Paper No. 91 (Florence: UNICEF).

Koenker, D. (1985) 'Urbanisation and deurbanisation in the Russian revolution and civil war', *Journal of Modern History*, vol. 57, no. 3, September.

Kohn, S. (1932) *The Cost of the War to Russia. The Vital Statistics of European Russia during the World War, 1914–1917* (New Haven, CT: Yale University Press).

Konovalov, V. (1989) 'Legacy of the Afghan war: some statistics', *Radio Liberty Report on the USSR*, vol. 1, no. 14, 7 April, pp. 1–3.

Krajick, K. (2001) 'Russia's prison meltdown', Moscow Centre for Prison Reform (MCPR) website at <www.prison.org/english/article1.htm>

Krementsov, N. (2001) 'The war on cancer and the Cold War: a Soviet case', in I. Löwy and J. Krige (eds), *Images of Disease. Science, Public Policy and Health in Post-War Europe* (Luxembourg: European Communities).

Krivosheev, G.F. (2001) *Rossiia i SSSR v voinakh XX veka. Poteri vooruzhennuikh sil. Statisticheskoe issledovanie* (Moscow: Olma-Press).

Lambroschini, S. (2001) 'War in Chechnya continues to grind on', *Johnson's Russia List*, no. 5, 16 February.

Lane, D. (1991) *Soviet Society under Perestroika* (London: Unwin Hyman).

Lapina, A.I. (1969) *Organizatsiia borbui s tuberkulezom v SSSR* (Moscow: Meditsina).

League of Nations (1922) *Report on Economic Conditions in Russia* (Geneva: League of Nations).

Lebedeva, N.S. (1996) 'Chetvertuii razdel Polshi i Katuinskaia tragediia', in Y. Afanasiev (ed.), *Drugaia voina 1939–1945* (Moscow: Rossiskii Gosudarstvennuii Gumantitarnuii Universitet).

Leitzel, J, (1995) *Russian Economic Reform* (London and New York: Routledge).

Lenin, V.I. (1917) *State and Revolution*, in *Selected Works*, vol. 2 (Moscow: Progress Publishers, 1977).

Lenin, V.I. (1965) *Collected Works* (Moscow: Foreign Languages Publishing House).

Leon, D., Chenet, L., Shkolnikov, V., Zakharov, S., Shapiro, J., Rakhmanova, G., Vassin, S. and McKee, M. (1997) 'Huge variation in Russian mortality rates 1984–94: artefact, alcohol, or what?', *The Lancet*, vol. 350, 9 August, pp. 383–8.

Leslie, R.F. (1980) *The History of Poland Since 1863* (Cambridge: Cambridge University Press).

Lewontin, R.C. (1991) *The Doctrine of DNA: Biology as Ideology* (London: Penguin).

Light, M. (1993) 'Democracy Russian style', *World Today*, vol. 49, no. 11, pp. 228–31.

Lincoln, W.B. (1994) *In War's Dark Shadow. The Russians Before the Great War* (New York and Oxford: Oxford University Press).

Lisitsin, Y. (1972) *Health Protection in the USSR* (Moscow: Progress).

Lorimer, F. (1946) *The Population of the Soviet Union: History and Prospects* (Geneva: League of Nations).

Lutz, W., Scherbov, S. and Volkov, A. (1994) *Demographic Trends and Patterns in the Soviet Union Before 1991* (London: Routledge).

Lyudskie poteri SSSR v Velikoi Otechestvennoi Voine (1995) (St Petersburg: RAN).

McKay, R. (ed.) (1991) *Letters to Gorbachev. Life in Russia Through the Postbag of Argumenty i Fakty* (London: Michael Joseph).

McKee, M. and Britton, A. (1998) 'The positive relationship between alcohol and heart disease in eastern Europe: potential physiological mechanisms', *Journal of the Royal Society of Medicine*, vol. 91, no. 12, pp. 402–7.

Maddison, A. (2001) *The World Economy: A Millennial Perspective* (Paris: OECD).

Maksudov, S. (1989) *Poteri naseleniia SSSR* (Benson, VT: Chalidze Publishers).

Mandelstam, N. (1971) *Hope Against Hope: A Memoir* (London: Collins & Harvill).

Marchenko, A. (1971) *My Testimony*, trans. M. Scammell (Harmondsworth: Penguin).

Markuzon, F.D. (1955) 'Sanitarnaia statistika v gorodakh predrevolutsionnoi Rossii', in A.B. Burtakov (ed.), *Ocherki po istorii statistiki SSSR* (Moscow: Gosurdarstvennoe statisticheskoe izdatelstvo).

Marmot, M. and Bobak, M. (2000) 'Psychosocial and biological mechanisms behind the recent mortality crisis in Central and Eastern Europe', in G. Cornia and R. Paniccia (eds), *The Mortality Crisis in Transitional Economies* (Oxford: Oxford University Press), pp. 127–48.

Marx, K. (1867) *Capital, Volume 1* (Harmondsworth: Penguin and New Left Review, 1988).

Maskhadov, A. (2001) 'Open letter to the French philosopher Andre Glucksman', *Central Asian Survey*, vol. 19, nos 3–4, pp. 309–14.

Mawdsley, E. (1998) *The Stalin Years. The Soviet Union 1929–1953* (Manchester: Manchester University Press).

Mayer, A. (2000) *The Furies. Violence and Terror in the French and Russian Revolutions* (Princeton, NJ: Princeton University Press).

Maylunas, A. and Mironenko, S. (1996) *A Life Long Passion. Nicholas and Alexandra. Their Own Story* (London: Weidenfeld and Nicolson).

Medvedev, R. (1982) *Khrushchev* (Oxford: Blackwell).

Medvedev, Z. (1989) *Nuclear Disaster in the Urals*, trans. G. Saunders (New York: Viking Press).

Merridale, C. (2000) *Night of Stone. Death and Memory in Russia* (London: Granta).

Meslé, F. et al. (1996) *Tendances récentes de la mortalité par cause en Russie 1965–1994* (Paris: INED).

Mezentseva, E. and Rimachevskaya, N. (1990) 'The Soviet Country profile: health of the USSR population in the 70s and 80s – an approach to comprehensive analysis', *Social Science and Medicine*, vol. 31, no. 8, pp. 867–77.

Mikhalev, V. (2001) 'Poverty and social assistance', in L. Klein and M. Pomer (eds), *The New Russia: Transition Gone Awry* (Stanford, CA: Stanford University Press), pp. 251–68.

Milanovic, B. (1998) *Income, Inequality, and Poverty During the Transition from Planned to Market Economy* (Washington: World Bank), available at <www.worldbank.org/research/transition/pdf/BrankoEd3.pdf>

Mironov, B.N. (1999) 'New approaches to old problems: the well-being of the population of Russia from 1871 to 1910 as measured by physical stature', *Slavic Review*, vol. 58, no. 1, spring, pp. 1–26.

Moiseenko, V.M. (ed.) (1992) *Naselenie Moskvy: proshloe, nastoyashchee, budushchee* (Moscow: Moscow University Press).

Moskalenko, M. (1990) 'Beria's arrest: from the unpublished memoirs of Marshall Moskalenko', *Moscow News*, no. 23, pp. 8–9.

Moscow Centre for Prison Reform (MCPR) (2002) Available at <www.prison.org/english/index.htm>

Moscow Times (1999) 4 June.

Moscow Times (2001) 1 June.

Moscow Times (2002) 18 February; 16 May; 29 May, 13 September.

Moskalevicz, J., Wojtyniak, B. and Rabczenko, D. (2000) 'Alcohol as a cause of mortality in societies undergoing rapid transition to market economy', in G. Cornia and R. Paniccia (eds), *The Mortality Crisis in Transitional Economies* (Oxford: Oxford University Press), pp. 83–104.

Moskoff, W. (1990) *The Bread of Affliction: The Food Supply in the USSR During World War II* (Cambridge: Cambridge University Press).

Murray, C., King, G., Lopez, A., Tomijima, N. and Krug, E. (2002) 'Armed conflict as a public health problem', *British Medical Journal*, vol. 324, 9 February, pp. 346–9.

Murrell, P. and Olson, O. (1991) 'The Devolution of Centrally Planned Economies', *Journal of Comparative Economics*, vol. 15, June, pp. 239–65.

Narodnoe khoziastvo v1987g (1987) (Moscow: Finansy i statisitika).

Narodnoe khoziastvo v1989g (1989) (Moscow: Finansy i statisitika).

Naselenie Rossii v XX veke. Istoricheskie ocherki tom 1. 1900–1939 (2000) (Moscow: Rosspen).

Naselenie Rossii v XX veke. Istoricheskie ocherki tom 2. 1940–1959 (2001) (Moscow: Rosspen).

Nelson, L. and Kuzes, I. (1995) *Radical Reform in Yeltsin's Russia: Political, Economic and Social Dimensions* (Armonk, NY and London: M.E. Sharpe).

Novoselskii, S.A. (1958) *Voprosy demograficheskoi i sanitarnoi statistiki* (Moscow: Medgiz).

Ocherki istorii Tumenskoi oblasti (1994) (Tumen: Komitet po pechati i massovoi informatsii administratsii Tumenskoi oblasti).

Ofer, G. (1987) 'Soviet economic growth 1928–1985', *Journal of Economic Literature*, vol. xxv, no. 2, December.

Orlov, S. (2001) 'The Medicalised Sobering stations: a history of a unique Soviet practice', in I. Löwy and J. Krige (eds), *Images of Disease. Science, Public Policy and Health in Post-War Europe* (Luxembourg: European Communities).

Paniccia, R. (2000) 'Transition, impoverishment, and mortality: how large an impact?', in G. Cornia and R. Paniccia (eds), *The Mortality Crisis in Transitional Economies* (Oxford: Oxford University Press).

Patterson, K.D. (1993) 'Typhus and its control in Russia 1870–1940', *Medical History*, vol. 37, pp. 361–81.

Phillips, L.L. (1997) 'Message in a bottle: working class culture and the struggle for revolutionary legitimacy, 1900–1929', *The Russian Review*, vol. 56, January, pp. 25–43.

Pilger, J. (1992) *Distant Voices* (London: Vintage).

Polanyi, K. (1944) *The Great Transformation* (Boston, MA: Beacon Hill, 1957).

Polian, P. (2001) *He po cvoei vole ... Istoriia i geografiia preinuditelnostuikh migratsii v SSSR* (Moscow: OGI-Memorial).

Politkovskaya, A. (2002) 'Chechnya: new atrocities exposed', Chechen Republic Online, 28 March, at <www.amina.com/article/loot.html>

Pomer, M. (2001) 'Introduction', in L. Klein and M. Pomer (eds), *The New Russia: Transition Gone Awry* (Stanford, CA: Stanford University Press), pp. 1–18.

Pristavkin, A. (1998) 'Death penalty in Russia', available at Moscow Centre for Prison Reform (MCPR) website at <www.prison.org/english/index.htm>

Prowse, M. (2002) 'Is inequality good for you?', *Financial Times*, 7/8 December.

Radzinsky, E. (1996) *Stalin* (London: Sceptre).

Ransome, A. (1928) 'Russia', *Encyclopedia Britannica*, 12th edition (new vol. 3) (London: Encyclopedia Britannica Company Ltd), pp. 408–28.

Rashin, A.G. (1956) *Naselenie Rossii za 100 let* (Moscow: Gostatizdat).

Ratkovskii, I.S. and Khodiakov, M.V. (2001) *Istoriia Sovietskoi Rossii* (St Petersburg: Lan).

Reyes, H. and Conix, R. (1997) 'Pitfalls of tuberculosis programmes in prisons', *British Medical Journal*, vol. 315, 29 November, pp. 1447–50.

Rimlinger, G. (1961) 'The trade union in Soviet social insurance: historical development and present functions', *International and Labor Relations Review*, vol. 14, no. 3.

Rimlinger, G. (1971) *Welfare Policy and Industrialisation in Europe, America and Russia* (Chichester: John Wiley).

Robbins, RG., Jr (1975) *Famine in Russia* (New York: Columbia University Press).

Rosefielde, S. (1996) 'Stalinism in post-communist perspective: new evidence on killings, forced labour and economic growth in the 1930s', *Europe-Asia Studies*, vol. 48, no. 6, pp. 959–87.

Rosefielde, S. (2001) 'Premature deaths: Russia's radical economic transition in Soviet perspective', *Europe-Asia Studies*, vol. 53, no. 8, pp. 1159–76.

Russia Journal Daily (2002) 13 March, 20 October, available at

Rutland, P. (1990) 'Labour movements and unrest', *Soviet Economy*, vol. 6, no. 3, winter, pp. 345–84.

Ryan, M. (1995) 'Russian report: alcoholism and rising mortality in the Russian Federation', *British Medical Journal*, vol. 310, 11 March, pp. 648–50.

Sammut, D. (2001) 'Population displacement in the Caucasus – an overview', *Central Asian Survey*, vol. 20, no. 1, pp. 55–62.

Scherer, J.L. and Jakobson, M. (1993) 'The collectivisation of agriculture and the Soviet prison camp system', *Europe-Asia Studies*, vol. 45, no. 3, pp. 533–46.

Schwartz, L. (1986) 'A history of Russian and Soviet censuses', in R.M. Clem (ed.), *Research Guide to the Russian Censuses* (London: Cornell University Press).

Seely, R. (2001) *Russo-Chechen Conflict 1800–2000: A Deadly Embrace* (London: Frank Cass).

Semashko, N.A. (1946) 'Friedrich Erismann. The dawn of Russian hygiene and public health', *Bulletin of the History of Medicine*, vol. xx, no. 1, pp. 1–5.

Sen, A. (1981) *Poverty and Famines: An Essay on Entitlement and Deprivation* (Oxford: Oxford University Press).

Sen, A. (1993) 'The economics of life and death', *Scientific American*, May.

Sennett, R. and Cobb, J. (1993) *The Hidden Injuries of Class* (London: Faber & Faber).

Serge, V. (1996) *Russia Twenty Years After* (New York: Humanities Press).

Service, R. (1991) *The Russian Revolution 1900–1917*, second edition (Basingstoke: Macmillan).

Shelley, L.I. (1996) *Policing Soviet Society. The Evolution of State Control* (London: Routledge).

Shkolnikov, V., Andreev, E. and Maleva, T. (eds) (2000) *Neravenstvo i smertnost v Rossii* (Moscow: Carnegie Centre).

Shkolnikov, V. and Cornia, G. (2000) 'Population crisis and rising mortality in transitional Russia', in G. Cornia and R. Paniccia (eds), *The Mortality Crisis in Transitional Economies* (Oxford: Oxford University Press), pp. 253–79.

Shkolnikov, V., Leon, D., Adamets, S., Andreev, E. and Deev, A. (1998) 'Education level and adult mortality in Russia: an analysis of routine data 1979 to 1994', *Social Science and Medicine*, vol. 47, no. 3, pp. 357–69.

Shkolnikov, V. and McKee, M. (2001) 'Understanding the toll of premature death among men in Eastern Europe', *British Medical Journal*, vol. 323, 3 November, pp. 1051–5.

Shkolnikov, V., McKee, M. and Leon, D. (2001) 'Changes in life expectancy in Russia in the mid-1990s', *The Lancet*, vol. 357, 24 March, pp. 917–21.

Shkolnikov, V., Meslé, F. and Vallin, J. (1996) 'Health Crisis in Russia. I. Recent Trends in Life Expectancy and Causes of Death from 1970 to 1993'; 'II. Changes in causes of death: a comparison with France and England and Wales (1970 to 1993)', *Population: An English Selection*, vol. 8, pp. 123–54.

Siegrist, J. (2000) 'Place, social exchange and health: proposed sociological framework', *Social Science and Medicine*, vol. 51, no. 9, pp. 1283–93.

Simonov, N.S. (2000) 'Mobpodgotovka: mobilisation planning in inter-war industry', in J. Barber and M. Harriosn (eds), *The Soviet Defence-Industry Complex from Stalin to Khrushchev* (London and Basingstoke: Macmillan), pp. 205–22.

Siren, P. and Fowkes, B. (1998) 'An outline chronology of the recent conflict in Chechnya', in B. Fowkes (ed.), *Russia and Chechnya: the Permanent Crisis* (Basingstoke: Macmillan), pp. 170–82.

Sivard, R. Leger (1987) *World Military and Social Expenditures 1987–1988* (Washington DC: World Priorities).

Sliwinski, M. (1988–89) 'The decimation of Afghanistan', *Orbis*, vol. 33, no. 1, winter, pp. 39–56.

Smith, G.B. (1988) *Soviet Politics: Continuity and Contradiction* (Basingstoke: Macmillan).

Smith, R.E.F. and Christian, D. (1984) *Bread and Salt: A Social and Economic History of Food and Drink in Russia* (Cambridge: Cambridge University Press).

Solovev, Z.P. (1940) *Voprosii zdravookhrareniia* (Moscow: Gosizdat).

Solzhenitsyn, A. (1972) 'How people read *One Day*: A survey of letters', in L. Labedz (ed.), *Solzhenitsyn. A Documentary Record* (London: Penguin).

Sosnovy, T. (1952) 'The Soviet urban housing problem', *American Slavic and East European Review*, vol. xii, no. 2, December, pp. 288–303.

Stok, D. (ed.) (1995) *Kieslowski on Kieslowski* (London and Boston, MA: Faber and Faber).

Tarassevich, L. (1922) 'Epidemics in Russia since 1914: Report to the Health Committee of the League of Nations', *Epidemiological Intelligence*, no. 2 and no. 5.

Tauger, M.B. (2001) 'Natural disaster and human actions in the Soviet famine of 1931–1933', *The Carl Beck Papers*, no. 1506 (Pittsburgh, PA: Center for International Studies, University of Pittsburgh).

Taylor, A.J.P. (1965) *English History 1914–1945* (Oxford: Oxford University Press).

Tichonova, L., Borisenko, H., Ward, H., Meheus, A., Gromyko, A. and Renton, A. (1997) 'Epidemics of syphilis in the Russian Federation: trends, origins, and priorities for control', *The Lancet*, vol. 350, 19 July, pp. 210–13.

Townsend, P., Davidson, N. and Whitehead, M. (1988) *Inequalities in Health* (Harmondsworth: Penguin).

Townsend, P., Phillimore, P. and Beattie, A. (1988) *Health and Deprivation: Inequality and the North* (London and New York: Routledge).

TransMONEE (2001) Database, UNICEF IRC, Florence.

Trice, T. (2001) 'Rites of protest: populist funerals in Imperial St Petersburg, 1876–1878', *Slavic Review*, vol. 60, no. 1.

Trotsky, L. (1972a) *Problems of Everyday Life* (New York: Pathfinder).

Trotsky, L. (1972b) *The Revolution Betrayed* (New York: Pathfinder).

Tsentralnyi statisticheskii komitet (1905) *Ezhegodnik Rossii, 1904 g.* (St Petersburg).

Tulchinsky, T. and Varavikova, E. (1996) 'Addressing the epidemiologic transition in the former Soviet Union: strategies for health system and public health reform in Russia', *American Journal of Public Health*, vol. 86, no. 3, pp. 313–23.

United Nations (2001) *Demographic Yearbook 1999* (New York: UN).

United Nations Conference on Trade and Development (UNCTAD) (2001) *World Investment Report 2001: Promoting Linkages* (New York and Geneva: UN).

United Nations Development Programme (UNDP) (1999) *Human Development Report for Central and Eastern Europe and the CIS, 1999* (Geneva: UN).

United Nations Development Programme (UNDP) (2001) *Human Development Report 2001* (New York and Oxford: Oxford University Press).

United Nations Economic Commission for Europe (UN ECE) (1993) *Economic Survey of Europe in 1992–1993* (New York: UN).

United Nations Economic Commission for Europe (UN ECE) (2000) *Economic Survey of Europe*, no. 1 and nos 2–3 (New York: UN).

United Nations Economic Commission for Europe (UN ECE) (2002) *Economic Survey of Europe 2002*, no. 1 (New York: UN).

United Nations International Children's Emergency Fund (UNICEF) (1994) *Crisis in Mortality, Health, and Nutrition*, Regional Monitoring Report No. 2 (Florence: UNICEF International Child Development Centre).

United Nations International Children's Emergency Fund (UNICEF) (2001) *A Decade of Transition*, Regional Monitoring Report No. 8 (Florence: UNICEF Innocenti Research Centre).

United Nations International Children's Emergency Fund (UNICEF) (2002) *Social Monitor 2002* (Florence: UNICEF Innocenti Research Centre).

Vasil'ev, K.G. and Segal, A.E. (1960) *Istoriia epidemii v Rossii (materialy i ocherki)* (Moscow: Medgiz).

Velkoff, V.A. and Miller, J.E. (1995) 'Trends and differentials in infant mortality in the Soviet Union, 1970–1990: how much is due to misreporting?', *Population Studies*, vol. 49, pp. 241–58.

Vigdorchik, N.A. (1914) *Detskaia smertnost sredi Peterburgskikh rabochikh (po dannym ankety)* (Moscow: V. Rikhter).

Vinogradov, P. (1922) 'Russia', *Encyclopedia Britannica*, vol. 32 (new vol. 3) (London: Encyclopedia Britannica Company Ltd), pp. 308–40.

Vitaliev, V. (1990) *Special Correspondent. Investigating the Soviet Union* (London: Hutchinson).

Volkogonov, D.A. (1995) *Stalin: Triumph and Tragedy* (London: Weidenfeld and Nicolson).

Walberg, P., McKee, M., Shkolnikov, V., Chenet, L. and Leon, D. (1998) 'Economic change, crime, and mortality crisis in Russia: regional analysis', *British Medical Journal*, vol. 317, 1 August, pp. 312–18.

Waldron, P. (1995) 'States of emergency: autocracy and extraordinary legislation, 1881–1917', *Revolutionary Russia*, vol. 8, no. 1, June, pp. 1–25.

Wall Street Journal (2002) 'Putin's Generals', editorial, 4 October.

Wasserman, D. and Vdmik, A. (2001) 'Changes in life expectancy in Russia', *The Lancet*, vol. 357, 23 June, Correspondence, p. 2058.

Wheatcroft, S.G. (1991) 'Crises and the condition of the peasantry in late imperial Russia', in E. Kingston-Mann and T. Mixter (eds), *Peasant Economy, Culture and Politics of European Russia, 1800–1921* (Princeton, NJ: Princeton University Press), pp. 128–72.

Wheatcroft, S. (1993) 'Famine and food consumption records in early Soviet history, 1917–1925', in C. Geissler and D.J. Oddy (eds), *Food, Diet and Economic Change: Past and Present* (London: Leicester University Press).

Wheatcroft, S. (1996) 'The scale and nature of German and Soviet repression and mass killings 1930–1945', *Europe-Asia Studies*, vol. 48, no. 8, pp. 1319–53.

Wheatcroft, S. (1997) 'Soviet statistics of nutrition and mortality during times of famine', *Cahiers du Monde Russe*, vol. 38, no. 4, pp. 525–58.

Wheatcroft, S.G. (1999) 'The great leap upwards: anthropometric data and indictors of crises and secular change in soviet welfare levels, 1880–1960, *Slavic Review*, vol. 58, no. 1, spring, pp. 27–60.

Wheatcroft, S.G. and Davies, R.W. (1994) 'Population', in R.W. Davies, M. Harrison and S. Wheatcroft (eds), *The Economic Transformation of the Soviet Union, 1913–1945* (Cambridge: Cambridge University Press).

White, S. (1996) *Russia Goes Dry: Alcohol, State, and Society* (Cambridge: Cambridge University Press).

Wilkinson, R.G. (1992) 'Income distribution and life expectancy', *British Medical Journal*, vol. 304, 18 January, pp. 165–8.

Wilkinson, R.G. (1996) *Unhealthy Societies. The Afflictions of Inequality* (London: Routledge).

Williams, C. (1996) 'Abortion and women's health in Russia and the Soviet successor states', in R. Marsh (ed.), *Women in Russia* and Ukraine (Cambridge: Cambridge University Press), pp. 131–55.

Williamson, O. (1986) 'Vertical integration and related variations on a transaction-cost economics theme', in J. Stiglitz and G. Mathewson (eds), *New Developments in the Analysis of Market Structure* (London and Basingstoke: Macmillan), pp. 149–74.

Winiecki, J. (1991) *Resistance to Change in the Soviet Economic System: A Property Rights Approach* (London and New York: Routledge).

Wnuk-Lipinski, E. and Illsley, R. (1990) 'International comparative analysis', *Social Science and Medicine*, vol. 31, no. 8, pp. 879–80.

World Health Organisation (WHO) (2002a) *World Report on Violence and Health* (Geneva: WHO), available at <www5.who.int/violence_injury_prevention/main.cfm?p=0000000682>

World Health Organisation (WHO) (2002b) *European Health Report 2002* (Geneva: WHO), available at <www.euro.who.int/euopeanhealthreport/20020903_2>

Wortman, R.S. (2000) *Scenarios of Power: Myth and Ceremony in Russian Monarchy. Volume Two: From Alexander II to the Abdication of Nicholas II* (Princeton, NJ: Princeton University Press).

Yeltsin, B. (1991) 'Speech to Congress of People's Deputies', *Izvestia*, 29 October, translated in *Current Digest of the Soviet Press*, vol. 43, no. 43, pp. 1–6.

Yeltsin, B. (2000) *Midnight Diaries* (London: Weidenfeld and Nicolson).

Yevtushenko, Y. (1981) *The Poetry of Yevgeny Yevtushenko*, ed. G. Reavey (London: Marion Boyars).

Zemskov, V.N. (1991) 'Massovoe osvobozdenie spetsposelentsev i ssylnykh 1954–1960 gg', *Sotsiologicheskie issledovaniia*, no. 1, pp. 5–26.

Zhiromskaia, V.B. (2001) *Demograficeshkaia istoriia Rossii v 1930-e gody* (Moscow: Rosspen).

Index

Compiled by Sue Carlton